Television Disrupted

Television Disrupted

The Transition from Network to Networked TV

Shelly Palmer

AMSTERDAM · BOSTON · HEIDELBERG · LONDON
NEW YORK · OXFORD · PARIS · SAN DIEGO
SAN FRANCISCO · SINGAPORE · SYDNEY · TOKYO

Focal Press Is an Imprint of Elsevier

Acquisitions Editor: Angelina Ward
Marketing Manager   Christine Degon Veroulis
Development Editor: Beth Millett
Assistant Editor: Rachel Epstein
Cover Design: Eric DeCicco
Interior Design: Frances Baca Design
Composition: Umbrella Graphics
Illustration: James Millefolie

Focal Press is an imprint of Elsevier
30 Corporate Drive, Suite 400, Burlington, MA 01803, USA
Linacre House, Jordan Hill, Oxford OX2 8DP, UK

Recognizing the importance of preserving what has been written, Elsevier prints its books on
acid-free paper whenever possible.

Library of Congress Cataloging-in-Publication Data
Application submitted

British Library Cataloguing-in-Publication Data
A catalogue record for this book is available from the British Library.

ISBN 13: 978-0-240-80864-2
ISBN 10: 0-240-80864-9

For information on all Focal Press publications
visit our website at www.books.elsevier.com

Printed in the United States of America

06 07 08 09 10   10 9 8 7 6 5 4 3 2 1

Printed in the United States of America

Contents

For Debbie, Alexis, Brent and Jared
(and my cats Mozart and Newton)
—Shelly Palmer

Acknowledgments

This book would not have been possible without the help and support of my wife Debbie and my family. A special wink to my son Brent, who reminded me that the Bible was not copy-protected. Special thanks also to my other son Jared, who was very respectful of the fact that I needed lots of time to write this book. Kudos to my daughter Alexis and my son-in-law Andrew Zinberg for reading and critiquing the manuscript. And thanks to Mom and Dad and my brother Jason. This was a group effort and I truly appreciate everyone's help.

I am also grateful for the extraordinary knowledge and guidance from my friends and colleagues. Special thanks to Gali Einav, Charlie Jablonski, Alexandra Kenney, Lilia Aramayo, Barry Fischer, Mark Schubin (technical consultant extraordinaire), copyright guru Ray Beckerman, Esq., Lydia Loizides, Channing Dawson, Tim Halle, Steve Ehrlich, Stuart Lipson, Jim Turner, Martin J. Reingold, Angelina Ward, Beth Millett, Christine Degon, Rachel Epstein, and the "Justice League."

I owe a special debt of gratitude to my friend Rick Mandler, whose contributions to this work were invaluable. And a special thank you to Seth Haberman, who is, without a doubt, the smartest kid in the class.

I would also like to thank the executive committee and the members of the Advanced Media Committee of the National Academy of Television Arts and Sciences (The Emmy® Awards), which I chair. We are truly blessed to be part of an organization that recognizes the importance of change and accepts the challenges of industry leadership with dignity, grace and foresight.

About the Author

The business and technology of television is changing at an ever increasing pace. Shelly Palmer, Managing Director, Advanced Media Ventures Group, LLC is one of the experts leading the industry's rapid evolution. From developing advanced television services to implementing new Internet technologies, Palmer's pioneering efforts have made him the successful creator, producer, composer and television Renaissance man he is today.

Palmer is the Chairman of The Advanced Media Committee (and 1st Vice President of the New York Chapter) of the National Academy of Television Arts & Sciences (NATAS) the organization that bestows the coveted Emmy Awards. Palmer oversees the Advanced Media Technology Emmy Awards, which he created in 2003 to honor outstanding achievements in the science and technology of the new media-side of the business.

Along with his contributions to the advancement of television, Palmer is a pioneer in the field of Internet technologies. He is the inventor of Enhanced Television used by programs such as ABC's *Who Wants to Be a Millionaire* and *Monday Night Football*. In 2004, ABC's *Celebrity Mole Yucatan* received an Emmy in the category of Enhancement of Original Television Content. It was Palmer who led ABC's team of advanced media professionals and spearheaded the award-winning project.

Palmer is a popular speaker and moderator at technology and media conferences hosted by industry organizations and top tier colleges and universities, like: The Consumer Electronics Show (CES), The National Association of Broadcasters Convention (NAB), The National Show presented by the National Cable Television Association (NCTA), Telecom presented by the United States Telecom Association, Digital Hollywood, iHollywood, DV Expo and ITV Europe. He is a guest lecturer at Stern Graduate Business School at NYU, The Columbia Institute for Tele-Information (CITI) at Columbia University, The Graziadio School of Business Management at Pepperdine University, The Digital Content Lab at the American Film Institute and other top tier colleges and universities.

Over the last two decades, Palmer has enjoyed a highly distinguished career as a composer and producer. His professional vitae includes years of experience in television production and musical composition. He created and produced *HotPop*, a teen lifestyle and music show airing on Starz/Encore's WAM! As a prolific composer, Palmer was the recipient of the American Society of Composers, Authors and Publishers (ASCAP's) 12th Annual Film and Television Music Award for ABC's hit series *Spin City*. He was also recognized the following season in the category of "Most Performed Television Themes." Palmer's music credits include the theme songs for "Live with Regis & Kelly," "Rivera Live" and "MSNBC" as well as the digital debut of the "real" cat singing the classic "Meow, Meow, Meow, Meow."

Palmer is the host of *Media 3.0 with Shelly Palmer*, a weekly business news series, which can be seen on public television and online at www.media30.com. Palmer is a graduate of New York University's School of the Arts. He is the author of one of the most popular television business news blogs, www.EmmyAdvancedMedia.com, and a weekly columnist for www.Mediapost.com. For more information, visit www.shellypalmer.com.

Introduction

There's a business school case study about the fledgling airline business in the early part of the 20th century. According to the story, after the Wright Brothers flew their airplane, some entrepreneurs decided that they should fund an aircraft company. They thought about where to get the money and decided to seek out one of the richest, most powerful corporations in America. They arrived at the offices of a giant railroad company and made their presentation. The executives listened attentively to the pitch and then summarily dismissed the nascent aviators, telling them, "We're in the railroad business, not the airline business." When this anecdote is taught in school, the moral of the story is usually something like, "The dumb railroad guys didn't know what business they were in. They weren't in the railroad business; they were in the transportation business."

This story may be true or it may just be business school lore, but professors in business schools everywhere use this parable to illustrate how important it is to know what business you are in. If the common interpretation is correct, we are not in the television business; we are in the audience aggregation business. But the story may seriously oversimplify a very complex reality.

Obviously, the railroad company could have made a cash investment in the new technology. This would have yielded several benefits: they would have owned a piece of the future and, in any event, had a board seat and first hand knowledge of the progress and speed to market of a potential competitive product.

Or, the railroad company could have recognized the airplane as an important way to move people from place to place and embraced the brave new world. They could have started buying real estate for airports and converting their workforce — but wait, was there a way for steam engine mechanics to become gasoline engine mechanics? How about a way for railroad engineers to be retrained (no pun intended) as pilots? No. There was no practical way to transition the railroad company into an airline. The only real way for them to invest was with cash, a hope and a prayer.

There are some who take the logic of this business case and apply it willy-nilly to several modern businesses — like the television industry. Those who do, believe that there is no practical way to transition a television company into a media company ... and they would be wrong.

In this book, we are going to explore the transition from network television (the 20th century broadcast television industry) to **networked** television (the evolving network of wired and wireless Internet Protocol-provisioned servers and clients world-wide). The transition to networked television is also a transition to a multimedia world where audio, video, still images and text may be available to you anytime, anywhere on any device.

Throughout our journey, we will move effortlessly between various media. At times, this may feel like a book about the music business, then the television business, then the cable television business, then the art world ... get used to it. All television is media, but all media is not television. That is the overwhelming lesson here.

In these pages we will look at the similarities and differences between the histories and the probable futures of all of the media that makes-up the networked universe. In the end, we shall learn that the most disruptive forces come *All television is media,* from some of the simplest and most mundane *but all media is not television.* areas. We shall also see the true power of incumbent systems and how inertia remains the great stabilizer. We will also come to appreciate now, more than ever, that we live in a multi-generational time and that the power of youth (and aspiring to be young) can not be overstated.

Perhaps the most important thing you can take from this book is what you bring to it. Your professional knowledge will easily translate across disciplines and through the paper-thin barriers that used to prevent "thinking too big." You will come away from this writing with ways to label and discuss things you already knew but didn't know how to describe. And, if I have done my job well, you'll be able to tell the difference between an airplane and a locomotive.

Probable Futures

There are an infinite number of things that will never happen. Of course, there are a finite number of things that will happen and predicting them has been the bastion of soothsayers, wizards, pundits and other experts since the beginning of time.

As you well know, most predictions are simply wrong. In 1865, a Boston Post editorial espoused, "Well-informed people know it is impossible to transmit the voice over wires and that were it possible to do so, the thing would be of no practical value." A few years later in 1876, a Western Union internal memo included this prescient edict: "This 'telephone-thing' has too many shortcomings to be seriously considered as a means of communication. The device is inherently of no value to us."

These predictions might have been penned by layman, but even being a successful businessman doesn't seem to enhance predictive powers past a point. Ken Olson, president of Digital Equipment Corporation, is famous for his 1977 quote, "There is no reason for any individual to have a computer in his home," as is H.M. Warner, head of Warner Brothers Movie Studios, for asking, "Who the hell wants to hear actors talk?" back in 1927. Even being the richest man in the world does not seem to guarantee the quality of any given prediction, as Bill Gates opined in 1981, "640K ought to be enough [memory] for anybody."

Limited predictive power is not limited to observers. Sometimes (actually, very often) the inventor of a technology will not truly understand what they have invented or how it will eventually be used. After Alexander Graham Bell popularized the telephone as a device to speed business communication, Thomas Edison thought there might be a business in recording and playing back telephone messages. In 1877, a full 22 years before it would reach critical mass, the phonograph was invented to keep records of telephone conversations. The history of invention is replete with stories of unintended consequences, and this continues to be the case today.

Investing in and incubating early stage technology is not our subject. Profiting from the probable futures of television, media and entertainment is our goal. To achieve this, we will look back far enough to understand the present and think far enough into the future to understand what must change. In the pages that follow, we are going to look at technological, economic and sociological forces and how their interaction will probably impact the future. These probable futures can be predicted just a bit more accurately than possible futures.

You should use this book as a guide to help you think about tactics for the near-term and strategies for the long-term. If you apply your personal knowledge to the framework outlined here, you will be uniquely positioned to profit as we transition from network to networked television. And, if you share your knowledge with the people you work with (or want to work with), you are likely to reap even higher rewards.

Television/Computer Convergence: Old News!

The term "disruptive technology" is not new. Successful new technology, by definition, will disrupt, displace and ultimately replace existing technology. For obvious reasons, investors and technocrats who need to generate industry interest or buzz for a new product love to declare it disruptive. It is important to distinguish between emergent technologies that are "solutions in search of a problem" and those that are true paradigm shifters. This is easier said than done.

A few years back, "convergence" was touted as THE disruptive force. You could not open the business trades or even consumer press without reading something about it. Televisions and computers were supposed to converge. If they have, where are all of the new devices? They can't mean those media center computers they sell at the computer store, can they? Aren't they supposed to look like a computer and a television set combined? No. The future doesn't always unfold the way people imagine it.

The Jetson's view of your kitchen is not how your kitchen ultimately became computerized. However, there are a bunch of computers in the room. There is a computer in your toaster oven, one in your microwave, one or two in your phone, a couple in your electric stove, one in your dishwasher and one or two in your refrigerator. There probably aren't any computer terminals in your kitchen (although there might be), but your kitchen is almost completely run by computers that you don't have to think about. The fact is, "kitchen appliance/computer" convergence happened years ago (while you weren't looking).

So too is it with "television/computer" convergence. The content is converged at the server side in broadcast operations and engineering departments all over the country (as opposed to the client[1] side where everyone was expecting it). Over the past few years, broadcasters have been replacing their tape machines with computer video servers and using them, instead of videotape machines, to feed their transmitters. Of course, once video content is converted to a computer file, it can be sent to any device that can play it. So while broadcasters transitioned to digital video serving for efficiency and convenience, they also received the added benefit of being able to serve their content to any type of consumer device over any type of distribution network.

As a practical matter, "television/computer" convergence is technologically complete (although hidden from view), which makes the television industry hard for

---

1. A client is defined as a requester of services and a server is defined as the provider of services. A single machine can be both a client and a server depending on the software configuration.

non-technical people to understand. However, convergence leaves the industry uniquely suited to transcend its original form factor. Once audio/video content is digitized it can be distributed or multicasted to any type of device as in Figure 1.

The media consumer in Figure 2 has choices and selects devices based upon lifestyle and personal preference. Server-side convergence enables content distributors to profitably serve their media anytime, anywhere, to any device.

To be sure, there are more business rules, contractual and legal issues to deal with. We don't have to wait for some behavior-changing, hybrid, computer/television contraption to move the business into the digital age ... we're already here.

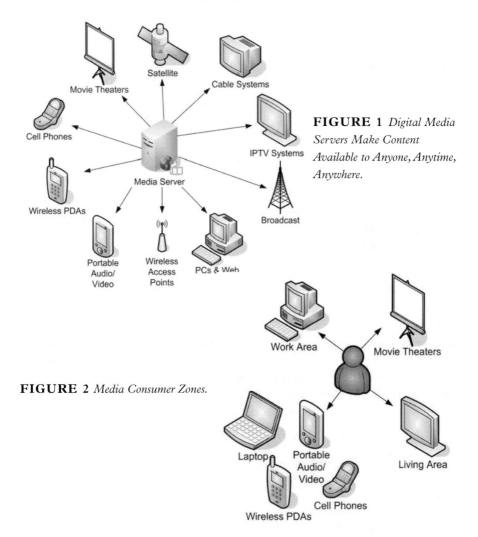

FIGURE 1 *Digital Media Servers Make Content Available to Anyone, Anytime, Anywhere.*

FIGURE 2 *Media Consumer Zones.*

About the Book

This book is divided into three general parts. To ensure that we're all on the same page, Chapters 1 through 4 lay the groundwork for the terminology and concepts in the chapters to follow. Depending on your interest and experience, it may be helpful to read this overview of the technologies and media covered in the book.

Chapters 5 through 8 review the existing technologies, paradigms, sociology and business rules in the broadcast world today and discuss some of the relevant issues and technologies.

The final section of the book, Chapters 9 through 12, looks toward the future and the challenges that lay ahead. Many of the industries, companies, technologies, business rules and statutes involved in the discussions here are at cross-purposes, and we will examine how those changes may impact the future.

> Perhaps a better title for this book would be "The Coexistence of Traditional Network Television with The New, Inherently Two-Way, Digital, Internet Protocol-Provisioned, Wired and Wireless Networks Which Will Continue to Grow Until This New Networked Technology Ultimately Disrupts and Replaces Most (But Not All) of the Old Network Technology." It is a better description because new technologies rarely instantly replace old ones and, more importantly, old learned behaviors are rarely instantly replaced by new ones.

A Note About Terms-of-Art and Technical Descriptions

Throughout this book you will see words that look like English, but are actually terms-of-art (technical terms) that have very specific professional definitions. In many cases this will cause confusion across professional disciplines. For example, the term "network" has a very specific meaning to a broadcast engineer, a different meaning to a program director and still a third meaning to a corporate IT director. Wherever possible, I try to define these terms contextually, in footnotes or in the glossary. This book is not attempting to be a technical manual in any sense; the goal is to give the reader a cross-disciplinary look at a group of technologies, business models and consumer trends that are all on a collision course.

Because I am covering areas that are emerging and evolving every day, it is very difficult to find ways to describe every system that will satisfy everyone's vocational preferences. Many systems and technologies that are cited as new or emergent have actually been around for decades (or longer), but they are mentioned or featured in the pages of this work because market conditions make them newly relevant.

Lastly, it is important to realize that there are very few technological absolutes. So, in my quest to simplify the technological descriptions herein, I am going to leave out lots of stuff that doesn't help us understand the bigger picture. I apologize in advance to the rather large constituency of hard-core techno-geeks who will consider this an unforgivable sin.

The Advanced Media Committee of the National Academy of Television Arts & Sciences (The Emmy® Awards)

As current chair and a proud member of the Advanced Media Committee, I would like to tell you why you should become a member. First of all, we're the nice people who bring you the Emmy® Awards. Being part of the committee entitles you to become part of the Advanced Media Technology Emmy® Awards process. If you qualify, you may be asked to join a blue ribbon adjudication panel or to become a judge. Membership gives you access to the leading edge of media technology and to all of the industry's "best practices" organizations who compete to be honored for their content, creativity and execution each year. Aside from producing the annual Emmy® Awards Gala, we also host many events, seminars and social gatherings throughout the year to encourage and facilitate dialogue between industry professionals. If you want to keep your finger on the pulse of advanced media, if you have something to learn or something to teach, we will welcome you with open arms. For more information, please visit www.advancedmedia-committee.com.

Who Should Read this Book

This is a book for media, entertainment and telecommunications professionals who are being forced (by constant technological change) to think about their businesses in new ways. Among other important topics, it covers:

- TV for telephone execs
- Telephone for cable TV execs
- Internet for TV, cable, satellite and telephone execs
- Mobile devices for everybody

In the following pages you will learn that:

- The sky is not falling.

- There is no "silver bullet" or single solution (and there really never has been).

- New media rarely completely replaces existing media.

- You can position yourself perfectly to take advantage of this exciting time of transition and change.

If you think of your customers as "access lines," "subs," "unique users," or "TV households," you need to read this book!

Who Should Not Read this Book

Academics and analysts looking for reference material, rigorous Socratic arguments or theoretical pontifications should not read this book. This book is written as a multi-industry overview with a simple thesis: The world is getting more complicated daily and to sort it out, we need to know a little bit about the technologies and organizations that are making it so. In certain cases, we can make educated guesses about the future.

1 The Businesses of Television

Wonkavision ... my very latest and greatest invention. Now, I suppose you all know how ordinary television works. You photograph something and then the photograph is split up into millions of tiny pieces, and they go whizzing through the air down to your TV set where they're all put together again in the right order.

— Willy Wonka, *Charlie and the Chocolate Factory*, Roald Dahl, 1964

From a technology perspective, Willy Wonka had it just about right. But very few people think of television as a technology, and there is no reason for them to. Television (from the Greek word, *tele*, and the Latin word, *visio*,) literally means far-sight or far-vision. Modern American network television lives up to that name. For more than 50 years, it has been the best, most efficient way to communicate with the largest possible audience. This probably won't change anytime soon. What is changing is our definition of a large audience and the value we are placing on it.

Ratings and demos, the *lingua franca* of the television business, are giving way to new types of ROI calculations. Production and distribution are quickly becoming democratized. And, every day seems to herald a new, world-changing technology and the portent of a new paradigm to accompany it.

Before we can jump into discussions about all of the things that are changing (hourly at this point) in the television business, we have to cover some basics and learn some vocabulary. If you know how television stations, television networks, cable networks and satellite networks came to be, and you have a pretty good idea who all of

1

the players are, you can skip to Chapter 2. Otherwise, let's look at a brief overview of mass media in the United States.

There Are Two Kinds of Television ...

There are several different consumer value propositions embodied in the modern media world. For television, they break down into two basic categories — "free," which is known as "advertiser supported," and "subscription," which means you pay for the media you use. Of course, nothing in the media business is ever that simple, so let's review the subtle (and not so subtle) variations of these two themes.

Free Analog Television

Free over-the-air television is supposed to be free. But, like so many things in life, it's not really free. You need to own a television monitor, a television tuner (you can purchase a television receiver which combines both elements — we commonly refer to television receivers as TVs,) and a television antenna. If you live within the coverage area of a local television station, you can use your television tuner to tune into that specific channel and watch whatever content is being broadcast free of charge. Oh, and you need electricity too. So, free over-the-air television is mostly free, except for the cost of the equipment, any maintenance fees and electricity.

As far as analog television technology goes, not much has changed since December 23, 1953. That's the day the Federal Communications Commission (FCC) authorized the use of the NTSC (National Television Systems Committee) standard of 525 lines of resolution per second for color broadcasts in the United States. In order to provide this mostly free service to viewers, a local broadcaster must obtain an FCC license to broadcast on a particular channel (frequency) from a specific geographic location.

Broadcast Networks

Since the broadcast coverage area of a local television station is physically limited by the power of its transmitter and the location of its antenna, as shown in Figure 1.1, the only way to cover the entire country with broadcast television is to create a "network" of local television stations. This has been accomplished by several organizations with familiar names, like NBC, ABC, CBS and FOX.

In today's mass-mediated world, the television networks own some of their own stations, cleverly referred to as "O&Os" (owned and operated). Stations that carry the network feed but are owned by other companies are known simply as affiliates. As you

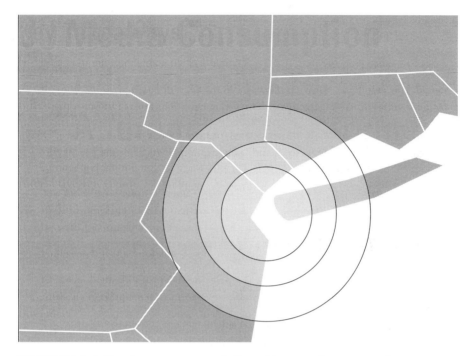

FIGURE 1.1 *Broadcast coverage area is dictated by transmitter power and geography.*

may have guessed, every station owned by a network station group does not necessarily carry that particular network. For example: the NBC Universal (which owns both the NBC and Telemundo Networks) does own a bunch of NBC and Telemundo O&O's, but they also own independent KWHY in Los Angeles. And, as you may also have guessed, there are station groups (such as Hearst Argyle and Advance Newhouse) that are completely independent but own stations affiliated with several different networks.

Designated Market Areas (DMAs) are used by Nielsen Media Research to identify TV stations whose broadcast signals reach a specific area and attract the most viewers. A DMA consists of all counties whose largest viewing share is given to stations of that same market area. The entire continental United States, Hawaii and parts of Alaska are covered by 210 non-overlapping DMAs, as shown in Figure 1.2. Table 1.1 shows the top 10 DMAs in the nation.[1] (Visit www.televisiondisrupted.com for complete listing.)

---

1. NSI® and DMA® are registered trademarks of Nielsen Media Research, Inc. Nielsen Media Research is a trademark of Nielsen Media Research, Inc.

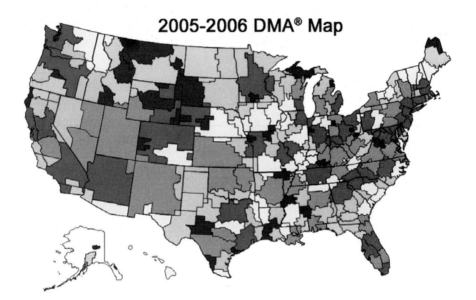

FIGURE 1.2 *The nation's 210 DMAs roughly correspond to the broadcast coverage areas of the television stations serving each of the markets.*

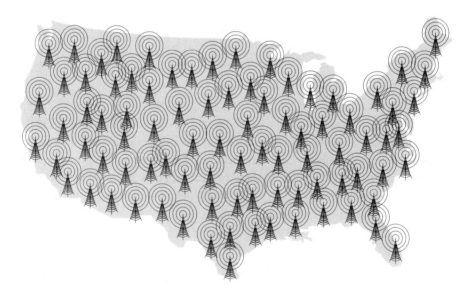

FIGURE 1.3 *Each broadcast network still has approximately 200 affiliated transmitters located in most of the 210 DMAs – that's one transmitter per channel.*

RANK	DMA	NUMBER OF TV HOMES	PERCENT OF THE U.S.
1	New York	7,375,530	6.692
2	Los Angeles	5,536,430	5.023
3	Chicago	3,430,790	3.113
4	Philadelphia	2,925,560	2.654
5	Boston	2,375,310	2.155
6	San Francisco-Oakland-San Jose	2,355,740	2.137
7	Dallas-Ft. Worth	2,336,140	2.120
8	Washington, D.C.-Haggerstown	2,252,550	2.044
9	Atlanta	2,097,220	1.903
10	Houston	1,938,670	1.759

TABLE 1.1 *Top 10 DMAs.*

If you think about it, the infrastructure of a modern television network is extremely large. Each station has offices, studios, engineers, a transmitter and an antenna to carry just one channel. Multiply that capital expense by the roughly 200 affiliates each network has, adjust for market size, then multiply by the number of different networks available in each DMA and you start to understand why television has become a multi-billion dollar industry.

Since television stations currently offer only one analog commercial channel (they will all have multiple digital channels after the mandatory conversion to digital), the multi-channel universe familiar to many consumers is brought to you by your local cable operator, cable over-builder,[2] direct-broadcast satellite service (DBS), or telephone company (telco). The FCC refers to these content suppliers as "multi-channel video programming distributors," or MVPDs. For our purposes, we describe anyone who runs a proprietary network for the purposes of delivering some form of video to consumers as a "system operator."

---

2. In the late 1990s, the FCC ended the practice of licensing sole cable TV operators in a given market. To increase competition, they allowed additional cable systems to come into existence. The companies that were formed to exploit this ruling were known as "over-builders."

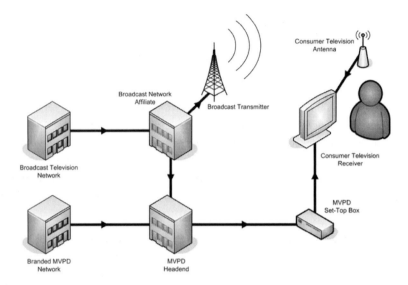

FIGURE 1.4 *A simple model with broadcast television and a system operator bringing hundreds of channels to the consumer.*

Cable networks (HBO, ESPN, A&E, CNN, etc.) can feed system operators directly. However, in order to be available through a system operator, a broadcast television network (NBC, ABC, CBS, FOX, etc.) must retransmit their signals from their local affiliates to the system operators.

Free Analog Television Models

There are two basic types of free over-the-air television: commercial and educational. Of the almost 1,800 television stations in the United States, roughly 1,400 are commercial and about 400 are educational (FCC, June 2005 Broadcast Station Totals).

Back 50 years ago, when the modern business model of commercial television began, the owners of commercial television stations (and networks) made a pact with the American people: You get to watch this interesting content for almost free if you agree to watch some commercial advertisements. Also, we'd like it if you went out and supported the advertisers because they pay us a bunch of money to broadcast the spots and we need them to come back and do it often. This may be a grossly oversimplified view of commercial television, but it is ultimately accurate. Today, of the 110 million television households, approximately 15 million still use antennas to receive free over-the-air television.

Free Digital Television

Just to complicate this issue a bit more, the FCC has mandated that all broadcast television signals in the United States be converted from analog to digital by early 2009 (but the date will probably change). Television stations have been allocated a range of frequencies in the spectrum to be used for DTT (Digital Terrestrial Television) broadcast. They have the option to use this digital bandwidth for HDTV (High Definition Television) or SDTV (Standard Definition Television) or anything else they choose, as long as they fulfill their obligations to the FCC for local broadcasting and live up to the requirements of their broadcast licenses.

You can get up-to-the-minute information about this or any statistic in this book by visiting http://www.TelevisionDisrupted.com.

Unfortunately, consumers who use an antenna to receive digital broadcast transmissions are going to have a different experience than they had with analog broadcast television. Analog television is broadcast using an FM signal and, although the best picture is achieved with a clear line of sight between transmitter and antenna, acceptable signals can be achieved even in sub-optimal situations. Sadly for antenna users, digital television signals are more complex than the analog television signals that they are replacing. Multipath[3] issues prevent optimal broadcast digital terrestrial television coverage in cities like New York where tall buildings block each other and receivers are in close proximity to the transmitting antenna.

Lastly, digital television is not backwards-compatible with analog television. This means that after the switch, everyone will have to have a digital television tuner, digital television set or a digital-to-analog converter (DA) attached to an antenna to use their current technology analog television sets to receive free over-the-air television signals. Broadcasters estimate that there are 73 million television sets (that's sets, not households) in American homes not hooked up to cable or satellite services and that rely on over-the-air broadcasts.[4] After the switch, these television sets are going to become landfill unless they have a DA. There is going to be a business here for somebody – and a cost to consumers one way or the other.

---

3. Because there are obstacles and reflectors in the wireless propagation channel, the transmitted signal arrives at the receiver from various directions and over a multiplicity of paths. Such a phenomenon is called multipath. It is an unpredictable set of reflections and/or direct waves each with its own degree of attenuation and delay. http://users.ece.gatech.edu/~mai/tutorial_multipath.htm)

4. Reuters. "House approves new digital-TV deadline," 19 December 2005. http://news.com.com/House%20approves%20new%20digital-TV%20deadline/2100-1025_3-6000804.html

Digital TV Is Not Necessarily HDTV

Contrary to popular belief and understanding, all digital television is **not** high defini-tion (HDTV), although all current-technology HDTV is digital. There are many reasons consumers are confused about HDTV and digital television technology. First and fore-most, the industry has done a particularly poor job explaining why consumers should care about it. A trip to the local television retailer is like a trip to an alien planet. You'll hear lots of gibberish spoken by the salespeople and what can be deciphered is information, not knowledge.

There is confusion about the very inconsistent, sub-optimal reception quality of ana-log television. Although analog television can theoretically deliver 525 lines of resolu-tion, consumers almost never experience it. The signal can be (and is) degraded at many points during its journey from television transmitter to consumer television receiver. This is not true with a digital picture. Because digital television is sent to you as data and converted to a picture just before you view it, you either see a per-fect digital picture or you see nothing.[5] There are no bad digital television pictures.[6] So when you compare a standard definition (SD) digital television signal to a SD ana-log television signal, the digital signal will almost always look significantly better. So much better, that digital SD pictures are often confused with HDTV pictures unless the two are played side by side.

You only see an HDTV picture when your HDTV-compatible monitor is connected to an HDTV tuner or HDTV set-top box and then, only the channels that are being trans-mitted in HD. You are not seeing an HDTV picture on any of the other channels. Nor will you see an HD picture when you play a regular DVD on a flat screen HDTV-ready monitor unless the DVD and the DVD player are clearly marked Blueray DVD or HD-DVD (the two competing high definition DVD formats). A regular DVD looks great on a big, flat-screen HDTV monitor, but you are not seeing an HD picture, it's just a full-resolution SD picture seen the way it's supposed to be seen. Still confused? So is everyone else. That's one of the biggest problems facing consumer electronics man-ufacturers and the other proponents of HDTV.

---

5. Digital video can experience drop-outs and other problems with transmission and playback which will distort or disrupt the viewing experience. If you can see a complete picture, it is usually a very good one.

6. This is not strictly true. Digital television pictures can be over-compressed by transmission engi-neers attempting to minimize bandwidth requirements. A digital television picture that has been poorly encoded, trans-coded, up-converted or improperly digitized can have degraded visual quali-ty. However, because the picture is digital you either see it or you don't.

Hybrid Subscription

Don't people with cable get free over-the-air television? Yes, they do. Only, it's not free. System operator subscribers pay a fee each month for the pleasure of having better signal quality (over cable, fiber or satellite) — which translates into a better picture and, nowadays, more channels. But, consumers also see advertising. How did this hybrid model become the most popular form of subscription-based entertainment in America? After all, you were only supposed to have to watch advertisements if the content was provided free ... weren't you?

Cable Television

A little history: In the early days of cable, there were no premium channels or important cable-only content. Cable's consumer value proposition was simply the promise of a better picture. Unless you are older than 40 or happen to use an antenna to receive your television signals, it is probably hard for you to imagine what the world was like in the days when everyone had antennas. Back then, if you lived close to the television transmitter you could use an indoor antenna, lovingly referred to as rabbit ears. But, if you lived in the suburbs or more rural areas, you had to have one of the big rooftop models like the Dual Dipole with screen reflector, the Amphenol Stacked Array, the Ten Element Yagi or my favorite, the Finco Bedspring.

All of these antennas had one thing in common ... they provided sub-optimal picture quality. This created a rare situation for engineers; an actual problem that needed a solution! The solution was cable, and people couldn't wait.

The First Cable Company

Formerly known as Community Antenna Television, CATV started in the late 1940s when John Walson erected an antenna on a Pennsylvania mountain top and connected it by cable to his appliance store back in town. His goal was to receive clear television signals from three Philadelphia stations. In the late spring of 1948, Walson connected some homes that were located along the path of his antenna cable and the first cable television system was born.

Back in the 70s, if you lived in an average television household, the TV was on over six hours each day. Even by today's standard (American households watched over eight hours of television per day in 2005, according to Nielsen Media Research) that's quite a bit of TV. So just about everyone wanted a better picture. Towns were willing to grant monopolies and other financial incentives to entrepreneurs who would take the risk to wire a neighborhood, and wire they did.

	(IN MILLIONS)
Total Television Households	110.2
Cable households	73.2
Satellite households (DirecTV and Dish)	22.2
Antenna Households	14.8

TABLE 1.2 *The Television Universe.*

Sources: *National Cable Television Association, Industry Overview: Statistics & Resources; Yahoo! Form 10-Q for DirecTV Group Inc.; Yahoo! Form 10-Q for EchoStar Communications Corp.*

Today there are an estimated 73 million cable television households, which account for about 66 percent of the total estimated 110 million television households (see Table 1.2). You can find more complete listing of industry statistics at www.televisiondisrupted.com for the most up-to-date information.

Part of the consumer value proposition of cable television was a higher signal quality (yielding a better picture) than you could achieve with an antenna. So, it stands to reason that the first, most important content you could find on cable was the retransmission of local television signals.

Must-Carry Rules

In 1972, when cable was still very young, "must-carry rules" were designed to ensure that local broadcasters would not lose market share to fledging cable networks that were competing with them for the limited number of available cable channels. Over the past few decades, must-carry has been ruled unconstitutional and has been revised several times.

Must-carry rules may not apply to every new broadcast frequency allocated for DTT.

The original version of the rule specified that cable companies provide channels for all local broadcasters within a 60-mile (later reduced to 50-mile) radius from the center of the cable company's footprint. Obviously, the primary issue was the requirement of the cable systems to carry broadcast television signals at all. However, there were important marketing and promotional issues as well. If a station is broadcasting on channel 2 it may be known in its DMA as channel 2, but it is more likely that it would be known by a promotional hook such as, "NewsChannel 2," "Eyewitness 2" or "2 on your side." These slogans serve the dual purpose of branding the station's news products and as a mnemonic for the channel number. Imagine the consumer confusion if your broadcast signal was found at channel 2 and your cable channel was 14. The need for must-carry was also a need to preserve market share and reduce consumer confusion. Or was it?

> A brash, young media mogul-in-the-making named Ted Turner had a vision for WTBS-TV, his little television station. He wanted to make it a "Superstation" available on cable systems all across America. So, in the mid 80s, Turner Broadcasting sued the FCC on the constitutionality of must-carry. In two decisions, 1985 and 1987, the U.S. Court of Appeals found that must-carry rules violated the First Amendment.

Whether intended or not, this decision had a major impact on the business models for small UHF (ultra high frequency, channels 14-83) stations. Cablers could now replace them with stronger brands like superstations as long as they provided an A/B to allow access to local broadcast signals. But, cable operators still needed content, so when room in the channel lineup became available, you started seeing local UHF stations all over the dial. Broadcast Channel 18 could be found on Cable Channel 34, etc. Although not optimal for marketing purposes, this was very important because traditional television antennas would not tune in the UHF spectrum. (Yes, you need a special, additional antenna to receive UHF.)[7]

Must-carry rules[8] and the related "retransmission rules" were still in effect as of the 1996 Telecommunications Act and, as you can imagine, are still being challenged by cable operators nationwide. This fight is going to truly get heated up as we approach the

---

7. UHF signals are inherently less efficient in the conversion of radio waves to the electrical signals used by the television receiver, and are subject to more losses from some environmental conditions than VHF signals. A separate, specialized antenna is required to receive UHF television signals.

8. There were additional Must Carry revisions, including the 1992 Communications Act, which continued the must-carry requirement for local and public television stations but allowed cable operators to choose between overlapping signals within a 50-mile radius. So, if there were two network affiliates in a market, the operator could choose which one to carry. In 1994, the FCC truly confused the issue when it gave television stations a choice of being carried under the "must-carry" rules or under a new regulation requiring cable operators to obtain retransmission rights in order to carry a broadcast signal. Retransmission was considered a big win for broadcast stations as it gave them more negotiating power against the cable operators.

date for the final conversion from analog to digital broadcast television. This is because it is unclear if the FCC will mandate that cable systems carry all of the channels that local stations will be able to broadcast after the mandatory conversion to digital.

This battle will be fought in court and in the marketplace. Remember, many media conglomerates own cable systems, local stations and some networks as well. The lesson to be learned from the history of must-carry is that disruptive technologies can have a dramatic impact on the status quo. We are likely to see companies that are otherwise sworn enemies band together to tackle this next phase of the must-carry fight.

Digital Cable

Although the FCC's mandate to convert all analog television stations to digital television stations seems to have nothing to do with the cable television industry, technical guru Mark Schubin recalls that it was the cable industry's desire to switch to digital that actually caused the FCC to mandate DTT in the first place.

Mark Schubin's Brief History of Digital Television

When the FCC established its inquiry into advanced (not digital) television (considered synonymous with HDTV) in 1987, all of the submissions it received were for analog systems. There was one hybrid analog/digital system from Zenith, but the function of the digital part was simply to reduce power levels, not to provide any sort of computer compatibility. Meanwhile, there were already moves afoot in the cable industry to squeeze more programming into existing bandwidth using bit-rate reduction and digital modulation. By early 1990, General Instrument (successor to the Jerrold line of cable equipment and predecessor of Motorola's) had come to the point of comfortably being able to squeeze six streams of TV programming into a single 6-MHz cable channel. HDTV was said to involve five or six times the information of SDTV. So, at the last minute before the FCC closed the door to submissions, General Instrument submitted an all-digital system.

At once, the universe changed. All but one (NHK) of the other proponents said to the FCC, "Ooh! Can we be digital, too?" From that, the FCC inquiry gradually morphed from being about HDTV to being about digital, and, when the FCC issued its order in 1997, it specifically stated that, although all broadcasters would have to transmit digitally, none would have to carry any HDTV at any time. So digital cable is what caused DTT broadcasting in the U.S. As far as the other way around, all there   CONTINUED ▶

CONTINUED ▶   existed were the 16-VSB[9] (intended to compete with cable's already established QAM) and a handful of cable operators (Time Warner Cable of NYC) doing some initial experimentation with 8-VSB[10] for HDTV.

Others believe that the FCC was motivated by the spectrum needs of land mobile technology. Regardless of the inspiration, there is one simple reason that the cable industry wants all of its subscribers to be digital: bandwidth. Digital cable is conceptually similar to analog cable, in that it is like a big hose filled with television signals. Your set-top box decodes the signal and converts it from digital to analog so you can view the content. But an analog channel on a U.S. cable system occupies 6 MHz. On a digital cable system using 256-QAM, the same 6-MHz channel can carry close to 40 million bits per second. If TV programming is compressed to 3 Mbps, that's at least 13 channels of programming instead of one, even before taking advantage of such techniques as statistical multiplexing. If the cable operator decides to go to 2 Mbps, that's almost 20 channels. And, of course, the exact same 40 million bits per second may also be used for Internet access or telephone service.

Satellite Television

There are about 22 million homes that use Direct Broadcast Satellite receivers (DBS) to consume television (DBS, like cable, sells its services in a hybrid subscription model – you pay, but you also see commercials). Their services are available in places that cable cannot reach, but they also offer several differentiated products to entice consumers, including all digital channels, better navigation, built-in digital video recorders (DVRs) and, in the case of DirecTV, very desirable exclusive programming.

When Ku-band (18" dish) satellite television entered the U.S. marketplace (circa 1994), it enabled people who were outside the practical range of cable to enjoy "cable-like" features, including an expanded channel lineup and better picture quality. In fact, at that time, the pictures were even better than cable. Originally, cable operators offered analog signals to consumers and, although the picture was (in most cases) far better than you could expect from an antenna, the quality was extremely inconsistent (even from room to room). The technical reasons for this are part of the analog vs. digital religious debate and we won't waste time on them here. Suffice it to say, that there was an

---

9. 16-VSB is an abbreviation for 16-level vestigial sideband modulation, capable of transmitting four bits (24=16) at a time.

10. 8-VSB is the 8-level vestigial sideband modulation method adopted for terrestrial broadcast of the ATSC digital television standard in the United States and Canada.

opportunity to provide a better, more consistent viewer experience and satellite's digital technology was its unique selling principle.

> HBO was the first channel to broadcast its signals by satellite in 1975 when they showed the "Thrilla in Manila" boxing match between Muhammad Ali and Joe Frazier. For $1 million per year, HBO leased a transponder on RCA's Satcom 1 and transmitted their programs to cable systems that paid $10,000 for the installation of 3-meter dishes to receive in the C-band. About 5,000 of these C-band Direct-to-Home (DTH) systems were operating by 1980, and by 1985, this number increased to 735,000 while the price of these DTH systems fell to $3,000. Penetration rose to 66 percent of U.S. homes by 1998 through the subscription programming of 11,000 cable systems.[11]

With a digital receiver, you either have a digital quality picture or you do not. The service, like the system, is binary – on or off. So, all other things being equal, when you are receiving a signal, the digital satellite television picture is probably going to look better than an analog cable television picture. Yes, the satellite operators were using an old cable tactic against the cable operators – better picture (and sound) quality. The trade-off was that prior to 1999, it was extremely inconvenient, or impossible, to get local stations through your satellite system.

Not surprisingly, it was the local stations who did not want DBS systems to carry broadcast television signals. The original Satellite Home Viewer Act (SHVA) was supposedly designed to protect the rights of television programs, producers, and broadcasters against unlawful duplication. The real issue, of course, was potential loss of advertising dollars. Local stations had a problem with the idea that distant television network signals (stations that ate into their market share and potentially affected their advertising rate base) were being introduced into the market.

Until the Satellite Home Viewer Improvement Act (SHVIA) in 1999, all DBS operators had a problem providing local television signals to their customers. But since then, DBS companies have been able to offer local channels to over 90% of U.S. television households.

The cable industry sees DBS as its biggest competitor. The business models and consumer value propositions are similar, the quality of service is similar and the cost is similar, as illustrated in the competitive services chart in Figure 1.5. I will touch on the subtle, but substantial, differences between these two distribution methodologies

---

11. Satellite & Cable Television - http://history.acusd.edu/gen/recording/television3.html

throughout the book. But, for the purposes of this discussion, at its most basic level, satellite's hybrid subscription model is indistinguishable from that of cable – you pay a monthly fee and you get some premium channels without commercials but many, many more with commercials.

Pricing Models and Packaging

Broadcast television does not generally offer its products to consumers using a "good, better, best" value/pricing model, but system operators do cater to customers with different needs and different budgets. There's the "premium movie package" or the "platinum bundle" and other offerings to entice consumers to spend more of their media dollars with a specific company. For the most part, these are marketing schemas and do not truly represent the core consumer value propositions of the business.

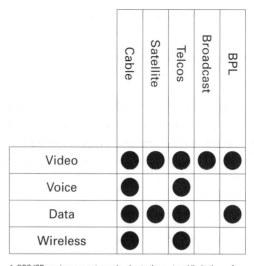

	Cable	Satellite	Telcos	Broadcast	BPL
Video	●	●	●	●	●
Voice	●		●		
Data	●	●	●		●
Wireless	●		●		

1. DBS ISP services are not pupolar due to the cost and limitations of the service. It is used almost exclusively in rural areas where consumers have no other choice.

2. Cable Operators are working with Telephone Companies to create MYNO's so they can offer branded wireless experiences to their customers.

FIGURE 1.5 *Media and Entertainment Competitive Service Matrix.*

When packaging content for consumers, the television business can use several alternative distribution channels (sometimes referred to as "windows," reflecting the sales vehicle's temporal restrictions). Outside of the traditional linear channels, the four most popular ways that content owners purvey their wares to consumers are subscription, pay-per-view, rental and purchase. Each method can be accomplished in a retail environment (yes, theatrical motion pictures are technically pay-per-view) or electronically.

Subscription

There are several organizations that use pure subscription models as revenue streams. The obvious ones are the premium cable services such as HBO, Showtime and Starz. These networks are available through most system operators and versions of their content will be available wherever subscriptions can be sold. They don't sell traditional spot or commercial advertising. However, many of these services have original programming divisions that have robust businesses selling product placement or other types of sponsorship opportunities.

Subscription is often discussed when financially modeling streaming video and some Internet-based businesses. For whatever reason, the only successful pure subscription-based content businesses in America seem to be HBO and the other premium channels (some of which are still all movies, all the time) and businesses that provide one of the "Four G's": girls, God, games and gambling. (A fifth "G," gay, has developed a significant following in recent years.) But, you can simply place the subscription businesses into their actual business categories: pornography, religion, video games (casual and console) and gambling.

Pay-per-view

Pay-per-view (PPV) has been around since the late 1970s. The modern version of PPV is simple: you select a program, pay for it, and watch it. There are several technological versions which we will discuss in more detail later. As business models go, PPV is extremely good for adult movies, pretty good for major sporting events (like boxing) and a nice business for wrestling, extreme fighting, concerts and, of course movies. Depending on the content, the consumer value proposition is a combination of access and convenience.

Rental

Renting content is a relatively new phenomenon in the United States. As a population, we are much more accustomed to owning. However, the advent of the consumer video cassette recorder (VCR) back in the late 1970s created a need and a market for video home system (VHS) video tapes. Sadly, these tapes were extremely expensive to purchase (even by today's standards). It was not unusual for a single movie to have a $79.95 retail price. In the early 1980s, the solution started to appear all over the country in the form of neighborhood video rental shops. By the 1990s, those shops had all but disappeared (at least in major metros) and were replaced by major chains like Blockbuster. Today, the rental market for video still exists although the form factor has changed (DVD's have all but replaced videotapes).

A Word About Physical Copies

There is nothing quite like holding a physical copy of something in your hand: a book, CD, DVD, vinyl record, etc. Physical copies of music, sometimes CONTINUED ▶

CONTINUED ▶   referred to as phonorecords by the copyright office, have been collec-
tor's items for more than a century. And, to look as far back as history will allow, there
was a serious collection of scrolls at the Library of Celsus in the ancient city of Ephesus.
To create a pirate copy of a scroll, all a second-century techno-geek had to do was to
pound a wet mat of woven papyrus into a thin sheet, let it dry in the sun, and find someone who could write.

Through the ages, physical copies of audio and video works have become easier and
easier to copy. In the 21st century, anything that you want to copy can be copied and,
more importantly, distributed at the touch of a button. Are digital video files rentable?
Certainly not in their most basic format. If you want to rent someone a digital video
file, you are going to have to invent packaging for it that combines value, convenience
and security. Sadly, the law of digital conundrums says you can only pick two of those
three attributes.

Purchase

For whatever reason, Americans love to own stuff. We like to own our homes, our
cars, our toys ... we like to own everything. Ownership is the American way. So, it makes
sense that consumers love to own their content. We've been buying sheet music since it
was invented, records since they were invented (although now they are practically
antiques) and, as soon as they were cheap enough — videos. Home video promotions
are everywhere. The Walt Disney Company is committed to reselling every title in its
library in every possible form factor: "This is a once in a lifetime chance to own 'Snow
White.' Get it today before it goes back in the vault forever." And, for $19.95
(discounted with an instant $5.00 rebate and with the coupon for two free bottles of
Pepsi), you will run to your local convenience store and pick it up.

As a consumer business model, purchasing is extremely strong. But it is increas-
ingly becoming a very dangerous proposition for content owners because physical
copies can be easily converted to digital files. Once a piece of content is converted to
an unencrypted digital file format, it is absolutely impossible to protect it. This is an
absolute truth. Yes, there are people who will pay for the convenience of having a
professional re-format content for a particular device. Yes, there are people who will be
happy to pay for a piece of content multiple times. But, at some point in the very near
future, a legally protected, copyrighted file of a piece of "evergreen" material will – as
a practical matter – become public domain.

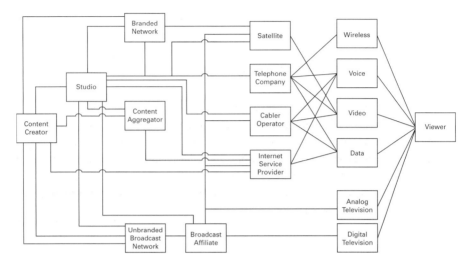

FIGURE 1.6 *From content creator to viewer via multi-channel program distributors, broadcasters and ISPs.*

System Operators

In this book, we will be spending quite a bit of time thinking about how consumers get to consume content, so it is instructive to study the diagram in Figure 1.6 and to truly understand the simplest version of the system operator world.

The first box on the left side of the diagram represents the original content and the people who create it. They can sell their wares to studios (Warner Bros, NBC/Universal, Paramount, etc.), directly to unbranded broadcast networks (NBC, ABC, CBS, FOX, etc.), to branded networks (MTV, ESPN, FOODTV, CNN, etc.) or to content aggregators who wholesale on-demand or broadband content.

Content can follow the old-fashioned, network path to the viewer from broadcast network to broadcast affiliate over the air to a rooftop antenna, but that is not how most people get their television media. Today, most households subscribe to a system operator (cable operator, satellite system or telco) to receive a combination of video, voice and data services. You should also notice the expanded role of the Internet Service Provider (ISP) in this diagram. They can be an excellent source of rich media content for consumers. I'll use variations of this diagram throughout the book to illustrate changes in the industry.

Big Media

The television business in the Untied States is dominated by a few very large companies. NBC/Universal, Disney, News Corp, Viacom and Time Warner respectively represent the television networks NBC, ABC, FOX, CBS and CW (which is a joint venture between Viacom and Time Warner). Depending upon who you ask, you will hear chapter and verse about how "good" or "bad" consolidation has been for the business. It's a meaningless topic — the business is overwhelmingly controlled by these corporations and will be for quite some time. The results of consolidation are easy to see in the business press, but they are less obvious — but probably more important — when consumers change television channels.

Television Business Components

There are three major components of the media business: form factors, packaging and distribution. Let's look at these components separately so we can use this nomenclature to describe how they combine to create value chains.

Form Factors

Although there are literally hundreds of media form factors, for television they fall into four main categories: shows, commercials, physical copies and master files. Other entertainment businesses have form factors too: books, newspapers, magazines, digests, photographs, portraits, paintings, concerts, plays, etc.

The most popular video content form factors are:

- Television shows (from 30 to 120 minutes or longer)

- Theatrical motion pictures (generally more than 90 minutes)

- Television commercials and promos (between 5 and 120 seconds)

- Advanced media formats (telescopes, showcases, pause trigger, speed bumps, etc.)

- Physical copy (DVD, phonorecord, CD, DualDisc, etc.)

- Master file (.wav, .mpg, .wmv, etc.)

Packaging

Modern television uses dozens of different business models to package and monetize form factors. They fall into several categories, including: playout attributes (schedule, dayparts), specific formats for commercial units and programming, etc. You package a form factor to make it salable.

The most popular television packaging options are:

- Linear day-parts (early morning, daytime, family time, prime time access, etc.)

- Pay Per View

- On-demand

- Subscription

- Ad-supported

Distribution

Traditional network television was developed to deliver linear programming using a fairly efficient one-to-many system. Alternatively, networked television systems offer one-to-one and optionally, non-linear distribution.

Linear Distribution Methodology

- Broadcast television – analog or DTT

- Cable Television – basic or premium

- Satellite television

- Internet Protocol Television (IPTV)

- IP Video

- Public Internet

Non-Linear Distribution Methodology

- Video On Demand (VOD, SVOD, FVOD, Near-VOD)

- Consumer-based time-shifted (personal video recorder, TiVo®, Media Center)

Technically speaking, all of the linear methodologies could be used to distribute non-linear programming as well. But in common practice, only cable, IPTV and the Internet are used to do so.

Linear Video – Good "Old-Fashioned" TV

Linear video for television (analog broadcast or DTT) and cable (basic or premium) is what most people think of as "good old-fashioned TV." Linear channels and networks can be found on all broadcast television stations, cable, satellite and IPTV systems. The unique attribute of linear television is that it is scheduled for you by the network or station programmers. Marketers sometimes refer to linear programming as "destination television" because you are supposed to watch the program when it is presented. (Of course, consumers don't always do what they're supposed to do.) When distributed over traditional networks, linear television is still the most efficient way to distribute emerging news stories, evolving stories that need continuous coverage, sports and other live events.

Since almost the beginning of the commercial television business, the industry has relied on two kinds of distribution licenses for linear video, "exclusive" and "non-exclusive." Exclusive distribution deals almost always define two specific conditions: duration of the exclusivity (window) and the geographic area (territory). Up to now, the temporal and geographic restrictions were significant and negotiable, but not unreasonably hard to define. For example: you can air 13 episodes of this particular show, nationwide on free over-the-air and basic cable/satellite from September to May of this year. You are entitled to re-run each episode two times during that period in the territory of the United States and traditional overlap areas.

The language of network television must transition along with the technology. The business needs new common currency, common packaging and new nomenclature to describe them.

These business rules evolved over the past half century. Show lengths (the form factor) became standardized in thirty-minute increments and dayparts (the packaging) were identified and named (morning, daytime, primetime, primetime access, fringe, late night, family time, etc.) Program categories matured and became part of our pop culture. Up to now, the only way to think about programs was in terms of "genre" (what they were) and "shelf space" (when they might air). When pitching a new program, the title of the presentation will often include a one-line subtitle like: "A one-hour, weekly, afternoon talk show" or "A half-hour, morning strip" (Strip shows air five days in a row and are said to be stripped across the schedule).

As George Bernard Shaw once said, "Every profession is a conspiracy against the laity." And, although it is true throughout this book, it is most ironic here, because in this case, the nomenclature is a conspiracy against the business itself.

The reason for this conspiracy is that every program director and producer (buyer and seller) in the television business thinks about the content in terms of its form factor, its packaging and its distribution. "This is a 'half-hour strip" — it can play in syndication from 10 a.m. until the noon news on an O&O and anywhere from 9 a.m. to noon on affiliates that don't run a three-hour network morning show." This conception of how the business works gets even more complicated when you add advertising units to the mix. The programming content of a half-hour show is actually 20 to 22 minutes in length. The remaining 8 to 10 minutes are used for advertising and promotion.

Advertising form factors come in lengths from five seconds to two minutes. A 30-second commercial is the standard "unit" and you will often hear industry veterans speaking about having some number of "units per show" to sell. For example: a "7/7 barter" split usually refers to a half hour show delivered to a station for free with seven units of advertising included from the syndicator or producer and seven units for the station to sell. Again, the entire business is based on the form factors, packaging and distribution methodology of television.

This is not just industry lingo. It is the actual currency of the television business. Industry professionals fully understand the value propositions of each of the common form factors, packages and distribution methodologies. They also understand the way the success of any particular endeavor is to be measured. ROI can take the form of ratings, brand awareness, sales lift, purchase intent, transaction or any combination thereof, but in all cases it is the common nomenclature and common packaging that enables commerce.

Random-Access Video – Good "New-Fashioned" TV

Thinking about television in terms of shelf space and dayparts is not a good way to approach networked television. In a playlist-based or on-demand world, the concepts have no meaning. How should we start to think about programming and advertising for networked television? If the show is the smallest cohesive unit of programming, then we must think about shows and the segments from which they are built. We must also consider promos and soundbites as meaningful units of communication.

Here we have a true obstacle. There are no common form factors, packaging or distribution methodologies for random-access or on-demand video. And, because of this, there is no common currency to do business with. To move the industry forward, we are going to have to develop nomenclature, measurement standards and a way to associate value with each of the component parts, thereby creating the "currency" of networked television.

One last point: people acquire video in a linear fashion, no matter how the video is stored, sliced or diced before it is presented. You can start, stop, pause and fast forward all you like, but in the end, if you are going to watch a video, it's going to be a linear presentation with a beginning, middle and ending.

This is the perfect segue into our exploration of the technologies that are most likely to disrupt the current financial models of the television industry. Over the next few chapters we will look at technologies that are being added to existing networks to enhance their value to consumers, and technologies that are offering alternative viewing and advertising experiences over the Internet. Then, we shall focus on the disruptive qualities of wireless networks and devices.

Key Takeaways

- There are two basic television business models: free (ad supported) and subscription.

- There are approximately 110 million television households in the United States. Between 85 and 88 percent are covered by cable and satellite, while approximately 12 to 15 percent are antenna-only broadcast homes.

- The FCC has mandated that all broadcast television be converted from analog to digital by early 2009, though this date will likely change.

- Nielsen DMAs roughly correspond to the broadcast coverage areas of television stations and there are approximately 1,400 commercial television stations in the United States.

- Because cable systems and satellite systems offer similar services, they fiercely compete for subscribers.

- Television content is packaged in one of these basic ways: free, hybrid subscription, pure subscription, pay-per-view, rental and purchase.

- The major components of the television business are form factors, packaging and distribution.

- Linear programming is scheduled for consumers, Non-linear programming is on-demand.

- There are highly evolved business rules and negotiable currencies used in the traditional television business, and these must evolve for networked, non-linear or on-demand businesses

2 Disrupting Television Using Existing Network Technologies

In this chapter, let's use the term "disruptive technology" to describe a system or methodology that allows the viewer to take control away from the programmers or distributors. Until the transition to networked television is substantially complete, the more control that consumers can exercise over their media, the less control the distributor is likely to have over the value chain. This imbalance is creating a challenge and an opportunity for the marketplace. The challenge is maintaining the relatively high income levels currently enjoyed by big media. The opportunity is for new business models and technologies to evolve that will shift the business paradigm.

Overview of Network and Networked Television

A quick review of the differences between network and networked television distribution is in order here. Then we can examine how the various technologies enhance the consumer experience while disrupting the time-honored financial models.

As we discussed in the Chapter 1, with a traditional network (broadcast or cable), when you tune in Channel 2, you are selecting one particular frequency, thereby ignoring all of the rest of the available frequencies. You may have hundreds of frequencies to choose from or just a few, but in every case they are all available to you all the time. The system operators push out signals and viewers with appropriate tuners tune them in at their convenience, as shown in Figure 2.1. Similarly, a rooftop antenna picks

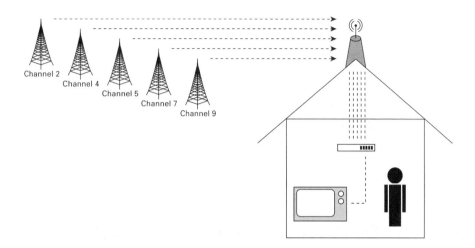

FIGURE 2.1 *Multiple network television signals can be received from one or many different towers at the same time; your television tuner lets you select the signal you want to watch. If you were to replace the towers and rooftop antenna with a cable, this diagram would be (more or less) depicting a traditional multi-channel cable system.*

up signals from all of the television transmitters in your area at the same time. Another way to think about this is that while selecting a particular channel to watch, consumers are deselecting all of the other available channels.

In a networked or IP-provisioned ("switched") system, you are getting only the data that is needed for the viewing experience you have chosen, rather than simply ignoring the "deselected" channels. As seen in Figure 2.2, this system is significantly more

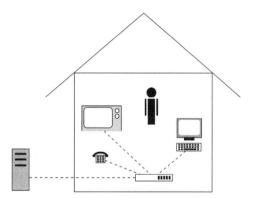

FIGURE 2.2 *A networked system uses bandwidth very efficiently since it only sends the digital data you need when you need it.*

efficient (from a bandwidth perspective) than traditional network infrastructure — although bandwidth efficiency does not necessarily equate to network efficiency.

Which system is better? Each system has strengths and weaknesses. Let's think of network vs. networked as "broadcast" vs. "on-demand." Consider how two different movie theaters might use the telephone to communicate with you. For a one-screen movie theater, a "broadcast" announcement that says, "Star Wars is showing at noon,

4 p.m., 8 p.m. and 10:30 p.m.; tickets are $10 each" is much more efficient than, "Press one for movie titles, press two for show times, press three for ticket prices." However, for a 15-screen multiplex, the "press-one-for ...," or "on-demand" announcements, make much more sense. Similarly, for shows like the Super Bowl, broadcast is the most efficient model. For an obscure piece of content like "Remlap's Sonata for Krumhorn," an on-demand system makes more sense. Of course, nothing in the real world is ever this cut and dried. In a networked system, viewing habits matter more than the number of channels available. For example, a household with two analog televisions and a dual-tuner DVR would require about one-fifth the bandwidth of a household with a single, heavy HDTV viewer.

Value-added Services Enhance the Viewing Experience

There are several technologies that are offered over, connected to or used in conjunction with traditional networks (broadcast, system operators and CDNs) with the goal of enhancing their consumer value propositions. It is the law of unintended consequences that makes them disruptive. These technologies include on-demand services, digital set-top boxes, digital video recorders, and interactive or enhanced television.

IPTV

One of the most misused terms in the business is IPTV. It stands for Internet Protocol Television. IPTV is not television using the Internet. It is television using Internet Protocol — an alternative method of distribution — a transport mechanism, nothing more. When deployed over private networks, the systems are not open to the public any more than a cable set-top box from a cable operator is open to the public.

Operator-deployed IPTV systems are designed to be walled gardens. (A walled garden, with regards to media content, refers to a closed set or exclusive set of information services provided for users. This is in contrast to providing consumer's access to the open Internet for content and e-commerce.) These IP-provisioned systems will be used by operators to achieve optimum bandwidth efficiencies while freeing up additional bandwidth to be used to provide a combination of television-like services, on-demand content, broadband connections, and Voice over Internet Protocol (VoIP telephone service) over a private, inherently interactive, two-way network. It is unlikely that a major system operator would choose to provide IPTV over the public Internet, at least not in the short term. There are too many quality of service (QOS) concerns; to say nothing of the problems with hacking and piracy.

Quality of Service

"What is your tolerance for rebooting your television set?" It would help to know the quality of service rating on the equipment.

Name	Percentage	Outage Per Year
3 Nines	99.9	8 hours, 49 minutes of outage per year
4 Nines	99.99	53 minutes of outage per year
5 Nines	99.999	5 minutes of outage per year

Commonly referred to as Three Nines, Four Nines and Five Nines, all telecommunications and electronics manufacturing companies use some version of this benchmark to determine the quality of their services.

It is probably more accurate to call IPTV over the public Internet "streaming video." In this book we will call it IP video, and Chapter 3 covers it in more detail. There are very few stand-alone or third party set-top box solutions in common use that display IPTV signals found on the public Internet. Those that are out there face the same challenges all new technologies have: distribution, cost-per-subscriber, and the aggregation of desirable content, to name a few.

Television provides a pretty good television experience. For broadcast business models, it is extremely efficient.

Many telcos have deployed IPTV-based television services. Some analysts predict that telco IPTV will ultimately enjoy a 20 percent market share. The telcos are hoping for over 25 percent of course, and cynics are saying it will level out somewhere in the 10 percent range. If the big telcos survive the build-out, we may see increased competition for features and significant downward price pressure on bundled services. We can also expect new, exclusive programming and a real effort to differentiate the telco IPTV product from other consumer media services.

Are we likely to see an IPTV product that mimics the current television experience utilizing the public Internet? We might, but it's highly doubtful. Television provides a pretty good television experience and for broadcast business models, it is extremely efficient.

IPTV should be as different an experience from television as television is from radio.

On the other hand, IPTV does offer an inherent two-way system that allows for census-based measurements and true transactional user experiences. These features are theoretically desirable and may give a competitive advantage to the companies that utilize IPTV distribution methodologies — or they could simply become commoditized or value-add feature sets that have no economic impact. It depends on how quickly IP-provisioned systems are deployed nationwide.

When thinking about disruptive technologies, keep in mind that sometimes existing technologies can be modified or adapted to compete effectively. This is the very definition of an arms race. Existing digital cable systems outnumber IPTV systems by several orders of magnitude. It unreasonable to assume that if there is a competitive advantage to any of the easily mimicked services of IPTV, that cable will not deploy a service that consumers might value over the option of switching service providers. More importantly, all system operators are equally interested and able to utilize IPTV as a delivery system for their content. Since losing customers is enemy number one for every cable company, we are not likely to see a time where cable operators let the telcos get too technologically far ahead.

Is the future of IPTV that limited? No. There are several models where IPTV systems will be used to create new audiences and new value chains utilizing upcoming video game platforms and portable video devices. Won't that change everything? No, it will change some things and the model cannot be built upon the current "me too" versions of IPTV in form or function. The new models will be more akin to aggregated Web sites than they will be to cable, satellite, or broadcast television systems. And, they should be as different an experience from television as television is from radio. In the meantime, let us not confuse "video over the public Internet" with "IPTV systems from the cable and telecommunications industries" — they just don't overlap.

Video On Demand (VOD)

The business models that are being proposed for VOD have the potential to seriously disrupt television, but the technology itself is actually interruptive. For all intents and purposes, you can think of VOD as "random access" television. Video is stored on a hard drive locally or on a server at a remote location; consumers can access any program at any time. These systems, when deployed by operators, are still walled gardens and programming, although time-shifted by the viewer, can be geographically controlled and temporally windowed by the rights holders. (In this case, the temporal window is measured as the time that a particular piece of content will be available on a given system, not the time of day it is to be viewed. Although, it is possible to restrict viewing of any video to a particular daypart, it generally doesn't make sense to do so.)

Other types of on demand business models include subscription video on demand (SVOD), free video on demand (FVOD) and near-video on demand (NVOD). NVOD is commonly found on satellite systems and older cable systems. This is where a PPV movie will be available on several different channels starting 30 minutes apart. It allows you to purchase the video and then wait no more than 30 minutes for it to begin. Some consumers actually like it better than VOD because it gives them time to go get their snacks together, use the rest room and prepare to watch a long-form piece. This last point is an important one. As we think about the transition from one technology to another, we must always keep in mind that consumer behavior is not always designable, nor do consumers tend to use technology as designed.

No one really knows if consumers like on-demand services on a full-time basis. The programming guides are tough to navigate and it's hard to discover new stuff the way VOD content is generally presented. It is easy to hypothesize that as soon as these problems are addressed, we will see a massive consumer acceptance of VOD. This would be a mistake. It is unclear whether this technology is sufficient to inspire a change in the learned viewing habits of several existing generations of television viewers. If this is a technology that only appeals to digital natives (kids born into the digital age), it may not be a particularly profitable short-term business.

To that end, there is much angst over the future of traditional television advertising associated with time-shifted viewing because it is extremely easy to fast-forward through any unwanted content. Absolutely no one knows what the average VOD user's tolerance for advertising might be. If you are going to the trouble of selecting your programming, will you want to watch a commercial? If so, what type would you be willing to watch? We'll discuss some probable futures for VOD advertising form factors in Chapter 10.

Consumer-Based Time-Shifted Television

What could be more disruptive to the business of television than putting complete control of television media into the consumer's hands? However, consumer-based time-shifted television (digital video recorders, TiVo, Media Center) is so similar to VOD that many consumers do not understand the difference between the two technologies. Digital video recorders (DVRs), also commonly called personal video recorders (PVRs), are devices that record random-access video to a hard drive. (For non-technical people, they are computers that look like set-top boxes, work like VCRs and have some cool extra features.)

The value proposition of DVR technology is that you can choose to record anything that is available on your system (broadcast, cable, satellite, IPTV, etc) and play it back whenever you wish. Content that is available to DVRs that are provided by system operators usually include some kind of rudimentary copy protection schema even if it is simply to disable certain outputs from the set-top box. On the other hand, third-party DVRs (which may include software running on a game console, PC or dedicated media center) can almost always accept and play back media obtained from anywhere. It is this system operator-bypass that is undermining the current business models in the extreme.

Consumer DVRs hit the market in 1999 when TiVo and rival ReplayTV introduced their first-generation boxes at the Consumer Electronics Show (CES). Far from being an instant success, the technology fascinated geeks, scared the hell out of commercial television executives and confused consumers; the latter being of utmost significance. Consumers just didn't get why they would need one. Ironically, now that DVRs are more widespread, the majority of people who have one say, "It changed the way I watch television." True enough, but communicating that value proposition to consumers remains an uphill battle to this day.

DVRs have been blamed by many television and advertising executives for the "death of the :30 second spot." First of all, the :30 second spot is not dead ... far from it! And, DVR technology is not the reason, nor is it the primary way, that American television viewers skip commercials. We will cover commercial skipping more fully in Chapter 10.

The Impact of Time-Shifted, Networked Television

"Where do you see this show?" said the program director to the producer. "Is it a daytime or primetime, perhaps late fringe or family time ... late night or a morning show?" In a time-shifted, networked world, these programming concepts and the financial models associated with them will cease to be relevant.

Since the Golden Age of Television, the television show has been the branded store of economic value for the industry. Network line-ups are solutions to technological restrictions, and they are forms that follow function. Given a choice, consumers will always choose to watch the shows they like, not the networks that carry them. This is why the "a la carte" cable arguments seem so unenlightened to people who believe in the near-term future of on-demand distribution. You will not distribute networks on-demand, you will distribute shows. By definition, all on-demand television is served "a la carte."

How will television networks survive? Actually, they will do just fine. There is much more to creating a successful television experience for consumers then creating linear playlists for dayparts. However, there may be a significant shift in the way money changes hands – on-demand content can come from many different sources –and the power will be in the promotion and long-term business relationships enjoyed by the networks.

The Death of the Walled Garden

Winston Churchill once said, "The farther you look back, the further you can see into the future." We don't have to look too far back to remember America Online's (AOL) humble beginnings as an online service. For those of you who were not tech-savvy in the early days of the Internet, the difference between the public Internet and an online service were profound.

The Internet

The public Internet was first proposed by J.C.R. Licklider of MIT in the early 1960s. It was conceived as a global network of computers to allow the sharing of scientific and military research. The project was conscripted by the Defense Advanced Research Project Agency (DARPA) in late 1962 and through the work of several now legendary scientists, like Lawrence Roberts, Leonard Kleinrock and Bob Kahn, evolved into the global network of computers it is today. That network, now called the Internet (or simply, the Net) is the transport system that packets of data travel over. Your e-mail, music and video files all live on individual storage devices (like the hard drive in your computer) and get from place to place over the public Internet.

This is not to be confused with the World Wide Web. In 1989, Tim Berners-Lee and a group of other big brains at the European Laboratory for Particle Physics (usually referred to as CERN) proposed the protocol that we now know as HTTP (Hypertext Transfer Protocol) and in 1991 the first World Wide Web pages or Web sites were put online using HTML (Hypertext Markup Language) which is still an extremely popular language for the creation of Web pages. In 1993, Marc Andreessen and his soon-to-be-extraordinarily-rich teammates at the National Center for Supercomputing Applications (NCSA) launched a browser called Mosaic (ultimately Netscape), which became the most popular Web browser until Bill Gates woke up and realized that Microsoft totally missed the evolution of the Internet and the World Wide Web. It didn't take Microsoft very long to corner the browser market with Internet Explorer, which is still the most popular browser in the world today.

Back in late 1992, the world was about to start moving at Internet speed. Delphi launched the first commercial online service. Although it had a workable e-mail client, it was still only truly suitable for early adopters.

For most consumers, the modern Internet Era starts circa 1995 with AOL, Prodigy and CompuServe. These were online services which did not use the public Internet. In those days, you dialed a number provided by the service and you entered a walled garden.

In AOL's walled garden, you could send and receive e-mail and you could find graphical pages that looked very much like Web pages, but they weren't. They were simply pages created by AOL to look like the Web. In the early days, this really didn't bother most people. You could hear perfectly smart people at cocktail parties all over America asking if you could "get something on AOL." AOL spent a great deal of time creating thousands of landing pages on thousands of different subjects. In fact, they had quite a nice business selling keywords. If you remember the early days of AOL, you couldn't type a URL (Uniform Resource Locator) into the address bar; you could only type an AOL keyword.

When, if ever, will Internet-provisioned systems operators be forced to open up their walled gardens?

Back then, the term keyword had a slightly different meaning. AOL assigned keywords to companies and products and sold them as direct addresses. So, AOL keyword LAWSCHOOL would take you to a custom micro-site developed for Kaplan Online/LSAT Law School. Type that same word into Google or AOL today and you'll get a list of 433,000 some-odd Web pages. AOL sold ads on major landing pages like EDUCATION and, as with the example above, created pages or micro-sites that looked like a client's Web site so that AOL users would think that they were actually on the Web. It was a very good trick.

This business model lasted a while. But, ultimately, it was doomed. The same people at the same cocktail parties started asking a question that by today's standards seems incredibly stupid, but back then demonstrated the power of marketing, "Can I get that on Netscape?" A question like that makes you shake your head today, but back in the mid to late 90s, a semi-disgruntled AOL user would have no way of knowing the vastness of the World Wide Web because their entire experience had been in the walled garden of AOL.

Dial-up users (in fairly large numbers) started to realize that you could use AOL to connect to the "real" Internet by simply using the AOL dialer and then opening up a browser (like Netscape or IE). Within a very short time, AOL was forced to let its customers enter URLs in the address bar that was formerly used only for AOL keywords. They had no choice. It was either open the walled garden or lose a significant part of their customer base. There is much more to learn from looking at AOL's journey, but now we must relate this learning to the present example.

It was a combination of market pressure and technological advancement that forced AOL to change its business rules. They simply didn't have a choice. Which begs the question, "When, if ever, will this fate befall the cable operators and IPTV operators?" Will there come a time when consumers have so many media choices outside the walled gardens of their cable or IPTV operators that they actually threaten the practical monopolies that the biggest media companies enjoy?

We can easily imagine a day when market pressure on the system operators is so great that they are forced to open up their walled gardens and let consumers experience all of the content that the Internet, Web and mesh networks have to offer. But, other technologies may solve this problem for consumers way before the system operators open the gates. Wireless networks, simple A/B switches and alternative wired competitors will offer early adopters enough choices to "move the needle" a bit. The two big questions are: When will the average consumer feel that they truly need access to the outside world? And, what – if anything – will the system operators do about it?

Interactive and Enhanced Television

Interactive television is, quite possibly, the most loosely applied term in the media business. It means so many different things to so many different people that recounting them all would require a separate writing! One of the earliest, and most annoying, interpretations of interactive television is the concept of "clicking on Jennifer Aniston's sweater." This hypothetical situation occurs when you are watching an episode of "Friends" on linear television and Aniston enters the picture wearing a fantastic sweater. You are supposed to pick up your remote control and click on it to activate the hypothetical interactive transactional engine (t-commerce engine) that will magically bring you all of the information you could ever want to know about the sweater and also allow you to buy it with one click. Ugh! This is only outdone by the popular favorite, "pick your own ending" for a dramatic hour or other type of show by clicking on one of three choices. Double-ugh! We will not speak of these absolutely ridiculous concepts again.

People are not trained to interrupt their viewing experience to interact with television shows and, for the most part, will not do it — no matter what the value proposition is. (We will talk about the concepts of lean-backward and lean-forward in chapter 4.) What people will do is react to television shows or, under certain circumstances, interact with an additional device that is more suited to the purpose of interaction while watching television. Here we are making a distinction between television (the technology) and television shows (the programming that people watch television for in the first place).

Over television (the technology), the concept of interactivity is as simple a picking up the remote control and changing channels. Any time a consumer takes control of their media, they are interacting with it. If the system has an intelligence layer and is smart enough to log and analyze the behavior, it is possible to offer excellent value back to the consumer in the form of collaborative filtering (recommending other shows he or she might find interesting) or simply using the data to offer dynamically created media experiences to the viewer. This level of interactivity does not ask the consumer to adopt any behavior that is out of the norm of the conventions of "couch potato-ing" and the technology is all but transparent to the consumer.

Then, there is the concept of enhanced television. In this case there are two methods which have enjoyed moderate success: one-screen and two-screen. One-screen enhanced television may include game play, information gathering, text or data services, additional rich media overlays, or any combination of any of these attributes all as part of a single-screen user experience. In this case, the single screen may be a television set, but it is just as likely to be a media center computer with a remote control. The difference between one-screen enhanced and one-screen interactive television is that enhanced television is usually a service that enhances a linear television programming experience and interactive television may just be part of a grid guide or other graphical user interface that allows the user to manipulate and value-add to their television experience.

Two-screen enhanced television uses a combination of a personal computer and a television set or a mobile device and a television set to allow viewers/users to interact with the programming. The enhanced programming experience can include literally anything that can be displayed on a computer screen in relative synchronicity with the television programming. Popular versions include fantasy football, voting and polling, home game play in sync with game shows, and live communities of interest developed around a show.

These early attempts at enhancements and interactivity are specifically built around the limitations of the existing network infrastructure. And, to achieve the relative levels of success that they currently enjoy, many compromises had to be made. For example: Most linear network programmers are very concerned with lead-in and lead-out (the sequencing of program to program in a line-up). The idea that a potential eyeball might be taken away from the next show completely prevents the programming department from sanctioning any programming enhancements that might offer additional information or program material, since accessing that material might impact ratings of the subsequent linear show. Obviously, these agendas are at cross purposes. Additionally, a great time to enhance a show is during a commercial break when most people are not paying attention anyway … oops! That's not really going to fly with network advertising executives. Of course, you can use the enhancements to help call attention to the advertisements just as easily as you can with the linear programming content. This actually works and, for the limited number of people who enjoy playing enhanced television games, is more effective than its pure linear counterpart. On the other hand, the enhancements that create the best user experiences are extremely disruptive to the financial model of network television. So, the idea of enhancing a show on a linear network or truly making it interactive is a better theory than reality. This is not going to change — ever!

What will change is the current network television model. The closer we get to an on-demand world, the closer we will come to networked television. And, the closer we get to networked television, the more important enhanced features and true interactivity will become.

Key Takeaways

- Consumer behavior is not designable, nor do consumers tend to use technology as designed.

- There are several probable futures where IPTV systems may be used to create new audiences and new value chains utilizing upcoming video game platforms and portable video devices.

- Consumer-based time-shifted television (DVRs, TiVo, Media Center) is so similar to VOD that many consumers do not understand the difference between the two technologies.

- There is much more to creating a successful television experience for consumers then creating linear playlists for dayparts. The network's power is their ability to promote their shows and their business relationships.

- At some point, system operators that provide IPTV systems over private networks may have to make the public Internet available through these systems.

3 Internet

On many levels, the Internet is becoming a meaningful threat to television's *status quo*. One could cite many reasons, but the two most prominent are democratized packaging and ubiquitous distribution. When taken together, they can exert a formidable disruptive force.

Packaging: Physical copies of content are easily converted (encoded, digitized, meta-tagged and stored) to digital files. To a computer, a file is a file is a file. Computers don't distinguish between audio or video or text or graphics, or anything else for that matter. A computer file can be very well protected – right up until the time that the media is used, seen or heard – at that point, it becomes virtually unprotectable. Unencrypted computer files might be thought of as the "final" form factor – once on the Internet, they are free for anyone who wants them.

Distribution: Broadband users have a fairly robust network with virtually worldwide distribution capabilities at their fingertips. As broadband penetration achieves critical mass, its value as a distribution technology is starting to rival (or even possibly exceed) that of the traditional network infrastructures. The value-add is two-way interactivity and the consumer relationship marketing (CRM) opportunities that accompany broadband. When you add video capability to this high-speed, two-way network, you start to see the foundation for a new generation of networked television technologies.

Broadband and IP Video

Broadband is defined by engineers to mean data transmission where multiple bits of data are sent simultaneously at different frequencies to increase the effective rate of transmission. Although this is the proper technical definition, most people are non-technical and don't use broadband as a term-of-art. So, for our purposes, we'll use the word broadband in a non-technical way to describe a relatively large, fast connection to a computer network or to the Internet.

Consumer broadband or "high speed" connections are available from several different sources. Here's a short list of the most popular telecommunications system formats:

- from telephone companies over digital subscriber lines (DSL)

- from cable operators over their existing cable infrastructures using a Data Over Cable Service Interface Specification (DOCSIS) modems to provide the connection

- from power companies using a system called broadband over power lines (BPL)

- from various wireless providers (some of whom are telephone companies) using systems like WiFi (802.11 specification) and WiMax (802.16 specification) and Evolution Data Optimized (EVDO)

But, by definition, the list is incomplete. Telecommunications companies are constantly working to upgrade and improve their systems.

There are also several types of fiber optic connections available: Fiber to the Premises (FTTP) or Fiber to the Home (FTTH) which are actually necessary for telephone companies (telcos) entering the IPTV business. And finally, there are industrial classes of service known as OC-carriers (Optical Carriers), T-carriers (E-carriers in Europe) and Digital Signals (DS), the generic descriptors for many classes of multiplexed telecommunications systems.

To view streaming video files, speak on a VoIP telephone, surf the net, watch some IPTV and play a network-based video game all at the same time, you need a very fast connection.

As you can imagine, each provider and their resellers have different grades of service, different qualities of service and, most importantly, different prices of service.

When you are browsing the Internet, you will not notice the difference between a 6 Mbps and 60 Mbps connection unless you have a blindingly fast computer equipped with a well-cached, professional-grade video card. However, if you are going to upload and download very large files (like video files) in real or faster than real time, you need the fastest connection possible. More to my point, if you wish to view streaming video files, speak on a VoIP telephone, surf the net, watch some IPTV and play a network-based video game all at the same time, you need a very fast connection.

Big "B" vs. Little "b": A short story about bits and bytes

A bit is a single character of data (a "0" or a "1"). A byte is eight characters of data. Therefore, eight bits make a byte. Megabits are abbreviated Mbps (notice the small "b"); megabytes are abbreviated MBps or simply MB (notice the big "B"). The math is very simple: 1 byte equals 8 bits, therefore: 1 MBps = 8 Mbps.

Just to complicate matters, networking hardware (like a network card or a router) is typically rated in Mbps (megabits). Confusingly, many computer peripherals (like hard disks and memory) are rated in MBps (megabytes). So, to transfer a file from your computer to a remote hard disk at 100MBps (megabytes), you would need an 800Mbps (megabits) network.

IP Video, Streaming Media and Progressive Downloads

In 1995, Xing Technology Corporation (acquired by RealNetworks on August 10, 1999) developed StreamWorks, the first live and on-demand audio/video delivery system over the Internet, also known as "streaming technology." Within a few years, RTSP (Real Time Streaming Protocol) servers were serving streams of live and pre-recorded digital audio and video files over the Internet. Streaming files are not downloaded to the user's computer; they are only made available for temporary viewing (sort of like traditional television). That being said, you can easily restart any audio or video stream and view the file as often as the rights-holder will allow.

Although often lumped into the same category, this is a very different technology than audio (.mp3) or video (.avi or .mov) files that can be progressively downloaded and viewed with media player software. A file that is progressively downloaded can be viewed after a portion of the file (but not necessarily the entire file) has been downloaded to your computer. It is possible to encrypt such a file with certain DRM restrictions, but it is not commonplace. Unlike a "stream," a "download" (progressive or otherwise) can be shared, e-mailed or otherwise distributed by uploading it to a server or making your hard drive available to a P2P network.

All of these technologies are collectively known as Internet Protocol Video (IP video) and they should not be confused with IPTV which we discussed in Chapter 2.

IP video is extremely popular. Almost every "rich media" Web site offers some kind of streaming media experience. There are hundreds of content aggregation sites that specialize in specific genres or cater to niche audiences with streaming audio or video offerings. Although a detailed description of all of the available media players is outside the scope of this work, you should be familiar with Windows Media Player, Apple QuickTime, Real One Player and some of the Flash and Java-based media players that are currently in use.

IP video has been hard for most rights-holders to monetize. The adult video industry has perfected both micro-payment and subscription models, but people don't seem to be willing to pay for other types of content using these financial models. What you mostly see with IP video offerings is a free-per-view model with traditional Web-based advertising surrounding it. This works well if the design of the Web site includes an embedded media player. In the best examples, the content (both the IP video and the Web page) is dynamically generated to achieve maximum audience relevance. Due to the graphic design and the intended purpose of windowed media players (media players that float as self-contained units in a computer screen window), they do not often lend themselves to the aesthetically pleasing or even meaningfully noticeable display of ordinary banner or billboard-style ads.

This makes the "real estate" around the player harder, though not impossible, to monetize with traditional Web advertisements. Obviously, there are several different types of media players and they can be designed in as many ways a people can imagine them. But that has not changed the financial reality. Outside of the four "Gs" (girls, God, gaming and gambling), the value of IP video is its ability to enhance marketing programs, offer additional pre-sales information, create consumer touch points, promote goods and services, and enable communities of interest.

IP video is disruptive to traditional networks when used to distribute original content in a one-to-one interactive environment. We are just beginning to enjoy and understand the benefits of this technology. As portable personal video is woven into the fabric of our lives (as well as the lives of a new generation of digital natives), the possibilities seem endless.

File Types and Extensions

There are literally dozens of popular computer file formats. Some require special software to open or for playback, others will open or play natively on personal computers.

Video

- .avi - Windows Media Format
- .m4p - MPEG 4 (iPod Video Format)
- .mov - Apple Quicktime Format

CONTINUED ▶

CONTINUED ▶

- .mpg (.mpeg) – Motion Pictures Experts Group
- .qt - Apple QuickTime Format
- .ram – Real Audio Media Format (Used for video too)
- .swf – Macromedia Flash Format
- .wmv – Windows Media Video Format

Audio:

- .aac – Advanced Audio Coding by Fraunhofer Institut
- .aif – Audio Interchange Format (Apple audio format)
- .mid – Midi (Musical Instrument Digital Interface)
- .mp3 – MPEG 1 Audio Layer 3
- .ra – Real Audio
- .wav – Wave File
- .wma – Windows Media Audio

Photo:

- .eps – Encapsulated Post Script
- .gif – Graphics Interchange Format
- .jpg – Joint Photographic Experts Group
- .png – Portable Network Graphics
- .psd – Adobe Photoshop Format
- .raw – Photo Format
- .tif – Raster Graphic Image Format

Document:

- .doc – Microsoft Word
- .pdf – Adobe Acrobat
- .ppt – PowerPoint
- .ps – Post Script

BitTorrent

IP video can also be considered extremely disruptive because of the unbelievable number of illegal files that are being created and shared. People often misquote a study by Cache Logic published in July, 2004, "The true Picture of Peer-to-Peer Filesharing."[1] The study says, "BitTorrent traffic made up 53 percent of all P2P traffic" by saying that

---

1. http://www.cachelogic.com/research/p2p2004.php

"53 percent of all Internet traffic is BitTorrent." The numbers are not quite as big as they are rumored to be, but they become truly impressive when you think about the reality that 99 percent of the files they are referring to are being traded without the rights-holder's consent.

Playout Software

One of the most exciting "legal" types of IP video distribution schemas is called "playout" software. These systems mimic the programming capabilities of traditional television systems. A broadband playout system allows programmers to encode video program material, commercials, interstitial material and promotional clips and schedule them for playout. When a user logs onto the Web site, they are treated to a 24-hour streaming video meant to mimic a television experience. These systems are generally resolution independent and can playout video in any format. Restricted only by bandwidth on the consumer side, you can also use these systems to distribute HD video over the public Internet.

The scheduler or channel manager can, in addition to programming a 24-hour day, offer any of the programming for on-demand viewing. These systems can be monetized in several different ways. They can be advertiser-supported or employ any kind of micro-payment or subscription schema that the content owner desires.

The most important feature of these broadband playout systems is control. A programmer can create a set of business rules that might restrict playout to one play per IP address unless a subscription is purchased or might restrict the region of the world where the content can be seen. Advertisers can make sure you never see their ads more than once per hour and not more than eight times total before they change their creative.

On the reporting side, broadband playout systems offer "television-like" CPM-based reporting. These are census-based metrics that tell the advertisers and program directors almost everything about the habits and behaviors of the viewer.

Many of these systems use an auction marketplace to price their advertising. This is a wonderful model for gross impression advertising against niche or target audiences. If a viewer is watching the Skydiving Channel or the Field Hockey Channel, you can reasonably assume that they are interested in those activities. An engaged viewer, spending quality time with a channel about their interests is usually worth more to an advertiser than a gross impression wasted on traditional one-to-many television.

The future of IP video is very bright. You will see more and more organizations, companies, creatives and ordinary people using this technology to express themselves over the public Internet. Most major content distributors are finding valuable ways to use IP video. This is way more than a trend — it is a powerful force for change.

Game Consoles and IP Bypass

Home video games have been around since Pong debuted in the 1970s. Video games have evolved into a thriving multi-billion dollar industry, an industry with which television desperately competes for viewers. For most of the past two decades, this has been competition for share of mind. After all, you have only so much free time and if you are playing a video game on your television set, you are obviously not watching a television program on it. There are a lot of leisure time activities that compete with television: nights out with friends and family, movies, music, playing sports, vacationing and anything else that might take your attention or time away from watching (even reading a book, heaven forbid!).

The latest generation game consoles are very specialized, powerful computers that may be the best "file-sharing" boxes ever widely distributed.

In the past few years, video game consoles have added a feature that has captured the imaginations of industry analysts and consumers alike. Both Playstation® and Xbox® can be plugged into the Internet to enhance game-play, update interactive aspects of the games and, most importantly of all — create online communities worldwide. It is very easy to play multi-player versions of many extremely popular games "live" with opponents or allies in the next room or in another country.

The latest generation game consoles are very specialized, powerful computers (by consumer standards) that, for lack of a better way to describe them, are the best "file-sharing" boxes ever distributed. To be sure, there are far more powerful computers in the hands of computer geeks and ordinary businesspeople all over the world. What makes these game consoles so interesting is the speed with which they are being brought to market and the fact that they have to be hooked up to television monitors (they don't come with screens). When the existing Playstation and Xbox users get their new models, they will know exactly how to use them! Plus, this user-base is heavily skewed to males ages 13 to 32, which is solid gold for an extraordinarily large segment of brand and lifestyle advertisers like quick-serve restaurants, soft drinks, cars, athletic equipment, electronics and many more. Will broadcast television sustain a significant economic hit from this probable future? I said I wouldn't make predictions in this book, but ...

Search

We live in a time where metadata may actually be more important than data. (Metadata is data that is used to describe other data.) Imagine that you had a hard drive capable of storing 10,000 movies and 1 million songs. They would be of little use to you without a way to search for them. So, the job of all search tools is to identify and deliver relevant results based on search criterion requested by users.

At this writing, Google, Yahoo! and MSN offer the most popular tools to search the Web. How they collect and sort their data and the actual search algorithms they use are considered "trade secrets." However, many experts find consensus in the notion that a Web page is still predominantly ranked by counting the number of links back to it. As one might imagine, there is a "secret sauce" component to page ranking, and maybe even a human being somewhere in the process.

The Web search business is extraordinarily profitable. There are several revenue models, and we can learn a great deal about how video files may be monetized in a networked environment by studying search on the Web.

When you enter a keyword or phrase into a search engine, the program returns a list of results, including short descriptions and hyperlinks ranked by order of relevance. How one creates a page that is returned at or near the top of these lists is the job of search engine optimizers (SEOs) and search engine marketers (SEMs). The big search engines will tell you that there is nothing you can do to make an individual Web page more relevant than to create it honestly and put it on a Web server. However, an entire industry of snake oil salesmen and charlatans has evolved to exploit the idea that having your site listed in the top five results on the first page of a search is worth whatever they charge. To be sure, there are legitimate SEO and SEM firms. There are some well-respected, well-understood techniques for increasing the likelihood that your site will enjoy favorable search results. For our purposes, let's just say that a well-crafted, truly relevant Web page on any given topic will show up at or near the top of the "free" search results area of a big search engine.

Paid search is a very probable future for video distribution.

In the "paid" search results area of the screen, you will find a list of hyperlinks that may be extremely relevant to your search criterion. This advertising real estate is sold to the highest bidder in a continuous online auction-style market that trades on the popularity of the relevant keywords.

Search engine revenue models are based on a time-honored retail concept: If a consumer asks for it, he or she probably wants it. And, if this was all there was to a search engine, it would be a good business. But there is much, much more.

Search results returned in the "free" area may contain links to very well constructed micro-sites that are relevant to your search but purely commercial in nature. In effect they are Web pages doing the job of infomercials. They look like valid Web sites with good information, but, in fact, they are commercial announcements for specific products or services and may not yield the true information you were searching for. There is a huge business in creating commercial landing pages and micro-sites. They are the equivalent of spam on the Web — you will certainly see this type of search engine abuse when video files become ubiquitous and searchable on the Web.

There is also room to work the system on the "paid" area of the search results page. Here, advertisers pay for the highest placement by bidding the most amount of money for specific keywords or phrases. They may pay for gross impressions, page views or click-throughs. However, there can be even greater revenue opportunities if users complete a transaction. Remember, if you can do it with one computer file, you can do it with another. To a computer, all files — whether audio, video, Web pages, text, photos and graphics — all look the same. So, paid search is a very probable future for video distribution.

Metatagging and Finding Rich Media

Metatagging is important because it is one of the main ways that search engines can help you find what you are looking for. With text (even closed captioning on video), it is pretty easy to create an algorithm that will extract keywords for use as metatags. With some programming creativity, it is possible to create more sophisticated algorithms that can extract key phrases or other meaningful combinations of words that will make searches faster and more accurate. What makes text searches relatively easy is the fact that the data is already in a language human beings understand.

But it is not as easy as it looks. Take some closely related terms: movies, films, flicks, flix, talkies, moving pictures, motion pictures, cine, and cinema. You cannot really collapse them into a single word without a potential loss of meaning. Certainly the social context would be affected were you to do so. You might enjoy going to the "movies" with a friend, but you might find the idea of doing the same thing with someone who referred to it as going to the "cinema" truly unpleasant.

You can, of course, metatag an object by hand. You can describe a picture of a girl on a motorcycle on a desert road as: girl on motorcycle, girl on motorscooter, woman on bike, woman on motorbike, woman on motorcycle, woman on hog, woman on Harley, girl in desert, girl on moped in desert ... too bad if your consumer searches for "motor cycling in the desert."

These are just some minor issues when dealing with the subtleties of language-based metatagging. Now, let's imagine the difficulties that automated rich media metatagging might encounter. Video cannot be searched by a simple program for keywords or phrases. To automate the process you will need pattern recognition algorithms for the video portion of the file and speech to text or sound pattern recognition algorithms for the audio portion. As you can imagine, the computer and programming power needed to accomplish these goals pushes the practical limits of current technology.

That being said, digital asset management, metatagging and rich media search engines are being developed everywhere. All of the major search companies are spending a great deal of time and money working on this complex set of problems. As this technology evolves, it will be incorporated into user interfaces that will ultimately help networked television reach its full potential as an emotionally satisfying viewing experience. Empowering consumers to easily find relevant rich media is the "holy grail" of networked television.

Really Simple Syndication (RSS), Blogs and Podcasts

The simplest way to think of really simple syndication (RSS) is as a way to syndicate Web sites. The specification was developed with a simple goal: Let publishers completely control publishing and subscribers completely control subscriptions.

When a Web page is published to an RSS server, an RSS feed is created. This feed can be seen by special blog-reading software as well as regular Web browsers. Without making this book a course on RSS, the result of using this XML-based specification is that content can be subscribed to and fed as opposed to being manually checked for and delivered. The original creators of the RSS spec thought they were creating a way for people to receive only e-mail and content that they really wanted. There are a literally hundreds of "feed readers" available for free download on the Internet. Most of the big portals feature the ability for you to subscribe to any feed and almost every major content publisher (and all bloggers) have the ability to publish using RSS.

The RSS specification that has spawned at least two extremely popular content form factors: blogs and Podcasts.

Blogs

Blogs (short for Weblogs), by definition, are user-generated content. This can be a private citizen, a corporate employee or any other type of computer user who has something to blog about. There are literally millions of blog pages on the Web and the vast majority of them are "made with loving hands at home." All blogs are Web pages, but not all Web pages are blogs. What makes a blog different from a Web site is the way it is published. When you create and publish content to a regular Web site, the content sits on a server and waits to be viewed. People can find a particular page on your site by accident, through a search engine or, of course, if you tell them about it. If you really want people to know about a particular page of content, you might e-mail them the link or even the entire page. When you create and publish a blog, everyone who has subscribed to your blog can see the new entry in their "feed readers." This automatic distribution is unique to RSS.

One remarkable feature of blogs is their almost uncanny ability to show up very, very high in the organic (free) areas of big search engines. This may have something to do with the way blog pages are created: they have unique content, page attributes and metadata. And, the content is usually very well-related and linked to other places on the Web that support it. As we discussed, the big search algorithms are well guarded trade secrets, and Google, Yahoo! and MSN swear that you can't "work" the system. However, blogs and pages that are fed using RSS make your content much easier to find. Not only does this make RSS a very effective syndication tool, it may well evolve into an important underpinning for subscription-based television distribution.

Podcasting

Now for the really interesting part: the RSS specification provides for an "envelope" in the feed. You, as content publisher, can put any computer file you want inside that envelope and it will be delivered with the rest of the feed. What does this mean? Well, if you take an audio file, like an MP3 file, and put it inside this RSS envelope, you have a Podcast.

What's in a Name?

In February 2004, Ben Hammersley wrote an article in *The Guardian* and used the term "podcasting" as a synonym for audioblogging. It was probably the first time the term was used in print. Podcasting is a portmanteau that combines two words: "iPod" and "broadcasting." It is a misnomer, since neither podcasting nor listening to podcasts requires an iPod or any portable player, and no broadcasting is required. Regardless, the term has become widely used to describe audio files available on the Internet.

This attribute of RSS has triggered the explosion of Podcasts and it is just the beginning. As I've said before, a file is a file is a file and computers don't distinguish between them. So if you like distributing audio files as Podcasts, you will probably love distributing video files or graphics or documents the same way. They just don't all have cool names yet ... but they will. Here's the tip of the iceberg:

- **Autocasting -** The automatic generation of podcasts from text-only sources.

- **Godcasting -** religious podcasts, typically Christian.

- **Javacast -** podcasting to mobile phones using J2ME Midlets.[2]

- **Learncasting -** delivering instructional content or academic support content.

- **Media RSS -** a kind of syndication of media files used by Yahoo!

- **MMScast -** podcasting to mobile phones using MMS.

- **Mobilecast -** podcasting to mobile phones.

- **Palmcasting -** podcasting to Palm devices like Treo and LifeDrive.

- **Punchcasting -** punching podcasts directly into smartphone devices.

- **Skypecasting -** recording Skype text, voice or video conversations.

- **Soundseeing tour -** podcast utilizing ambient noise and descriptions.

- **Streamcasting -** when an RSS feed contains a link to streaming media instead of a file, RSS becomes a way to control streaming syndication.

- **Vodcasting/Vidcasting -** video-based podcasts.

RSS Enables REP "Really Enhanced Piracy"

RSS feeds are an important tool for syndication. They also have the capacity to enable mind-boggling amounts of piracy. It's one thing to take a song make it available on your P2P network so your friends (or whomever) can download it. To do this, you will probably name the song file with a semi-recognizable name. The MP3 file spec allows for certain metadata, but file names say a great deal about what you may be downloading. File polluters and spoofers (who try to waste downloaders' time by uploading bogus data onto file sharing services) spend a great deal of time working with file names. When a song or a video has even a semi-recognizable name, it's pretty easy to identify.

You can add a pre-recorded video to a blog to create a vlog (video blog). There are several consumer Web sites dedicated to this form of communication. There is also some exceptional software from Serious Magic (www.seriousmagic.com) that makes vlogging as easy as blogging.

---

2. MIDP (Mobile Information Device Profile) applications are piquantly called MIDlets, a continuation of the naming theme begun by applets and servlets.

On the other hand, how might you identify what's inside an MP3 file called "Shelly Palmer's Weekly Countdown.mp3" or "The Shelly Show.mp3." The only way is to listen, or to search the metadata and hope for a comprehensive description of that episode. This doesn't seem to be a big deal until I decide to do a Podcast show that includes my 10 favorite songs in a row. Some would argue that a Podcast from a trusted source is actually more valuable (and therefore more damaging to the content owner's bottom line) than a single title because it has the added value of a "brand" associated with it. Imagine (no pun intended) distributing a collection of John Lennon songs this way. It's a piracy nightmare!

RSS: "Really Simple Stealing"

Jason McCabe Calacanis, CEO of Weblogs, Inc., likes to say that RSS also stands for "Really Simple Stealing." You can play the "home game." Here's how: Create a blog page with one of the zillion inexpensive blogging services. Subscribe to a bunch of relevant RSS feeds to populate it. Now, drop a link to Google's AdSense on the page. What have you created? A Web site that is, for all intents and purposes, an automatic money machine. The original goals of RSS were lofty but simple: create software that lets publishers completely control publishing and that lets subscribers completely control subscriptions.

When used as designed, RSS allows you to receive highly relevant content directly from the publishers as it becomes available. However, the same attributes that enable you to automatically subscribe to an RSS feed also enable you to embed the commands in a Web (or blog) page. This allows you to "sub-publish" someone else's work and make it look, smell and feel like your own. Not exactly what the software designers had in mind.

Not surprisingly, some of these "mash-up" blogs are extremely creative. The sites can include information from several blogs, search and information services and can be more relevant to a user than the original blogs. That being said, there are many, many more that are just created by cutting and pasting a few lines of code for the sole purpose of making money off someone else's creative. Now, most major news sites and many savvy user-generated blogs limit the RSS feed to a title with a short synopsis or an abstract that links back to the original work. But this in and of itself does nothing to prevent the monetization of mashing up other people's work by exploiting the RSS feeds.

The evolution of technology is an arms race. Every positive innovation seems to inspire some individuals to concoct ways to exploit it. Bloggers go to great lengths to get as many people to read their material as possible. Is this problem just a bunch of graffiti artists complaining about someone defacing their work? No, it's just one more example of the law of unintended consequences and a testimony to the inventiveness and unpredictability of the online community.

Online Media Providers

High-traffic Web sites are packaged several different ways, including search engines, portals and transactional sites. The lines between these business models, their unique selling principals and core businesses are blurring. Google may have started out as a search engine, but it is now a massive "eyeball aggregation" engine that connects people who want to be connected. This is also what Yahoo! and MSN do. In fact, it is what eBay and Amazon also do, though all of these organizations do it very differently.

It has been interesting to watch the evolution of the high-traffic Web sites over the past few years as they attempt to transform themselves into media companies. This kind of transformation will require significant changes in the infrastructure of the Internet and a new generation of personal devices to evolve along with it. As Ben Silverman, president of Reveille Productions, said at the Madison & Vine conference in 2005, "I don't go home, sit with my dad and watch my Google." He got a big laugh, but the Google guys may actually have the last laugh. In a world where metadata is as important as the data it describes, portals may take on the role of rich-media gatekeeper.

Display Ads

No description of the Web and Web advertising would be complete without a mention of the medium's most popular advertising form factors. Forgetting pop-up windows and other interruptive, intrusive and annoying tricks, there are a few time-tested ad units that are still in ubiquitous use: banners, billboards and skyscrapers. These may be still images, animated or even include some video elements. There are standard sizes which can be found on www.iab.org, the official Web site of the Internet Advertising Bureau, and they are sold directly as well as through rep firms at very negotiable CPMs. There has been much debate about the census-based metrics associated with this type of advertising. Because the advertiser (or its agency), in many cases, actually serves the ad to the Web site, the metrics are very accurately reported.

The Internet advertising model will most likely be the one copied when a significant amount of people start to use IP video offerings as a significant media source. By comparison, existing television network advertising models will seem archaic. The industry is moving as quickly as possible towards "best practices" measurability and accountability. And one probable future is the ability for video advertisers to serve — and measure — their own advertisements.

Key Takeaways

- To a computer, a file is a file is a file.

- If you wish to view streaming video files, speak on a VoIP telephone, surf the net, watch some IPTV and play a network-based video game all at the same time, you need a very fast connection.

- The most financially successful IP video models are the four "Gs" (girls, God, gaming and gambling).

- The latest generation of game consoles are very specialized, powerful computers (by consumer standards) that, for lack of a better way to describe them, are the best "file-sharing" boxes ever distributed.

- Paid search is one probable future for video distribution.

- RSS is a method of distribution where publishers completely control content and subscribers completely control their subscriptions.

4 Existing Wireless Networks

There are several types of existing wireless networks. We have wireless networks in our homes, there are companies that offer wireless telephones for communication (like mobile phones), and there are commercial wireless providers that offer private and public industrial networks of all descriptions. For our purposes, we must look at the technologies that are most likely to impact consumers in the foreseeable future. When thinking about wireless, try not to think only of telephone handsets. Wireless devices can take any shape and offer a combination of many different functions.

Mobile Phones and Devices

When discussing handheld communication over wireless networks, most people immediately think of mobile phones. We must call them mobile phones because cell phone is a term-of-art that refers to a very specific way that *There are close to 3 billion mobile phones currently deployed and the number is trending up.* the wireless signal gets from phone to phone. In the very near probable future you will see many different types of wireless phones and devices that use many different types of technologies to move data around, including WiFi, WiMax, EVDO and some new uses of old frequencies (like 700 MHz, where analog television signals used to live).

Mobile Phones

You often hear mobile phones referred to as the "third screen." This makes the bold assumption that television is the first screen in your media life and that the computer screen is the second one. There are only about 1.1 billion television households worldwide. There are few places on Earth where there are more computer screens than mobile telephone screens. The latest estimates say that there are close to 3 billion mobile phones currently deployed and the number is trending up. The concept of the third screen seems to be misguided – mobile phones certainly enjoy much wider usage than computers and they are trending towards unseating television as a primary communications device.

One of the biggest opportunities for mass-market interactivity and commerce is the computer in a mobile phone. Almost everyone has one and they know how to use it. The screens are easy to read and the communication in text, graphics or sound is inherently two-way. No matter what the application, mobile phones offer the most ubiquitous opportunity for one-to-one communication.

Will the trade take this idea too literally? What features would your fantasy mobile device include? The highest, best purpose for a mobile phone is voice communication, so let's make that a given. We also have to temper our fantasy with one undeniable reality – energy. Mobile devices run on internal power stored in batteries. When coupled with more efficient electronics, today's best battery technology can give you several hours of talk time. The actual amount of time you have to speak on a mobile telephone is a function of a combination of technical issues outside the scope of this book. However, until some major discovery occurs, every feature you add to a mobile device will reduce the amount of talk time. So, are we willing to listen to three hours of music, watch 30 minutes of video or spend an hour surfing the Web at the risk of missing an important call? There are practical limitations to all-in-one devices that must be thought through. That being said, there may be a gigantic market for small, efficient dedicated devices. Consumers will vote with their checkbooks!

Short Message Service

Short Message Service (SMS), commonly called "text messaging" or "texting," is a service that enables users to send messages of up to 160 characters to and from mobile phones. It is so popular in Europe and Japan that some nimble-fingered middle-school students can create and send text messages by typing with their thumbs faster than they can with a traditional keyboard.

In the United States, text messaging on mobile devices is continuing to gain popularity. Its current pricing makes it a good profit center for mobile service providers. The consumer value proposition is clear: quick, easy, short messages between friends. Message 1: "When will u b home?" Message 2: "10 min" is a much faster way to communicate this information than a telephone call would be.

Texting is a huge profit center!

According to "Maximizing the Value of Mobile Networks," a white paper by Cisco Systems, SMS and premium SMS are the biggest profit centers for mobile networks. Where basic voice can bring in about $0.12 per Megabit, SMS averages $65.10 and Premium SMS is an $81.38 per Megabit goldmine.

There have been, and there will be, many attempts to use a premium version of SMS for interactive communication. Premium SMS chat is basically a text chat between two or more mobile device users that carries a premium charge for each message. There are also many subscription-based information services that deliver customized messages using SMS. Why would anyone pay additional fees to use SMS? Popular premium services include dating, astrology, religious messaging, and interactive voting and polling.

The television industry has been trying to use SMS as an interactive profit center for years but there seems to be a limit to the value that consumers place on being able to interact with their favorite shows. The cost of basic SMS messages can be relatively high if used in volume, so there is quite a bit of user pushback when premium prices are attached to this function. To that end, the value of every viewer having immediate access to a personal communications device that can be used in sync or interactively with a television or radio show has yet to be realized in a meaningful way.

Fox's hit series *American Idol* solicited viewers in their fourth season to use SMS text messages (or a telephone) to vote for their favorite contestants. They received 41.5 million SMS votes (which is impressive because the SMS voting was only available to Cingular customers). This was a sharp increase from the third season, which only garnered 13.5 million SMS messages. However, to put this in perspective, there were more than 500 million total votes cast via regular telephones in season four, making SMS voting about eight percent of total votes cast. So, is there a television-related "killer app" that will drive SMS usage to new levels and create a true profit center? Not yet.

Multimedia Messaging Service

Multimedia Messaging Service (MMS) devices can send pictures, video, graphics and audio files individually or in combinations across both GSM/GPRS, CDMA and EVDO networks. Like SMS, MMS messages can be user-generated or sent in bulk from a server. This is a logical evolution from the text-based world, but it has limitations and, some would say, limited usefulness. No one would disagree that "a picture is worth a thousand words," but some things are better acquired in a short text message than in a multimedia presentation. On average, someone can silently read 160 characters of text in less than six seconds while it takes more than 12 seconds to listen to the same message read aloud.

The big opportunity for MMS is considered commercial. Coupons, offers, advertisements, commercials and promotional offerings almost always enjoy a better response when presented in colorful, multimedia formats. However, this type of content may be unacceptable to American consumers. Google Mobile Search is doing some advertising in Europe but the practice of MMS advertising in the U.S. is all but non-existent.

Will we see a time, in the near future, where there are advertiser-sponsored, free MMS mobile phones? Would you be willing to hear or watch a commercial every time you used your mobile phone, even if the mobile service was free? It's food for thought, but don't think about it too much.

Video on Mobile Phones

When video is distributed to a mobile phone, it is usually served as a clipcast or a stream. A clipcast is a short piece of video that may be cached in the device or is small enough to be downloaded quickly for viewing. This is made possible by distributing the content using third-generation (3G) EVDO networks. One major problem with clipcasting is the user interface (UI). For the most part, the UI is a deck with 14 character text choices. It is hard to decide which item to pick from a list where all of the entries say "CNN News" and offer no additional information for differentiation.

Another problem with the system is that the clips are relatively short, usually :30 seconds up to a couple of minutes. Phone company executives say the reason clips are short is because research tells them that's what people want to watch. Of course, there are no long-form videos to choose from, so the data may be quite skewed. Have you ever read a 500-page book in one sitting? Probably not. So, it makes sense that publishers should send you 20 pages at a time, right? It does sound absurd, but for now it's up to the consumer to reprogram their wireless video experience about every two minutes or so. Believe it or not, using this system (which is available today to 140 million people in over 50 major metros) is even more annoying than reading about it.

Somebody will ultimately put a pause button on a mobile phone. Or, at least develop a technology that allows you to start a piece of content from the place you left it. This will result in a more complete, emotionally satisfying experience for viewers, and they will respond by engaging longer with the content and the brands that support that content.

3G services, like Verizon's Vcast, have an additional problem — they are too expensive. It is not unusual for a mobile-phone-based video add-on to cost $15/per month. Whether consumers will pay this or not is anybody's guess. There is extreme downward price pressure on monthly mobile phone bills as the marketplace gets more and more crowded. However, premium content is always charged to distributors on a per-subscriber basis. So the content providers are going to be looking to raise their prices (when is the last time your cable or satellite bill actually went down?) while the phone companies are going to do everything they can to lower consumer costs. This, when combined with the highly annoying UI, makes clipcasting more of a parlor trick than a paradigm shift.

The other type of mobile phone video is streamcasting. This can be accomplished with a dual tuner handset. Qualcomm's MediaFLO system is an early example of a national footprint in the 700 MHz spectrum. Qualcomm actually broadcasts a television signal to the handset using a television transmission frequency and they multiplex the signal so you receive about 20 channels of linear video. These channels are programmed almost exactly like linear television and it is also unclear how much, if any, benefit this offers consumers over alternative video experiences.

One of the incorrect arguments against mobile-phone-based video comes from comparing the experience to a Sony Watchman portable, personal-sized television. These have been on the market since 1984 and they do not sell all that well. People often say that if there was a market for portable video, everyone would be walking around with a Sony Watchman, but this is not a good analogy. First of all, the Sony Watchman is an analog television receiver. It has an antenna, a tuner and a monitor and it only receives over-the-air television. Yes, the device is portable, but it does not offer the user any program storage or any control over the time of day that they may watch a program. Because linear television is programmed based upon daypart and geographic region, you are at the mercy of the time of day you are able to watch. Clipcasts on mobile phones can be user time-shifted and user-programmed. The only thing that a clipcast has in common with a Watchman is that they both have small video screens.

The streamcasting service, on the other hand, will look a great deal like good old fashioned television. The biggest difference will be the availability of premium channels like HBO and cable networks like MTV and ESPN. The addition of these premium choices may help the telcos move some handsets off the shelf at retail, but the user experience is still going to feel like watching linear television. Again, it is unclear whether consumers want or need a way to watch linear programming on a mobile phone. But, this won't stop content owners from making every possible piece of branded content available in the format. The "cool factor" is too great and the potential (though unrealized) is too inviting.

FCC regulations are a key factor in the future monetization of mobile video devices. For obvious reasons, the definitions of data and video are being hotly debated in Washington. Remember, all digital video is data but ... all data is not digital video! This reality is not lost on either side of the battle. Cable operators want to call streaming video sent over wireless networks (which is technically just digital data), video. This would require the wireless video providers to adhere to all kinds of FCC regulations that do not apply to transporters of ordinary data (whatever that is). Once again, technology has outpaced strategy, tactics, business rules and regulations. We'll just have to wait and see whose lobbyists prevail.

Portable Media Devices (Portable Video)

The main point of differentiation between mobile-phone-based video and portable or personal media devices (PMDs) is the delivery mechanism. For the most part, you download video content to a personal or portable media player. Most often, this is accomplished by connecting the device to a computer or directly to the Internet. This is not to say that there are not several devices with wireless (WiFi, Bluetooth, WiMax, EVDO, UWB, television antennas, etc.) connections to which you can stream or download video remotely. In fact, there are portable DVRs and handheld video devices of all kinds and new models with new features debut almost daily. But PMDs are too new for a standard to have evolved. Apple's Video iPod, Creative's PMDs and Sony's PSP all have different mechanisms and formats — it's tough to tell which type of device and which feature sets will ultimately capture the consumers' mind.

The Myth of Personal Video

You can now have all of your favorite music, all of your favorite photos and all of the video you could watch for a week or two stored in one device in the palm of your hand. For a great number of reasons, this may be a better fantasy than reality. Here are some things to think about:

- **Battery life:** After you miss the end of a movie you're really into, there is absolutely no way that you will listen to any music or show even one photo on your PMD if you have any intention of watching video on it. That bright little screen eats battery life, and TV shows and movies are long.

- **Navigation:** PMD navigation is almost OK for music and marginal if you add a couple of hundred photos. But add 30 videos, 50 podcasts and an audiobook, and you'll be in search hell.

- **Programming:** You need to dedicate some quality time to finding and loading your videos. There's not much properly formatted content available for any given system, so almost everything needs to be transcoded. This isn't hard to do, but it takes time — time that many people do not have. (File-sharing anyone?)

- **Fatigue:** I have some songs on my PMD that I really love, but I don't need to listen to for about another year. They are small files and it makes me happy to have them at my fingertips. I don't mind hearing them in shuffle mode, and I can easily skip over them if want to. I will not need to re-watch the "New York Minute" episode of "Law & Order" any time soon. It's just taking up space.

- **High-Focus Activity:** You can listen to music while you are doing almost anything, except listening to something else that includes music. Personal music has been a part of our culture since Sony introduced the Walkman in the 1970s. Not true with video, a high-focus activity. There are far fewer moments during the day when you can give your full attention to personal video than you can imagine.

Taking all of this into consideration, is there a market for "personal video" devices? Yes. Is there content that is more suited to this screen size? There will be. (That being said, TV is a "close up" medium and well-shot television shows translate nicely to small video screens.) Will someone have to figure out navigation? Absolutely! Will you ever really use a multifunction device for multifunctions? Only when batteries last for days instead of hours. Will these devices be much cooler and more useful when they are wireless (WiFi, UWB, wireless USB, WiMax, EVDO)? Significantly!

Is there such a thing as "personal video?" Absolutely. Just ask people you know who have a Video iPod or a PMD about how they use it. Everyone will have a different story about how "personal video" fits into their lives. Some people use it instead of DVDs for their toddlers in the back seats of their cars. Others use it in cabs or airports or commuting ... how people use personal video does not matter. The fact is, they use it. Is it a paradigm shift or a parlor trick? Only time will tell.

Great "Genre-Specific" Content Is Coming to a PMD Near You!

No new technology can ever realize its potential without creative evolution. There is an excellent opportunity for a new genre of creative to evolve here. In the 80s, MTV took an old concept, "the musical," and gave the creative community an opportunity to take it to another level. The music video genre, with its quick cuts and shaky camera work, inspired a generation of videographers, filmmakers and television professionals. It is pretty easy to look at mobile video devices with their small screens and "anything, anywhere, anytime" attributes and imagine several new creative approaches to exploiting the medium. And that's just what's happening all over the creative community. Production companies are creating tons of new, exciting genre-specific content — it's a great time to be in the creative side of the business!

Key Takeaways

- There are close to 3 billion mobile phones currently deployed and the number is trending up. The idea that mobile phones are the Third Screen seems to be misguided.

- SMS is an excellent profit center for the mobile service providers. The consumer value proposition is clear and usage is trending upward.

- There have been (and will be) many attempts to use premium SMS for interactive communication. It is not a great business in the USA.

- The big opportunity for MMS is considered commercial. Coupons, offers, advertisements, commercials and promotional offerings. So far, it is unrealized.

- Video distributed to mobile phones is usually served as a clipcast or a stream. Dual Tuner handsets will offer a television-like experience.

- FCC Regulations are a key factor in the future monetization of mobile video devices.

5 Emerging Networks

Some kinds of networked television systems work reasonably well over the public Internet. However, as our need to distribute IP video increases, new (more robust) networks will emerge to meet the demand. These may come in the form of private networks, tiered services from existing providers, new wireless technologies or any combination thereof. There are no hard and fast rules governing the evolution of this technology.

We can start to think about the future of the new networked paradigm by looking at some of the disruptive technologies that concurrently emerged with the Internet, starting with an overview of the value of compression and the ability to move small files quickly and inexpensively between network nodes. Then we will briefly analyze the various value propositions that might motivate such behaviors. Ultimately, this will help us make some reasonable observations about the probable futures of networked television.

Data Compression

Famed mathematician Blaise Pascal once wrote, "I have made this letter longer than usual because I lack the time to make it shorter." We've all been there. It is very difficult to find the delicate balance between brevity and unintelligibility. The ongoing quest for communicative efficiency has two goals: 1) compress as much information as possible into each data packet and 2) move the data packet as fast possible.

Luckily, some of the most significant advances in computer science in the past 20 years have been made in the area of data compression. As hard drives get bigger, we seem to have an unending supply of large files to fill them up with, as well as an insatiable need to move them around. The smaller we can make them, the faster we can move them, the faster we can move them, the better off we will be.

Data compression is both an art and a science, and as you can see in Figure 5.1, the need for data compression predates computers. When compressing data that describe static things like text or low-resolution graphics, you can use an algorithm to mathematically reduce the file size and get pretty good results. There are literally hundreds of data compression schemas in use today. You are probably familiar with WinZip (or Stuffit, if you're a Mac person). These popular file compressors take big files and make them smaller. It is quite common to compress a big file before you e-mail it to someone. In fact, depending on the e-mail system, it may be required.

FIGURE 5.1 *The need for data compression is not new. In the early 19th century, postage was charged by the sheet, so people wrote in two directions (compressing the data) to save money.*

Since a file is a file is a file, you can intuit that digital audio and video files can also be compressed. You would be right. There is not much need to go through and name all of the popular audio and video compression schemas here. They change constantly and each system has specific formats, codecs (a device or program that can compress and decompress multimedia files), resolutions and players associated with them. Suffice it to say that almost every online audio and video distribution system uses some form of data compression.

Encoding

But, as we said, data compression is both an art and a science. The "art" part of this process is the encoding phase. Audio and video files have different "aesthetic" reactions to data compression. You can't just compress an audio or video file that you care about and expect it to sound or look fine. Choices about resolution, codecs, filtering and many other encoding parameters have a dramatic effect on the quality of the encoded, compressed file. In case you are wondering, traditional television and cable systems use a format known as MPEG2 which is the standard by which future compression schemas will be benchmarked.

Dark Fiber

There is another, more macro, type of data compression that deals with speed of transmission and the maximization of available bandwidth over a network (as opposed to a single file). During the dot-com boom, several very large companies spent billions of dollars laying fiber optic cable all across America. Known as "dark fiber," these cables were not attached to any particular system; they were just light pipes laying in the ground waiting to be lit up with data. It never happened. To be sure, there are several gigantic fiber optic networks in use today. Almost all of the major carriers have their own systems (and back-up systems as well). During the build-out, something unexpected was developed – Dense Wavelength-Division Multiplexing (DWDM), which allowed multiple wavelengths to be combined into one optical signal. DWDM increased the total data rate on one fiber to one terabit per second (10^{12} bits per second). This data compression technology, and other subsequent compression schemas, cost the dot-com speculators billions of dollars because they created an extraordinary amount of over-capacity on the existing fiber optic networks.

There is an important lesson to be learned from this experience. Technology is fleeting. Technological edges or advantages can be extremely short-lived. And, as we all know all too well, the last half mile is the barrier to entry. In other words, getting fiber to the curb is not the same as getting fiber to the premises or fiber to the pillow.

Traditionally, innovations in audio have happened about 10 years before their video counterparts. This is just a bit of armchair wisdom, not a trend analysis. Later in this chapter, we will explore some of the profound differences between the audio and video businesses and the technologies that enable them. Let's take a moment to see if we can learn anything from the music industry that might help us prepare for what's ahead.

The Napster Effect

Back in 1999, an 18 year-old named Shawn Fanning spent about a week writing code for a file-sharing program he would call Napster. Depending upon who you ask, you will hear myth and lore about how this early, legendary software company either destroyed the music industry or how it freed a generation of music lovers from the tyranny of big corporate record companies. No matter which sides of the legal, ethical and moral debates you choose to empathize with, one thing is clear – the industry has yet to recover (as a practical matter, it never will).

The Recording Industry Association of America (RIAA), which represents most of the big record companies and a bunch of smaller ones, filed a lawsuit against Napster. The suit did not charge Napster with copyright infringement; rather, it alleged that the company's file sharing software contributed and facilitated copyright infringement by others. Napster lost the case.

Not everyone hated Napster

Some recording artists saw new opportunities with Napster. Dave Matthews, of the Dave Matthews Band, said, "Napster… is the future, in my opinion. That's the way music is going to be communicated around the world. The most important thing now is to embrace it, and that was the spirit by which we did this co-promotion."

At the center of the technology that Shawn used to create this gigantic, viral community of music users sat an index of available songs. This file server had an IP address and could be easily located by anyone with more than a casual interest in finding it. To shut down Napster, all you had to do was pull the plug – and that is essentially what happened.

Before we talk about why today's peer-to-peer (P2P) networks are significantly more difficult to dismantle, let us ponder the "Napster Effect."

Program directors are some of the highest paid, most respected professionals in the entertainment business. Their work is a deft combination of voodoo, the dark arts, magic, science and guts!

Before the death of Napster, circa 2001, you could walk into almost any college dorm room in America and find a desktop computer absolutely loaded with music files. A random walk through Warren Towers, the freshman dorm at Boston University, might have yielded several computers per floor with more than 3,000 songs on them. This may sound like a large number of songs, but it isn't. It is the equivalent of about 300 CDs, give or take a few. Most people can listen to 3,000 songs in a few weeks and in under two months, they will hate all of them for having heard them too often. More to the point, back then you had to create playlists and that meant you had to take the time to be your own program director.

Now, there are some people who have the time and the desire to create playlists and program music all day — they're called program directors. Every radio station, television station, movie theatre, concert hall, even the local bar down the street where your neighborhood garage bands play on Friday night has a professional program director. Their jobs are very, very simple: create a stream of content that aggregates a specific audience so that the organization they work for can convert the share-of-mind of that audience into share-of-wallet. By the way, just because something is simple to describe does not mean that it is simple to do.

The Four Attributes of the Napster Effect

- **Control** — Most people don't want to be active program directors all of the time.

- **Discovery** — Most people need a directed way to explore and discover new things.

- **Conformity** — Most people need to conform to the norms and social mores of their clans.

- **Identity** — Most people need to identify with their music and the communities of interest that surrounds it.

The Napster Effect would have appeared shortly after the novelty of Napster wore off. It's sort of like driving a standard shift car in New York City. You appreciate the control, but after a while, it's just too much work. Waiting for the Napster Effect to appear would not have prevented any files from being downloaded nor any copyrights from being violated. However, it might have given the recorded music companies time to offer up a legal, emotionally satisfying, alternate business model; perhaps one that was more consumer-friendly than suing its customers. There are those who will argue that the lawsuits have worked and that there is less illegal file sharing because of them. Maybe. But we'll never know how different the world might have been had the recorded music industry been willing to embrace the technology.

It should be noted that, when queried, most seasoned recording industry executives will tell you that it is not their job to move the industry forward or lead the technological revolution. Their jobs are to make a profit each quarter and, in the case of publicly traded companies, to increase shareholder value to the highest possible extent. If it were possible to take advantage of any new technology and accomplish their primary objectives, they would be happy to do so. This is just another stunning example of business rules and strategies lagging behind technological innovation.

MP3 Files and Compression

The digital audio files that captured the imagination of the primordial file sharers were medium to low fidelity Motion Pictures Expert Group Audio Layer 3 files, or MP3 for short. The format, which offers up to 12:1 compression, quickly became a favorite of computer users who, at the time, had relatively low bandwidth Internet access and small hard drives. These files were "ripped" (the act of transferring files from a CD) to MP3 files using free, downloadable software and then could be shared freely between computer users.

Today the concept of ripping and "burning" (the act of transferring files to a CD) is commonplace. The feature is in almost every computer-based audio player including iTunes, Windows Media, Real and QuickTime. Most of the encoding programs allow users to choose a compression ratio and resolution for the final audio files. These audio resolutions range from 32kbps to 192kbps, with the higher number yielding better quality audio. Surprisingly, even the highest quality MP3 file sounds significantly worse than the CD from which it was made -- sometimes remarkably so. This phenomenon of consumers opting for convenience over quality is the subject of engineering debates and audiophile conventions worldwide. It may account for the abject failure of extremely high quality audio formats like DVD-A or SACD.

Another important kind of consumer compression was introduced with the QuickTime 7. That's the version of QuickTime that shipped with the first video iPods. Pull down the export menu and you will notice that anything you can watch with QuickTime 7 or higher can be exported (compressed and ready to view) to "Video for iPod." It is this kind of "so easy, anyone can do it" innovation that is facilitating the evolution of networked television.

The Fate of Audio and Video File Sharing

Is there going to be a "Video Napster"? Aren't all files sharable over the Internet? Yes, although it won't be technically like Napster, and yes – all files are sharable over the Internet. However, there are some differences between audio and video files that will have a profound impact on the timeline and ultimate method of file sharing. These differences are worth a few moments to examine.

File Differences and Quality

The most obvious way in which audio and video files are different is their size. Audio files, especially MP3 files, are small by modern standards, and they can be moved easily between computers. Video files are much, much bigger than audio files, so we rarely see full screen, full bandwidth IP video in a computer environment. By comparison, a traditional system operator television picture offers a quality that is orders of magnitude better than anything the average consumer is likely to see streaming over the Internet. This will eventually change — it has to.

In the mean time, the question is: How much quality will American television viewers sacrifice for convenience in video? They have an unbelievable tolerance for it in audio — nobody knows if there is a video equivalent. It's truly anyone's guess.

If IP video viewers are willing to put up with small, grainy, low-contrast, less colorful pictures that aren't really full motion, we could see a sea-change in the very near future. Certainly for some emergent content like news and sports, the technical quality is not always the most important attribute. For a breaking news story, some audio is better than no audio and some picture is better than no picture. However, for categories like entertainment, there is little evidence that people are willing to sacrifice picture quality the way they are willing to sacrifice audio quality. Big screen and HDTV sales are on the rise while small, CRT screens are on the way out.

The Audio Paradox

When purchasing a home theater system, most consumers seem to be more interested in high-quality audio components than when they shop for stand-alone audio products (like MP3 players). This makes perfect sense. We are trained to become audiences. This training is accomplished over the literally thousands of hours we spend watching television and movies throughout our lives. Part of this training is knowing when the sound matches the picture. Want a really weird experience? Hook up a 5.1 Surround Sound home theatre audio system to a 13-inch standard definition CRT television monitor. You will know that the sound is much bigger than the picture and it will really bother you.

When thinking about the future, we have to forget about technological limitations. Things like compression algorithms and file formats change daily. For example:

If you have the time, you can download HDTV quality video files using BitTorrent and other P2P networks right now — it may be an overnight process, but the software does the work while you sleep. At some point you will be able to do it in real time. Although invention is not innovation, you can be sure that every technology you can think of will make it to market if it actually solves a problem.

So is there a video lesson to be learned from the file sharing hell that the audio business finds itself in? As we have said over and over again, a file is a file is a file, and computers don't differentiate between them. To that end, if you can move one piece of data over a P2P network, you can move another. It is not a question of whether or not video files will be traded as easily as audio files; it is simply a question of when.

 According to JupiterResearch, a division of Jupitermedia Corporation, HDTV will experience significant growth in the U.S. over the next five years. At the end of 2004, HDTV sets made up 21 percent of overall TV sales; that number will rise to 70 percent of overall TV sales by the end of 2010. Additionally, 63 percent of TV households in the U.S. will have an HDTV set by 2010. (http://www.jupitermedia.com/corporate/releases/05.10.06-newjupresearch.html)

Playback

The simple act of trading a file is not very meaningful if you don't have an emotionally satisfying way to play it back. This is where most experts who disagree on this topic find the biggest chasm. There are some people who believe that having a video file is, in and of itself, a goal and once accomplished, the industry is powerless to monetize that content ever again. The other camp will tell you that just having the file is practically useless if you don't have the appropriate technology for convenient playback. This is one area where audio and video are completely different. Personal audio is a fact of modern life. We've had personal audio players since Sony introduced the Walkman in the 1970s. Is there a market for personal video? There well may be, but it has not yet been demonstrated at scale.

So a good question might be, is there a setting where an average television viewer would choose to watch a video? The answer is usually phrased citing the two modes of usage that, to date, have separated computer users from television viewers: 2-foot vs. 12-foot or, as it is more commonly referred to, lean-forward vs. lean-backward experiences. This is where most pundits and soothsayers are forced to predict that technology will converge on the consumer side. Someday we are supposed to view a mythical box that will bring the best of television and the best of a computer together in one device. This "media center" will become our "entertainment portal," and file sharing of video will decimate the industry. This is not a probable future of television. But, not because there won't be media center-type black boxes for sale everywhere. It is because the living room media experience for which they are built is slowly ceasing to exist. And, more importantly, the incumbent system operator will not relinquish control of whatever living room still does exist without building a moat around their walled garden.

Consumers are transitioning from viewers to viewers. But they are doing so with small, disparate, dedicated technologies that fit their lifestyles, not the other way around. Convergence may ultimately occur in the living room, but it will probably start in a less centralized place. (See "The Myth of the Media Center" in Chapter 8.)

Audio and Video Are Not Analogous

When discussing the ultimate fate of the television or movie business, you often hear people waxing poetic about how the recording industry's fate will soon befall video-based businesses. It may, but it's doubtful. If it does, it will have nothing to do with the file-sharing concepts and the analogies that are usually drawn. The economies of scale between a music production and a major motion picture are so disparate they can almost never be mentioned in the same context as their audio counterparts.

The Psychological Effect

First let's deal with the sociology of music, cars, beer, clothes, movies and television. People wear their clothes, beer, cars and music, and they watch movies and television. If you doubt this statement, look in your closet, your driveway, your refrigerator and your music collection. These are the trappings of your clan. You define them and they define you. They tell everyone in the world who you are, what you're about, who you hang with and — most importantly for this exercise — how to get your attention. Music is extremely personal, so are all of your lifestyle choices. This is one, very rare, instance where you can use yourself as a "test market of one" for a concept. You and all of your friends can laugh about watching a bad television show or movie, because you claim absolutely no ownership of the content or creative concept. This is not true when you are using your personal playlist to entertain your friends. It is not true when you dress, when you offer a friend a beer or when you drive up to someone's house in your car.

Psychological ownership of music makes it vastly different from movies and television. In many ways, music is a fashion accessory to your lifestyle, while television and movies are no more than temporary destinations. Like a bad restaurant, you never have to go back to a bad movie or television experience again. You don't have to listen to a song you don't like again either, but you won't frequent the places that keep playing them. To continue the metaphor, you don't associate a movie theatre with a particular kind of movie and you don't associate your local affiliated television station with a particular kind of show.

Then there is the all important "critical listening" factor in music. While most people really know a quality movie or television show when they see it, they have no idea what makes a quality song. They only know if they like it or if they don't! Why does this matter? Because the democratization of music production has put "world class" sonic quality literally onto everyone's computer. Can an average person tell if a mash-up was done by Eminem or his friend down the street? Go ahead, do the test. The results will surprise you. This is a very good thing for the evolution of the creative musical process, but it is not a good thing for professional musicians at all.

If most people are bad at making watchable videos, they are absolutely terrible at singing in tune or composing music. In practice, this comes down to simple marketing and salesmanship. If you don't hear the difference, there isn't one.

Lon T. Palmer, president of Freeport Music, tells a story about a man who was in the market for some new stereo speakers. After several hours of "critical listening" the man said, "This pair (pointing to a particular set) sounds like I'm sitting in the orchestra at Lincoln Center … this pair (pointing to a different set) sounds like I'm sitting in the mezzanine at Carnegie Hall. I like to sit in the orchestra at Lincoln Center, I'll take those." What the salesman knew that he didn't was that the speakers were identical except for the color of their enclosures and the model numbers which indicated only that difference.

That famous Rolling Stone magazine cover said it best: "Perception is reality." The customer believed there was a difference between his two choices and, much more importantly, he had a preference for one over the other. It is this very real, peculiar attribute of music that separates it from other types of media.

Audio and Video Production

So, to summarize — music is a commodity. It can be manufactured very inexpensively by almost anyone, almost anywhere. And, of utmost importance to this argument, most people cannot differentiate between the most expensive and the least expensive work product.

Conversely, it takes an army of talented creative people to manufacture a professional television show or motion picture: writers, directors, producers, camera operators, actors, art directors, wardrobe wranglers, set designers, set builders, script supervisors, hair, make-up, editors, graphic artists, composers, musicians, post-production supervisors… the list goes on and on. You might have all of the skills individually, but you probably don't. And, even though you can make a video or a movie with a home video camera and the post-production suite of programs on your laptop, absolutely everyone who watches it will know it was "made with loving hands at home."

How does this relate to file sharing and piracy? There are several different schools of thought. One is that you won't invest too much time in something that you don't plan to use very often. The technology for practically innocent manipulation of video files does not really exist. You have to really want to move a video file to do it. And, more to the point, you need much more equipment, expertise and free time than the average person actually has. So taking the time and energy to download a movie or show may just not be a good use of time and resources.

Another concept is that people have much more respect for high-end motion pictures and television shows than they do for music because they can really tell the difference in video production value. Most people will not settle for a free low-quality video experience when a high-quality one is fairly inexpensive. Movie files are large and, in the illegal file sharing world, you don't know what you are really downloading until you are done downloading it. There are already movies legally available for 99-cent downloads that are guaranteed to be virus-free and exactly as advertised. Again, respect for time, value and convenience is a good weapon against piracy.

Is this to say that video and movies are not going to be pirated? Don't be silly. People are going to trade them like baseball cards — but not all people, not every movie and not all of the time.

Peer-to-Peer Networks

It was easy to shut down Napster. All you had to do was disconnect the index server from the network and it was over. That's because Napster was based upon a client-server network architecture where there was a central server with client "nodes" attached to it over the Internet, as in Figure 5.2.

Unlike a client-server network where each node is connected to a central server, a peer-to-peer (P2P) network relies on the computing power and the bandwidth of equal peer nodes that function as both "clients" and "servers" simultaneously, as seen in Figure 5.3. As each peer is added to the network, it brings along computing power, bandwidth and storage that it can share with everyone, which increases the total capacity of the system as it expands. It is the distributed nature of P2P networks that make them powerful. Should a

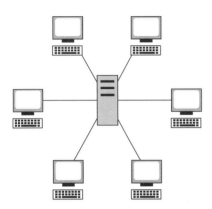

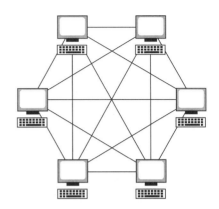

FIGURE 5.2 *Client-Server Network: This type of network can be easily shut down because each network node is connected to a central server.*

FIGURE 5.3 *Peer-to-peer networks do not have central file servers; since each node is connected to more than one other node, they are very hard to shut down.*

single node fail, peers can find replicas of the data on multiple other peers. This ability to find data without relying on a central server makes P2P networks very hard to shut down.

BitTorrent

One of the most powerful P2P networks is BitTorrent, an application created by programmer Bram Cohen. The protocol makes it possible to distribute very large files without incurring a massively large bandwidth bill to go with it. Torrent files are broken up into small pieces and distributed across the P2P network to achieve the reduction in server and bandwidth costs. BitTorrent has become one of the most popular (and controversial) ways to distribute files over the Internet since it is suspected that a large proportion of the files that are transferred using the system are traded without appropriate compensation to the rights-holders. There are outlandish claims about the number of files that are transferred using BitTorrent. Many people believe that these numbers can be used as a barometer to estimate the amount of piracy going on in the P2P space. You will also hear people say that since music files are relatively small, the large bandwidth usage must indicate that large files (like movies) are being traded freely over BitTorrent. We have seen no studies and have no empirical data to disprove these assumptions.

Wireless Mesh Networks

Simply stated, a mesh network is a communications network that has two or more paths connecting any individual node. If you have a wireless router and a bunch of

Content   **Contact**

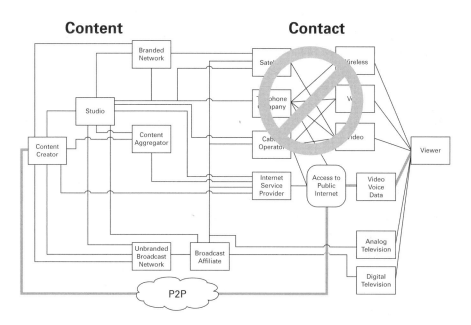

FIGURE 5.4 *Mesh and P2P networks have an opportunity to bypass the system operators and go straight to the consumer.*

wireless connections in your house, you already have a primitive mesh network. On the horizon are very large, wireless mesh networks that will connect entertainment centers in automobiles and wireless devices of every description. The unique quality of a mesh network is that it is not centralized. Each individual network node simply connects to the node or nodes that are closest to it. This makes the network "self-healing," because a node can malfunction or drop out without having any effect on the other nodes around it. The working nodes simply find other nodes to connect to. Imagine a swarm of automobiles on a highway all wirelessly connected to each other. Traffic information would be real time. Your car could even tell the car behind you that your brakes were applied with more than usual force which might keep you from getting rear-ended. The applications are practically endless.

Media and entertainment mesh networks are going to pop up everywhere. There's no way to stop them. How they are exploited and how the power is harnessed will have a significant effect on how media is distributed in the coming years.

While there are some ambiguities about what can legally be done with these evolving infrastructures, there is no ambiguity at all with respect to the power of distributed computing and how much it will change the world in which we live.

Content vs. Contact

If you examine Figure 5.4, you will notice that we have divided our traditional distribution diagram into two areas: content and contact. All of the content providers are on the left side of the diagram and all of the contact providers are on the right. Traditional contact providers are the system operators. They not only provide voice and video, they provide data access as well. The cloud on the bottom of the diagram marked P2P represents the entire world of mesh networks and the file sharing space.

Many system operators fear that there is a real chance that consumers can bypass traditional broadcast network infrastructures and use their personal data connections to obtain content virtually free of charge. This fear is well placed. Should a significant number of heavy media users choose to bypass traditional networks for even half of their media consumption, the system operators would feel the financial impact.

Key Takeaways

- Compression is a fact of networked life. How audio and video files are compressed has a significant effect on their quality when played back.

- Napster was a client-server file sharing network; that's why it was easy to shut down. Mesh and P2P networks are decentralized, which makes them extremely hard to shut down.

- The value of professional program directors should never be underestimated.

- To a computer, audio and video files are the same — but video files are much, much larger.

- Piracy issues for video will be different than they are for audio — this has more to do with the sociology of usage than technology.

6 Content, Storytellers, Gatekeepers and Related Skills

When people say "Content is king," they don't mean your content — unless you happen to be holding the rights to distribute games from major sports franchises, episodes of hit prime time television series or reruns of big off-network sitcoms. Saying content is king is like saying hits are important. It is an absurd, overused, oversimplified way of communicating the idea that good business models revolve around the "business of hits."

However, since the financial barriers to entry of the networked television business are significantly lower then those of the network television business, the economics of the "business of hits" is being redefined. And, the inherent two-way nature of the technology that enables networked television has some added benefits for storytellers.

Storytelling

Somewhere back in time, we learned how to listen to a speech. And, whenever the concept of an imagined performance first occurred to someone, the concept of an audience sitting quietly and paying attention was not far behind.

Whatever it was that caused the first people to gather around a speaker, or compelled a crowd to experience an event as a group, still lives in us to this day. Because it does, an in-person report about a fire in a distant part of a prehistoric savanna and a televised report about an identical fire occurring today would be astonishingly similar.

Although separated by thousands of years, the stories would share many attributes. They would both have beginnings, middles and endings. They would both follow a story arc that included a rising action, climax and falling action. They would both contain the essential story elements of who, what, when, where, why and how. And, finally, they would both be set using some combination of the only three story lines in existence: man against himself, man against man, and man against nature.

We do not instinctively respond to stimulus by sitting quietly and passively observing; we learn to do it.

However, there would be one profound difference in the narrative. In our prehistoric in-person report, the audience would be able to ask questions and interact with the reporter. In our modern, televised report, the technological limits of television would prevent any such interaction. Our modern reporter would have to craft his or her narrative to anticipate the audience's questions or assemble a small group of people who could mimic the interaction to the emotional satisfaction of the distant television audience.

Story-Listening

Today, people have a fairly well-developed sense of how they are supposed to behave during various types of communication experiences. These are commonly called the conventions of a particular medium. The conventions of reading, theater, movies or television all require an audience's willingness to accept the limitations of the medium for the sake of their own enjoyment.

The seminal point here is that all of these conventions are learned behaviors. We need to be trained to understand when the images we see are real and when they are works of fiction. Anyone who has ever comforted a frightened child with the phrase, "It's only a movie," knows how powerful, but realistic, two-dimensional moving pictures can be. How many of us have been awakened by a nightmare evoked by a fictional character or event? We know they are not real because we have been taught that they are not real — but they have the power to affect us deeply.

Conversely, we are taught when an image is real. When the President addresses the nation or when the news covers a disaster, the images may look like works of fiction, but we know they are real — we know because we have been taught.

Most of us know the difference between "fake" reality and "real" reality – although it has been the subject of some controversy. There have been lawsuits brought against the people who make and distribute television, claiming that specific programs caused their clients to lose touch with reality and commit crimes or risk their lives. Just about since the day it was empanelled, the FCC has been receiving

Today, if even a handful of major television news channels decided to play a hoax on the people of the United States by reporting a fake terrorist attack or some other doomsday scenario (as Orson Wells did on October 30, 1938, with his radio play "War of the Worlds"), there would be an instant breakdown of basic social services and complete chaos would ensue. These television news sources are trusted for their respective brands of "real" reality, and nobody is trained to believe otherwise.

complaints from lobbyists and ordinary citizens about how television improperly reflects our society.

It is this learned behavior and the conventions of watching television that sets the stage for the eminent transition from network to networked television. What confuses most people is the lumping of all kinds of content into one bucket. Shows that were created for the network television model are different from shows that are just starting to be created for networked television. Yes, it is all "content," but the value of any given work is directly related to its ability to adapt to the new paradigm.

The Value of Content

Is a dial tone content? Probably not. But a television test pattern is content and, as you well know, sometimes it is more interesting than the "paid" programming (such as infomercials and shopping shows) that passes for content on the myriad channels that can't afford "real" programming. Real programming is also a grey area. What is real programming? Reality programming is real, so is emergent news, so is a very well-produced shopping channel. In fact, even a poorly produced infomercial is considered content these days. So let's just accept the idea that anything that fills up media space is content.

Part of the disruptive nature of digital technology is the impact it is having on the relationship between content and value. As we transition from network to networked television, the store of economic value in any particular piece of content may shift based upon how and when it is viewed and how well it can be protected. Let's take a look at some genres and make some educated guesses about how they might be valued in a networked television future.

News

Emergent news has a very short shelf life. It is only interesting until the story is reported. Then, it's all about follow up. You may need to reference yesterday's news for archival purposes, a follow-up story or to repurpose it for a documentary or year-end wrap-up. But, as a practical matter, nobody cares about yesterday's news.

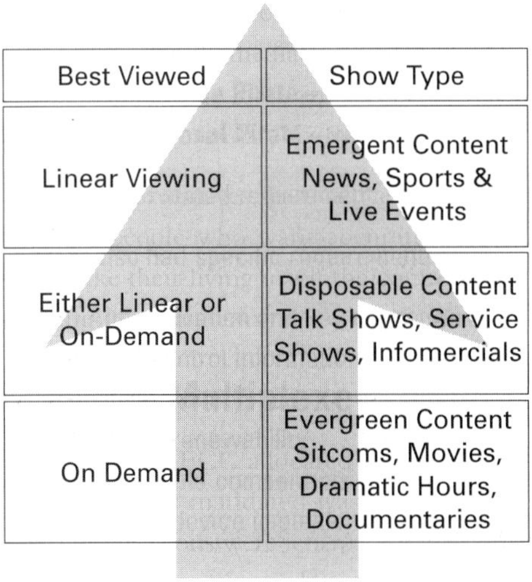

Best Viewed	Show Type
Linear Viewing	Emergent Content News, Sports & Live Events
Either Linear or On-Demand	Disposable Content Talk Shows, Service Shows, Infomercials
On Demand	Evergreen Content Sitcoms, Movies, Dramatic Hours, Documentaries

FIGURE 6.1 *Content Value in a Networked Universe.*

The value of content is different when it is distributed in a networked environment. It may be measured by when or how it is best viewed or by its susceptibility to piracy.

Because emergent news is usually served up fresh, it has a very high value to people who care about the subject. Sadly, it has a very low value to people who don't care about the subject and, more importantly, it has almost no residual value. On our scale of content value, news is close to the top.

Sports

Live sporting events could also be considered emergent — the content has significantly less value after the game is played and the score is known. However, the shelf life is a bit longer because of ancillary opportunities like highlight films, compilations and other forms of exploitation. On the content/value scale, sports also sits very near the top. On balance, news and sports share many of the same attributes, and viewers will consume news and sports media in very similar ways. There are news addicts that are as addicted to news as sports fans are to sports. And, there is a great deal of money to be made packaging these two categories in form factors that people want.

Disposable Television

Interestingly enough, disposable TV is not necessarily the most emergent or timely; it's just the fastest to go stale. Examples include infomercials that no longer pull their weight, talk shows that look dated or feature topics that are no longer in vogue, and service shows whose subjects have been rendered irrelevant because of new technology or methods. These shows typically have a relatively short shelf life, but they can be extremely profitable for the businesses that create and use them.

Entertainment

Near the bottom of the scale sits movies, sitcoms and television dramatic hours. The value propositions for these three types of entertainment could not be more different. But, in this context, they are similar because they embody a form of packaged, non-emergent entertainment. The shelf lives for this group can be very, very long. Both old and new, classic movies are coveted. From "Fountainhead" to "Psycho" to "Jaws" to "Star Wars" to "Flashdance," there is big money in hit movies. After their theatrical release, they are distributed via PPV, DVD, airlines, premium channels, network television, and syndicated television or cable — each new distribution window is a new profit center for the hit.

Network television shows can also enjoy a long and profitable "off-net" life. You will find episodes of "Star Trek," "Seinfeld," "Gilligan's Island," and "Spin City" or monster franchises like "CSI" or "Law & Order," to name a few, in DVD box sets and broadcast syndication worldwide. Here, the problem is digital distribution. As the public Internet becomes more available and file sharing services become commoditized, there is little hope of maintaining the value proposition or sales structure of these back catalogs.

Concepts Are Worthless — Packaging Is Priceless!

Production and distribution are now fairly well democratized. But there is still a great deal of value in the old infrastructure. To test this theory, try to sell the "concept" of a music show to MTV, or a news show to CNN, or a kids' show to NICK. They won't be interested in your concept. They might be interested in your talent (if you have any) but they have "best practices" distribution networks and all of the production capability they could possibly need. Your concept is meaningless to them unless you have some exclusive rights that they can't get without you. These rights may be an on-camera personality or production technique that is unique to you or a script that blows them away or, more usually, a package of all of the above that looks like a winner.

Even with all of that going for you, you have about a one percent chance of success. Many people make the mistake of thinking that since production and distribution are democratized, anyone can make a show, put it up on the Web and get people to see it. This is mythology. There is a reason the number one advertiser on television is television, as shown in Table 6.1. The promotion departments of every network, station,

	DOLLARS IN BILLIONS		
	2002	2003	2004
Total advertising revenue (including value of unpaid TV promos)	$ 133.8	$ 143.9	$ 157.6
TV self-promotion	$ 14.7	$ 16.1	$ 17.1
Percent of total ad revenue	11.0%	11.2%	10.8%

TABLE 6.1 *TV Advertises Itself More than Any Other Ad Buyer.*

Source: *TNS Media Intelligence, AdWatch 2005*

There's an old adage in the business, "When the ratings are up, it's the programming, and when the ratings are down, it's the promotion." Don't believe it. There are no ratings without promotion, because nobody can watch a show they don't know about. Making a show and putting up a Web site without promotion is like tacking your business card to a wall of 5 billion business cards. The card is available, but nobody is likely to find it.

operator and show work full time, 24/7 to get your attention.

As discussed in Chapter 3, there are several ways to promote your show using the Web, blogs, RSS and CRM in conjunction with traditional advertising and marketing. It is becoming almost imperative that contemporary media organizations use a combination of every possible media channel to promote their content. This is true, of course, for advertisers as well.

The Sociology of Content Gatekeepers

We've super-sized a generation by feeding them at QSRs (quick serve restaurants). We've told them that what they are eating is called a hamburger, so should we be surprised if they do not recognize ground sirloin on a sourdough bun as the same food-stuff? Or if they do recognize the genus (hamburger), should we be surprised that their tastes have evolved (or devolved) to a point where they will show a marked preference for MickyD's over a classic "21 Burger?"

Who Are the Gatekeepers?

Since the advent of technology, there have always been significant monetary barriers to entry for almost every creative outlet. You needed a printing press to make books, a recording studio to make music, a film studio to make films, etc. You also needed crafts-

Tastes change and art evolves, but in the before-time, they had help and guidance from gatekeepers.

people (back then they were politically incorrectly referred to as craftsmen, but at that time, all machines, boats and hurricanes were female — crazy times, they were!). The organizations and businesses that could effectively field an infrastructure and efficient distribution channels became the gatekeepers of their respective domains. To stay in business, gatekeepers needed to have a better than average ratio of hits to flops. So, they evolved rules (and bureaucracy) to filter out things that would not sell to the masses. That was then.

Personal computers and the Internet have removed the financial and technological barriers to entry, which has effectively removed the role of the gatekeeper.

Not to worry, you say: Brands and branding do the same job. No, they don't. Brands may represent what is supposed to be good, but brands are not gatekeepers. What's the difference? Well, gatekeepers prevent lots of bad ideas from being realized. Brands simply apply labels to stuff that fits into a brand strategy that does nothing to limit the amount of worthless creative that clogs up our world.

You may think that there is no such thing as worthless creative, and you'd be right! After all, if someone has taken the time to create something, shouldn't we give it the respect it deserves? Actually ... it's up to you. You are the world's foremost expert on the subject of what you will like or respect. And in this particular case, it is 100 percent about you!

Without gatekeepers, you will have to filter all of this stuff yourself. You will have to trust your own taste, and you will have to be your own program director. Of course, you could crawl into the cocoon of a trusted brand — but then where would you get new stuff that's truly leading edge? Are we sociologically ready to keep our own creative gates? And, more importantly, what are the social implications of a world without gatekeepers telling you how to think and what you should feel? Not only is this sociologically unprecedented, it is wonderful fun to think about.

Computed Gatekeepers

What makes it fun is that some new technologies are slowly starting to replace human gatekeepers. In Chapter 3, we introduced the concept that, in a networked universe, metadata may actually be more valuable than data. This idea is central to the business model and consumer value proposition of every rich media digital asset management system. Amazon's collaborative filtering system is a great example of an automated gatekeeper. Phrases like, "Customers who bought this book also bought ..." sell lots of books. Even a simple "Top 10" list is a very effective sales tool in the right environment.

Automating a recommendation can yield excellent results but there are deeper and more interesting approaches emerging. On top of the list is social tagging, where people not only create metadata for their personal use, they share it with others and — while doing so — create communities around the subject or point of interest. There are a few versions of this collaborative tagging technique in use. The idea of "tag clusters" or "tag clouds" is the process of allowing users to create their own taxonomies that feed a central community taxonomy to create a "folksonomy," which, as simply as it can be described, is a collaborative description of a given object.

Folksonomy

On www.vanderwal.net, Thomas Vander Wal (who coined the term folksonomy) describes it as "the result of personal free tagging of information and objects (anything with a URL) for one's own retrieval. The tagging is done in a social environment (shared and open to others). The act of tagging is done by the person consuming the information. The value in this external tagging is derived from people using their own vocabulary and adding explicit meaning, which may come from inferred understanding of the information/object. The people are not so much categorizing as providing a means to connect items and to provide their meaning in their own understanding."

We are going to see great strides made in interactive, behaviorally driven and collaboratively created rich media gatekeepers in the very near future. They may do a much better job of reflecting audience needs, wants and desires than their human counterparts could ever imagine.

The Philosophy of Content Form Factors

"Form follows function" is the gist of the functionalist philosophy of design. The concept is that you probably can't use a computer monitor as a fork and vice versa. So, the design of something should follow its form. Uber-architect Frank Lloyd Wright turned the concept into a religion and admonished, "Form follows function — that has been misunderstood. Form and function should be one, joined in a spiritual union." Look around you. Our world is replete with examples of this fundamental construct. There are so many examples of the functionalist design philosophy in so many areas of our lives, we sometimes mistake things for what they seem to be as opposed to what they are.

Functionalist Design Philosophy

The first musical recordings were "recordings of performances." The form followed the function. Someone sang or played and someone else recorded the performance. The concept was astoundingly simple: capture the performance for other people to hear. It was a logical extension of the way we consumed music from the beginning of time: one to one in a living room, one to a dozen in a wealthy patron's music room, one to 100 in a recital hall, one to 500 in a concert hall, one to 15,000 at an arena, one to a zillion using the magic of recording technology.

The term "recording artist" is one of the most abused terms in the business. Although everyone in the biz likes to call themselves recording artists, there actually is an entire school of modern-day recordings that cannot exist outside of the recording studio or the form of digital audio workstations. In this case, the function follows form.

Because the philosophy of an audio recordist was to authentically reproduce what a live audience would experience, a great deal of time and money was spent attempting to recreate the sensation and emotional power of attending a live performance. Somewhere on the road to this goal the industry took a gigantic turn. With the advent of sound-on-sound recording and sound-with-sound recording (multi-track recording systems), musicians and producers started to "perform" recordings. They made recordings using equipment and technology to create sounds and performances that could not actually be performed by musicians (live, dead or recorded). This is not a semantic exercise, it was a fundamental change in the way music was created and realized.

It's not just music. Look at old films of stage plays or ballets. The directors locked down the cameras and let the movement on stage do the work. In the post-MTV, post-"Star Wars" world of quick cuts and video effects, the editor and special effects directors are actually characters in many films and videos — so much so that the storylines could not exist without their work.

Visit the sound stage of a modern movie production; you may only see green screens, harnesses and camera dollies. Actors who are speaking to each other on screen may never actually meet in person. Entire characters are created with computer graphics and never exist except on the finished film. In fact, some A-budget movies require so much video compositing that the actors actually never see the sets until they attend the premiere.

These transitions are actually quite new from a historical perspective: about 45 years old for music and somewhat less for film and video. However, this unusual reverse design philosophy is popping up everywhere. We can call it the "Formist School." Here function completely follows form. It's a DVD, it's a Flash movie, it's a mash-up, it's a re-mix, it's a video stream, it's a rich media site... it simply can't exist in any other form.

Some students of arts and letters will argue that oil paintings can't exist in any other form factor either. This may be true from a purist's point of view, but in reality, oil is an artist's medium, not a form factor. An oil painting can be reproduced as a photograph, a photograph on canvas (some of which would fool a curator's eye), or shown in a video or slide presentation or PowerPoint deck. You cannot demonstrate the features of a DVD experience without the functionality of a DVD player. Nor can you demonstrate the features of a rich media Web site or a GUI without the hardware for which it was designed.

The Democratization of Production

How much money does it take to produce a television show? That's like asking how much is a car? A television show can cost literally any amount of money and take anywhere from real time to years. But we don't need to concern ourselves with high-budget productions; they are usually funded by people or companies that have a value chain associated with high-budget productions. It is a highly evolved, self-regulated system. The question is always, how little can you spend to realize the production concept? And, more to our point, is there a way to make money (or at least get paid) for making the show?

Much has been said about the disruptive nature of the democratization of production tools. Inexpensive digital cameras are ubiquitous. And, to be sure, daily advancements in desktop audio and video post-production software — coupled with the constant downward price pressure on personal computer solutions — have seriously commoditized production ability. But ... it has done absolutely nothing to commoditize production capability.

The average American 25-year-old has watched more than 36,000 hours of television. Nielsen puts the number at about 4.5 hours each day. That qualifies almost any American television viewer as the undisputed expert in what they personally like to watch and how much attention they usually pay to production values (the quality of the elements in a show, including video, graphics, music, sonic quality, sets, lights, actors, costumes, number of cameras, etc.). The importance of production values is relative to the content. In an emergent news story, any image is better than no image. You would be willing to put up with pops and clicks on a reproduction of an old Enrico Caruso recording because the content is so much more important the production quality. However, you might not be willing to watch a one-hour prime time drama that was shot with home video equipment and that didn't have a music track or any enhanced sound effects. Even if the story was compelling, you would instantly know that the production values were well below your usual preferences, and the lack of production values would seriously impact your decision to watch.

The cost of a production is substantially related to how many people it will take to produce the show, not the cost of the equipment used to produce it.

Equipment is usually rented, not because it is unaffordable, but because production companies are not in the business of owning equipment.

Does low-cost, high-tech equipment lower productions costs? Does the advent of prosumer technology disrupt and democratize production technique? No. Not really. On an average shoot, the cost of equipment rental is not material to the budget. A professional cameraman has the same day rate no matter what camera he is shooting with. You will still need a lighting director, gaffer, grip(s), etc. The production will still need actors, hair and makeup, wardrobe, sets, catering, a grip truck, a director and on and on.

This is not to say that an average person could not walk into an electronics or computer store, spend under $10,000, and walk out with the equipment necessary to produce a broadcast-quality show. It is done everyday. However, having the equipment to produce a broadcast-quality show and actually producing one are two very different things.

Back in 1998, the year that the MiniDV digital videotape format was introduced, people were espousing the virtues of this new breakthrough technology. Finally, the consumer electronics industry had put a digital video camera capable of making near-broadcast quality images in the hands of anyone who wanted one. That April, on a panel presented by the Emmy Advanced Media Committee, Fred Siebert (principal of Frederator) put the issue into perspective in his own special way: "… yeah, they can buy cameras … but most people suck!" The audience laughed hard because Fred was right. Without talent behind the camera, it is just a very expensive paperweight.

But all production technology is not hardware. Post-production software and graphics, editing, compositing, sweetening and animation programs are becoming democratized as well. The impact of this technology is just beginning to be felt. In the hands of digital natives, production software is a great equalizer. We are going to see the volume of "professional looking" work product increase exponentially. To paraphrase Fred Siebert, most of it may still suck, but some of it won't. This is because software on a personal computer can be mastered by an individual. You can look forward to some wonderful creative work done by people who, until recently, could not overcome the financial barriers to production.

Networked Producers and Content Creators

Notwithstanding size or success, there are basically two types of production entities: independent and distributor-affiliated. An independent producer is a person or company that can produce a show but must find a third party to distribute it. A distributor-affiliated producer is part of an organization which includes distribution. In practice, there are business agreements that blur the distinction between the two, such as "first look" deals or wholly-owned subsidiary studios that are free to sell to other networks, etc.

Regardless of whether a producer is independent or distributor-affiliated, producers are really manufacturers. They manufacture their product and wholesale it to a distributor. The distributor may be one of the giant media conglomerates or it might be a corporate client who simply wants to make DVDs and send them out to sales leads. Up until very recently, the vast majority of producers were in the wholesale business and sold their products almost exclusively business-to-business (B2B).

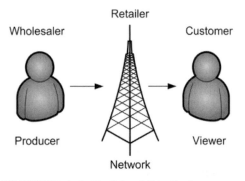

FIGURE 6.2 *Traditional Distribution.*

In the traditional model, producers wholesale their shows to networks for distribution to viewers. This is a classic two-step distribution model.

B2B businesses have a very specific type of sales force. Typically, they have a small group of high-value clients, a larger group of medium-value clients and an even larger group of low-expectation, low-profit clients which they don't pay too much attention to. B2B sales people are highly specialized and the sales technique, no matter what the industry, is based upon personal relationships.

If producers are wholesalers in the network television business, then the networks are first-tier or master distributors. Television networks package their products as if they practiced a business-to-consumer (B2C) business model, but they are actually in the B2B business as well. They aggregate content and package it for final distribution to consumers through affiliated local television stations, cable or satellite operators or other B2C businesses like system operators.

Who Owns the Customer?

When all network programming was one-to-many, linear, and with temporal and geographic restrictions, the question of who owned the customer did not have meaning. More accurately, customer ownership could be claimed by anyone who benefited from a relationship with the viewer. An advertiser could say that they were creating advertising for their "core audience" and they would be right. A programmer or content creator could say the same thing. Everyone in the value chain could claim a relationship with the viewer and be technically correct.

In theory, this is still true (even in a networked environment). However, in practice, "he who owns the billing relationship owns the customer." Therefore, then as now,

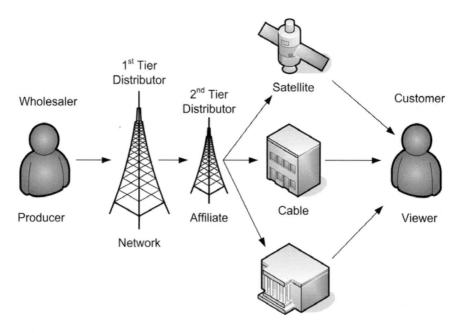

FIGURE 6.3 *Who Owns the Customer?*

The customer billing relationship is the key to a modern content distribution system.

producers bill networks, networks bill advertisers (and second-tier distributors), system operators bill consumers. Producers own their relationships with the networks, networks own their relationship with the advertisers and their distributors, and system operators own the relationship with the consumer.

This starts to get complicated as soon as you add new technology to the mix. Let's start with the current, old-fashioned, business model as just described. The network pays a producer for the rights to distribute a show. In order to make a profit, the network sells some of the available advertising to its clients. The network allows its second-tier distributor to sell some of the available advertising (usually, but not always to local advertisers) and the second-tier distributor (like a cable or satellite operator) may pay the network on a per-subscriber basis for the right to carry the network and request a few available spots to sell as well.

So in a traditional model, you might have advertising from a network, local affiliate and operator in a given show. You may also have some product placement or branded content in the body of the show that the producer keeps or shares with any of the other stakeholders in the value chain. As complicated as this may sound, this is the simplest business model for television distribution in the United States and it is not going to get any simpler.

Technology Changed the Rules

In 1960, the skills required to become President of the United States changed forever. That was the year John F. Kennedy debated Richard M. Nixon on television for the first time. When reminiscing about Kennedy's win, pundits love to cite that he was tanned and good-looking, with great hair and professionally applied make-up, while Nixon appeared pale and had a nervous demeanor and sweaty brow. They say that Nixon won on the radio but Kennedy won on TV. No matter how you look at it, after 1960 everyone running for public office had to be extremely video-aware to succeed.

In 1980, MTV signed on with a video entitled "Video Killed the Radio Star," and they weren't kidding. It was no longer acceptable just to be a good musician; you also needed to be a good-looking, video-savvy entertainer.

After the new paradigms emerged, not only was every politician and musician required to have video skills, they were required to have expert ones.

The Transition of Skill Sets

As a practical matter, the technological transition we are experiencing is trivial when compared to the sociological transition that must accompany it. To succeed and prosper during and after this technological transition, almost every organization along the value chain will have to fundamentally change how they do business.

Producers will need new skills and new infrastructure to take advantage of networked television's new business rules and interactive technology.

For example, as previously described, almost all producers are manufacturers/wholesalers. Their sales relationships are with distributors. In a networked television world, the technology allows for a significant disintermediation of the master distributors.

In a non-linear universe, the broadcast network brands become almost meaningless to consumers. After all, people watch shows, not networks. The programs are the brands, and producers are empowered to become B2C companies. There's only one problem. Most producers do not have the skills or infrastructure to take advantage of this technology.

A production company has a few key executives who have strong relationships with their master distributors. Post-transition, they will have to have highly successful consumer relationship management systems in place or they will not be able to even marginally exploit a networked world. They will have to modify their organizations and transition from wholesaler to retailer. Many of them won't be able to do it. So you can easily see a new kind of intermediary evolving to help producers take advantage of the networked world. They may be an evolved version of traditional networks, but they probably won't be built on the old infrastructure. Are Google, Yahoo! and MSN the new networked distribution channels? They are well-positioned to help producers make the transition.

Key Takeaways

- One-to-one storytelling has changed little over the years, but the conventions of one-to-many storytelling are learned behaviors. This is important as we transition to networked, inherently two-way, television.

- Content has different value (and revenue potential) in an on-demand, file sharing, networked world than it did in the past.

- Professionally packaging all of the elements required to complete a project is still the best way to bring a piece of content to market.

- Ubiquitous, democratized production capability has flooded the Internet with content representing a very wide quality delta. As the gatekeeper's role is assumed by the proletariat, we may experience interesting sociological changes.

- Networked technology offers content creators direct access to their customers — they will have to develop the consumer-relationship marketing skills to fully realize new business opportunities.

- Billing relationships will ultimately dictate much of the changes to the existing business rules.

7 Networked Value Propositions

One of the big promises of networked technology is the "redistribution" of wealth. This is usually grossly overstated by supplicants and adepts of the anti-establishment free bits and bytes crowd. In a zero-sum version of the future, they predict that free files will obliterate profits and that all data (intellectual property and content) will flow unfettered through a myriad of mesh networks worldwide. As egalitarian as this might sound, it is a highly unlikely scenario.

Owing to its inherent two-way nature and built-in data-collecting capabilities, networked technology does have the power to help businesses explore new marketplaces and potentially find profits where none existed before. This chapter takes a look at databases, long tail content, walled gardens, physical form factors and the socio-techno divide.

Databases

A database is an organized collection of information, and collecting information is one of the best things that two-way, interactive systems can be programmed to do. The store of economic value embodied in any particular database is a function of the knowledge that can be ascertained by querying the information stored therein. So, in a networked environment, we can expect to see large amounts of data that can be monetized in many different ways.

Databases can contain user preferences of all kinds, playlists, behaviors, records of transactions and user profiles, to name a few. Databases can ask for user input or can self-assemble based on the way users interact with the system. All networked television systems will make extensive use of databases and this book cannot possibly cover all of the ways they will be used. However, there is a type of consumer database that has had the attention of the television industry for quite some time. It is the database associated with a very profitable use of the medium known as "direct response" television or DRTV.

Direct Response Television

You are probably familiar with infomercials and the :120 second direct response television spots hawking everything from cutlery to indoor grills. And, of course, you are familiar with QVC, HSN and all of the other shopping channels. These DRTV businesses count their customer databases amongst their most valuable assets. Why? Most people will never buy anything directly from a television advertisement or a shopping channel, but the ones who do are literally worth their weight in gold.

The way you monetize this type of database is often referred to as "upsell." Have you ever wondered why DRTV spots will often offer to double consumers' orders for the same price or give them the merchandise virtually for free? Upsell. Once you have captured the consumer's contact and credit card information, you can use that information to attempt to sell them anything. They are DRTV buyers and they now belong to a very exclusive demographic club – yours!

Networked television may entice direct response advertisers to reallocate money from their non-television budgets to exploit the paradigm.

Part of the unrealized promise of interactive television and the future promise of networked television is the conversion of the billions of non-television direct response advertising dollars into DRTV or networked DRTV dollars. Alas, this is one of the other great myths of interactive television.

For years, television advertising has been bought on a "waste" model. We will cover this in Chapter 10. Although DRTV advertisers buy a fair amount of "gross impression" or waste model television advertising in various form factors (such as :30s, :60s, :120s and infomercials), they have evolved methods to measure (within the limits of the technology) their cost-per-lead, cost-per-order or any other metric they wish to associate with success. They can even calculate the amount of loss-per-order or "opportunity cost" they are willing to accept to capture a qualified lead for upsell.

Traditionally, the bulk of DRTV advertising dollars has been spent on direct mail and print advertising, with only certain categories profiting from the use of television. Can networked television succeed where broadcast interactive television failed? We are likely to see many new and interesting kinds of database marketing as we transition from network to networked television. The lure of the direct response dollars is an exceptional motivator.

The Tale of the Long Tail

The Eskimos have 27 words for snow... The Great Wall of China is the only manmade object you can see from space... More than 20 percent of value is locked up in the "Long Tail." These are all myths that have such romantic power, you just want to believe them; but they are still myths.

In October 2004, Chris Anderson, editor-in-chief of Wired magazine wrote "The Long Tail," a brilliant article. In it, Anderson argues that products that are in low demand or have low sales volume can collectively make up a market share that rivals or exceeds the relatively few current bestsellers if sales and distribution costs are low enough. Because the article was well-written and the premise seems to make sense, people started adding the phrase "long tail content" to their PowerPoint decks and using the term to ascribe all kinds of magical attributes to previously unsalable content. Not a disaster, just kind of fun to watch — in a schadenfreude kind of way.

In 1906, long before the long tail, Italian economist Vilfredo Pareto created a mathematical formula to describe the unequal distribution of wealth in his country. He observed that 20 percent of the people in Italy owned 80 percent of the wealth. In the 1940s, Dr. Joseph M. Juran attributed his own observation of "vital few and trivial many" to the 80/20 rule, which he called "Pareto's Law" or the "Pareto Principle."

As a practical reality, the 80/20 rule applies in almost the entire observable universe. Twenty percent of the distribution embodies 80 percent of the substance. Fill in the discipline, fill in the variables — it holds up time and time again. If you look at a P&L from any company in the media business, 20 percent of the content will account for 80 percent of the revenue. Why should anyone ever consider thinking about this another way?

Zipf's Distribution

There is an excellent reason to move away from the 80/20 rule: the media business is a business of hits. Hit television shows, hit movies, hit records, and so on, and when you draw a diagram to illustrate the demand for "hit" content, the resulting curve looks like a long tail (hence the title of Anderson's article).

This curve is known as a Zipf's Distribution, and it is a "1/f function." In other words, and as shown in Figure 7.1, given a set of Zipfian distributed frequencies, sorted from the most common to the least common, the second most common frequency will occur half as often as the first. The third most common frequency will occur one-third as often as the first. The nth most common frequency will occur 1/n as often as the first. This is an experimental law, not a theoretical one and it is based upon the observations of Harvard Linguist, George Kingsley Zipf. He noticed that the frequency of use of the nth-most-frequently-used word in any natural language is approximately inversely proportional to n.

So, a Zipf's Distribution is a very useful tool if you are trying to calculate the amount of equipment you are going to need to deliver VOD content. It's a great way to determine how many of each item to order for the "best seller" list. It's a good indicator of how many DVDs you'll need of the most popular titles in your rental establishment. But it does nothing to tell you about the actual value of any of the items.

An item can be most popular because it is free. It can be most popular because it is less expensive and considered a better value. A Zipf's distribution is an excellent way to plot a demand curve and, if properly applied, the insight gained can be very useful.

Results

The problem with the long tail is not with the math, or even with the idea; the problem is the way people interpret (or more precisely, misinterpret) Anderson's concept. With regard to content (audio and video on the Internet), there is a pretty good theoretical argument to be made for the value proposition of the long tail. After all, in theory, it goes on forever and it is full of valuable things like old Sidney Bechet and Bunk Johnson recordings. These artists, by default, have a place on the long tail.

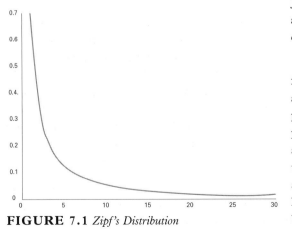

FIGURE 7.1 *Zipf's Distribution*

But, how will consumers find this long-tail content, and if they do, who will get paid? Promotion and micro-payment schemas are an absolute requirement for this type of sale, and they come at a cost. Consumers may have heard of these guys and even be willing to search for their stuff, but who has heard of the 70s disco band "Demon Rum," whose recordings are also on the tail? Just because these properties are in your catalog, does the long tail guarantee you a profit if you invest in encoding and storing them?

Take a movie that already exists. Retain counsel (internal or external) to get all of the appropriate clearances for reduction of the work to digital files. Rent a film chain and color correction suite for the day. Make a digital video file of the entire movie. Down-convert it to every usable format for current distribution and then create files in every resolution required from 56k up.

There is a very real point where marginal cost exceeds marginal gain and it happens very close to the borderline of the top 20 percent of the selections available on the long tail.

Now the fun starts. Create meta-tags and descriptions that are meaningful to search engines so people can find the file. Add a DRM wrapper so you can get paid. Come on, take a guess ... how much have we spent on this single title? For a feature-length motion picture, it might easily be $15,000 sitting on a server ready to go. Now remember, we don't know who wants to watch this movie, we are just sure that in time, according to the Zipfian distribution, every movie will be watched. Add the cost of money to this equation and multiply by every title in your library. Does it still sound like a good idea?

You will probably want to do an analysis to determine which movies are the best investments. Which will bring the best return in the shortest time frame? In other words, you'll need to determine which movies are in the top quintile (top 20 percent of the curve) of revenue producers to determine if the content is worth encoding at all.

But isn't the long tail an accurate way to look at content usage? Yes, it is. And it's great if the content can be encoded and stored at a very low cost. It's just not a profitable way to look at a back catalog that was not created with the long tail in mind. It is never less expensive to prepare content for long tail distribution than it is during the original production process. If you know that one day you will want to store your content online and make the files available for electronic distribution, you can easily take advantage of the long tail. However, after the fact or with existing material in non-digital formats, there are very real costs associated with encoding and storage. When you calculate those costs and the cost of capital, the value chain (or lack thereof) is clear.

So, as it has been for time immemorial, the 80/20 rule is the clear winner for modeling return on investment in the information age or any other. No disrespect intended to those who have been spinning the tale of the long tail.

The Value of Walled Gardens and Form Factors

Computer files may be the "final" form factor, but that is not stopping media companies from trying to extract every last bit of value from each file. Because most media is delivered through walled gardens or physical copies, even files can be resold. This is especially true where service providers control the entire distribution channel (like some cell phone carriers do). Table 7.1 illustrates how many times consumers may pay for the same piece of content.

On top of all of that, if the media company has their way, you will pay $12.95 per month for the subscription to HBO which will broadcast the movie and the concert on their linear and VOD channels and ultimately, part of your basic cable or satellite package will go to pay a per subscriber fee to Music Choice where you will hear the song. You might also pay $12.95 per month to a satellite radio company where you can hear the song and, if Apple continues its dominance over the personal music player world, you could ultimately purchase a co-branded Video iPod with the complete collected works of this artist (including this song) for about $300

Download the song on iTunes	$0.99
Download a portion of the same song to use as a ringtone	$2.49
Use a portion of the song as a ringback tone	$1.99
Purchase a download of the video of the song on iTunes	$1.99
Purchase a still image of the artist of the song to use as wallpaper	$1.49
Purchase the DVD of the movie featuring the song	$14.99
Purchase the CD which includes the song	$19.99
Watch a PPV or VOD of the movie featuring the song	$3.95
Watch the HD version of the VOD concert featuring the song	$6.95
Total revenue from one content source	**$54.83**

TABLE 7.1 *Revenue streams from the same content source.*

Compatibility and Portability

Any time a consumer wants to move their files to a new device, the media company wants to charge another fee. Consumers put up with this now, but they won't for long. When you switch cell phones, your provider can sometimes move your phone book from the old phone to the new one, but not always. When they can't, you are doomed to a few hours of hunting and pecking with your thumbs to re-enter the data. When you subscribe to a set of video games on your cell phone and you switch to a new phone, you have to re-subscribe to every game. People put up with it, but they are not happy.

How many times can you sell the same master file? There doesn't seem to be any limit. You just have to keep the walls in the walled gardens up and keep the formats incompatible. In fact, it seems like a pretty good business.

How long will it take for consumers to realize that they are paying for the exact same thing over and over again? When will they insist on portability? And if it is not available, when will they take matters into their own hands? More to the point, when will certain consumer electronics manufacturers decide to capitalize on this model and enable ordinary people to truly "own" their media? These are just a few of the questions that will be answered during the transition from network to networked television.

The Socio-Techno Divide

According to the Teens and Technology (Pew Internet & American Life Project, July 2005), less than 73 percent of teens living in households earning under $30,000 annually use the Internet. This is in stark contrast to their upscale counterparts, where 90 percent of teens from families earning more than $30,000 a year go online and, at the highest income levels, households earning more than $75,000 a year, 93 percent of teens go online.

To some, these statistics suggest a significant socio-techno divide, since fewer low-income households afford their children the Internet access that higher income households do. What the study does not say is that household broadband access is not required to be part of our mass-mediated culture. According to Generation M: Media in the Lives of 8- to 18-Year-Olds (Kaiser Family Foundation Study, March 2005), more than 80 percent of teens live in a household that has cable or satellite television and a computer. So the vast majority of digital natives do have access to some level of interactivity.

And then there's wireless access: 45 percent of all teens own a mobile phone and 33 percent have used a mobile phone to send a text message. Pagers and mobile phone usage in low-income households makes up quite a bit of the difference with regard to access to interactivity.

There is a concept that broadband penetration will cause a sociological divide as measurable media metrics allow marketers to concentrate their efforts on the wins they can count while ignoring the rest of America that doesn't have high-speed access – but this will probably never happen.

Almost anyone who is interested in being part of the "digital media experience" can afford to get in the game.

Bandwidth is a commodity, and it is going to become less and less expensive as time goes on. Mobile devices, not personal computers, are already the computer of choice for the vast majority of computer-illiterate Americans, and these devices are practically (and literally) given away. The downward price pressure on distribution networks is almost unbearable. To be sure, there are (and will be) other socioeconomic forces that cause dramatic class distinctions, but the exclusivity of media penetration is not on the list.

Chapter 8, "Media Consumption," moves to the most important aspect of any content delivery system, the consumer. After all, what good is a network with no one to use it?

Key Takeaways

- The practical exploitation of transactional databases is a goal of networked television, although pricing based on actual response metrics is extremely dispassionate and represents a seriously two-edged sword.

- The 80/20 rule is the best way to evaluate ROI for back catalog. A power law like a Zipf's Distribution is an excellent way to evaluate demand.

- Walled gardens are valuable assets, but as consumers acquire new, more powerful technology, they will start to push back.

- Broadband is a commodity and will become even less expensive in the future.

8 Media Consumption

The way consumers consume media is one of the most researched aspects of modern life. Understanding how humans use communication, respond to brand messages, value premium services, and acquire and consume consumables is more art than science. But this has not stopped the scientists from attempting to quantify every aspect of the process.

It is always impressive to witness an analytical mind trying to understand and describe the mind of an artist. It takes on many forms. Tone-deaf music critics, visually jaded movie critics, art critics who couldn't draw a straight line with a ruler and, yes, market analysts who haven't the foggiest notion of the intuitive, artistic nature of marketing.

Quantifying and Comparing Media Consumption

Be that as it may, there are some times when it is helpful to graph, plot or otherwise attempt to describe the indescribable. One scale that does this is the Advanced Media Consumption Index. (AMCI, created by Advanced Media Ventures Group, LLC, and used with permission, http://www.amvgllc.com) This scale describes the media form factors in common use in the United States and assigns a number value to each (see Figure 8.1).

99

On the lowest part of the scale, we have a person who lives "in the middle of nowhere." It could be Bob, a 39-year-old who lives in a remote cabin in the backwoods. The media Bob consumes consists of a weekly trip to town where he catches up on the local gossip, gets supplies and reads a fax copy of the summarized front page of last week's *New York Sunday Times*. Bob has a transistor radio somewhere in the cabin, but its batteries died a few years ago and he keeps forgetting to get new ones. He has no television, no magazine subscriptions and very few books. Bob is a creature of the backwoods and he doesn't consume very much media.

Some would argue that this should be a "one" on the scale and "zero" should indicate absolutely no media exposure. But, in the 21st century in the United States of America, it is absolutely impossible not to consume some kind of media at some point in your life. Even Bob encounters a small portion of media each week.

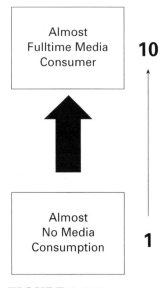

FIGURE 8.1 *The Advanced Media Consumption Index.*

On the opposite end of this scale is Jonathan, a 32-year-old Wall Street derivatives trader. He has quite a collection of media consumption touchpoints:

Work

- Two mobile phones

- A PDA

- A Bloomberg terminal

- Three computer monitors

- Five television sets tuned into the five major cable news channels going all day long

Home

- A Bloomberg terminal

- Three computers

- Six HDTV monitors (in different rooms)

- Daily home delivery of the *Wall Street Journal, Financial Time*s, *The New York Times* and *The New York Post* (for fun)

- Monthly subscriptions to *Forbes, Fortune, FHM* and two dozen controlled circulation trade and business publications

- A DVR in every room

- Cable for his broadband

- Satellite television (so he can get NFL Sunday Ticket)

- Six telephone lines: three are VoIP, one is a POTS line (Plain Old Telephone Service), and two are an ISDN pair (legacy Internet backup) from the local phone company

- Current generation video game console in the bedroom and in the living room; both are connected to the Internet

- A local area network and a storage area network

- WiFi in every room as well as Cat 6 wired connections to a very serious server

Jonathan has a personal Web site, eight e-mail accounts, and blogs about his business and one of his passions, wine. Jonathan is a "10" on the AMCI and as soon as someone figures out a way to implant a WiFi chip in his brain, he will have it done.

With respect to media consumption, everyone in America falls somewhere between these two extremes. What's interesting about this scale is how unimportant the actual definitions of each media consumer are. Technology is fluid and people use it as needed to consume media, so any way you want to define an avid media consumer and a nonconsumer is fine for our purposes.

Media Consumption Form Factors

What is important is the theory that the higher up on the scale you are, the more important the form factors of your media become to you, as shown in Figure 8.2. Someone who is a seven on this scale will demonstrate a set of preferences not only for which media they consume, but the form factor with which they consume it. So, for example, Jonathan (our 10 from the previous paragraph) will not only know which model of PDAs are available, he will have a decided, reasoned preference for one over the other.

The converse is also true. Bob, our backwoodsman who tips the AMCI at 1, really doesn't care what form the single page summary of last week's news takes. Was it faxed, snail mailed, carrier-pigeoned, on thermal paper, laser paper, copier paper, newsprint? Bob doesn't care.

When thinking about the future (near or far) and how people might adopt technology or, more importantly, change their behaviors or preferred form factors, you have to add another layer to the AMCI: target demographics. Before making an investment in a transition technology or betting on a media-based behavioral change, you need to know where your core audience sits on this scale. Some people believe that early adopters occupy the top 20 percent of the AMCI, others think that early adoption is technology-specific and cannot be predicted.

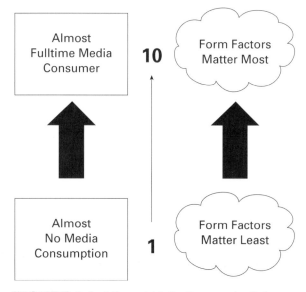

FIGURE 8.2 *Advanced Media Consumption Index with Form Factor Overlay.*

One important note about early adopters: No matter what the industry, they rarely indicate anything about potential success or failure of any particular technology. Most technology marketers know this. On the other hand, most media consumers must consume media before it goes stale - so early adoption of a media technology or form factor may be an excellent indication of future success. Remember, marketing is more "art" than "science."

Applying the Pareto Principle to the AMCI

As in most observed media indices, Pareto's Principle (the 80/20 rule, discussed in Chapter 7) applies here. Eighty percent of the media is consumed by 20 percent of the population. But it is not the top 20 percent of this scale. The counterintuitive notion about the AMCI is that the top quintile of this scale does not necessarily consume more media than the fourth quintile; they just consume it differently.

Jonathan, our derivatives trader, consumes an unbelievable amount of media each day, but he only has so much time to do it. Jennifer, a 14-year-old ninth grader from a Midwest suburb actually spends more time than Jonathan consuming media; she just

There are dozens of research studies that quote the average number of brand impressions an average person might encounter each day. The median for a city dweller is about 3,000 images daily. We live in a mass-mediated culture, and the messages are inescapable.

doesn't have as many gadgets to do it with. That being said, she has a television set, a video game console, a mobile phone, wireline phone, a computer and an MP3 player. She's probably a seven on the AMCI, but she may actually consume more media than some of the 10s do, because she has more free time.

The AMCI is a useful tool for any type of forecasting. You can create your own and get syndicated research or download public domain research from Web sites to add the appropriate layers to build your model.

Consumers as Video Program Directors

On-demand technologies ask consumers to become their own program directors. We have discussed the role and value of professional program directors, but there are legitimate times that consumers are willing to be their own program directors. A few examples include entertaining friends at a party, collecting music or videos for a trip, or for content lovers, personalizing their media experience. We could probably list dozens of reasons why a person might choose to be his or her own program director.

The key problem with on-demand technology is not desire; it is complexity. It's just too hard for the average person to do. Now, making a playlist in iTunes could not be simpler. But, putting your iPod in shuffle mode is actually easier, and it is also the path of least resistance.

There are other factors that help with playlist creation. Recommendation engines and collaborative filtering like Amazon's "if you like this … you might also like …" are good ways to help people pick the right stuff for their playlists. Consumers can also skew shuffle modes, setting them to play the content they manually play the most more often than the content they play less often.

Of course, all of this technology requires consumers to collect all of their media into one place. Amazingly, almost everyone can now carry their entire music collection with them. If you purchase a 60GB player, it would be very, very hard for you to fill it up with current technology compressed audio files.

We usually think of playlists in terms of music, but we shouldn't. We should be thinking about this in terms of content or media. Imagine living in a world where you could carry your entire video collection with you. Or, more likely, pick from a list of any video you ever heard of (and many you'd never heard of) for immediate download.

You can already carry a great deal of video with you as individual files. As the list grows, how will you choose to consume it? Will you make a habit of creating playlists for yourself? Will someone sponsor them in order to help you offset your costs? Will trusted brands make the playlists for you? When downloading a show, which brand will be more important to the consumer experience: The Apple Store or the ABC television network? As consumers start to purchase and legally download shows, how will they prefer to do it?

Playlists and Advertising

An on-demand "playlist with commercials" might come with free content. In the linear world, it's called television and radio. Program directors use playlists in traditional network programming. Trusted linear (as opposed to on-demand) playlists can be found in the TV Guide under channel names like Nick at Nite, The Disney Channel, MTV, The History Channel, etc. These are branded networks and they make a promise to viewers: if you watch, you will be treated to a group of programs that are informative, enlightening and entertaining on the topic(s) for which the network is best known.

There is no term to describe a "playlist with commercials" in the non-linear world – but there will be soon. Imagine downloading a playlist and agreeing to listen to the commercials in their entirety. This may sound like a twisted "back to the future" use of new technology, but it is not. Content is expensive to produce but sponsors are willing to pay for it if consumers are willing to listen to their messages.

So imagine a system where consumers get free downloadable content for their non-linear system, if they agree to watch or listen to ads. If consumers skip the ads, will they have to pay? Obviously, this particular system does not yet (and may never) exist. But, it is going to be important to learn how to deal with consumers who create their own media environments. Will they subscribe, purchase, steal or rent? These questions will be answered by combining simple technology and a simple business model.

Consumers and Their Privacy Issues

In order to give a consumer the best possible viewing experience, networked television systems will need to know as much about them as possible. The technology to accomplish this is built in to the network. By definition, networked television is two-way and interactive.

There are going to be significant privacy issues in the era of networked television. These issues may end up bifurcating the networked system into information haves and have-nots. People willing to share their information with the network will have an enhanced experience, while people unwilling to share their information will have a diminished experience. The legal battle will be very similar to the anti-spyware regulations that the Web world has gone through, since the technology is almost identical.

Anything, Anytime, Anyplace

In a networked television universe, the concepts of time and place do not exist. There are no geographic boundaries and there are no pre-defined start times. Every program is accessible everywhere and available on demand. This non-linear technology cannot have a big impact on mainstream television until the business culture starts to think of this in terms of a true paradigm shift, not a parlor trick they simply pay lip service to.

The availability of on-demand technology will not, in and of itself, turn television viewers into "viewsers." It is only the true needs of consumers and their willingness to change their behaviors that will fully empower the exploitation of this technology. We are going to see hundreds of companies come and go over the next few years as consumer behaviors and on-demand technology evolve into a profitable system. However, we cannot predict which version of on-demand technology and which set of consumer behaviors are likely to merge to form this ecosystem.

It is also important to consider that there is more than one technological way to fulfill the goals of the "anything, anytime, anyplace" ideologues. Using a traditional cable system with legacy broadcasting technology and DVRs, you could deliver about 210,000 two-hour movies per week. Deployment of new technology is not the only barrier.

The Fantasy Paradigm

In an on-demand, networked universe, a show can be any length, a commercial can be any length and consumers can view anything at any time, from anywhere on any device. However, there must be profitable economic models for content creators and distributors or it will remain a fantasy.

VOD and the Single Channel Universe

How often have you channel surfed up and down your entire cable or satellite television system, looked at every guide listing and come to the conclusion that you had 500 channels and nothing to watch? You're not alone. Almost everyone has felt that frustration at some point in their television lives.

Part of the problem is the way linear television is programmed. Networks and stations break the day up into dayparts (see Chapter 1) and they program for the audience that they think will be watching at that time. As with all things statistical, you can fairly accurately predict what a population might want, but not what an individual will want – so, television programmers just guess and use various sample-based metrics to determine their success.

When coupled with the notion that people don't really like to go out to video rental stores, the cable industry came up with the idea of creating VOD. In theory, this technology solves two problems at once: you'll be able to find the one program you want to watch and end those undesirable trips to Blockbuster Video. That's the theory. You have to wonder just how much research the cable industry did before they decided to spend the billions of dollars they've spent building VOD. Was there really a consumer need for this service? Is there?

The questions are moot because the systems have been built and, as one would suspect, VOD lives up to its name. It is, in fact, video on demand. You can choose from a bunch of titles, press a button and within a few seconds, the video will start playing.

The initial VOD offering is so unbelievably limited in its capabilities that the door has been left wide open for entrepreneurs to exploit the public Internet and to create IPTV offerings that will be much more desirable and consumer-friendly than current VOD.

The cable industry uses this technology as a unique selling principle for its services because it requires two-way interactivity and satellite cannot offer it. Although IPTV systems can, the telcos are creating IPTV offerings that are almost identical to cable, so average consumers will not be able to tell one system from another.

Television on Demand Might Have Been a Good Idea

TVOD (which does not exist) would be a system that mimicked a television experience while allowing users to pick programming in a VOD environment or, better yet, through a graphical user interface that helped sort out the video offerings. It would also allow television commercials of various lengths to be inserted in the video stream on the fly. This would mean that instead of "baking" commercials into the programming (like they have to be with VOD) a place-holding technology would mark the spot where a television commercial would run and the creative would be pulled from a server as needed. This would allow advertisers to keep their commercials fresh and relevant to viewers no matter how long the show stayed in the TVOD system.

CONTINUED ▶

CONTINUED ▶

TVOD would also have the option to let viewers "drill down" through an ad by clicking the select button on their remote control. This drill-down or telescoping feature might take viewers to a longer form piece of content or, perhaps a special offer or some other type of programming that was relevant to the viewers total TVOD.

Navigation Is the Holy Grail

In the zillion-channel, walled-garden television universe, we have local stations (but probably not their digital tiers), the broadcast networks they are affiliated with, branded networks, local public access offerings, VOD and PPV. And to navigate this cornucopia of media choices we have a grid guide.

Grid Navigation

The grid displays a channel number, a four-letter description of the channel, the time of day and the title of the show (or a truncated title or single word mnemonic). We can navigate this guide using the directional arrows on the remote control.

Grid guides are not good. Even the best versions leave much to be desired. It may be the least emotionally satisfying way to learn about what's on, but it is a moderately efficient way to find something, if you know its approximate location on the grid. The problem is that you can't search effectively. When you do search, space limitations require several button presses to get the few lines of description that the guide offers for any given show.

 Some large content providers, like Discovery Networks or The Walt Disney Company have enough content to fill up an entire mosaic with their own offerings. But an all-Disney mosaic would not give consumers of kids programming a useful guide to other popular choices such as Fox Kids, Nick, and WAM!.

Mosaic Barker Navigation

Mosaic barker channels can be found on cable and satellite systems and they look and work pretty much the same on both. What you see is a screen divided up into six or eight tiles with a miniature television screen in each. Some of the pages are themed, like sports or drama or comedy, etc. Some allow you to control which channels are shown in the tiles of the mosaic.

There are various navigation techniques employed on mosaic pages, but most let you focus on a particular tile with the remote control to play the audio from that tile. Some allow you to preview the channel by clicking, others just let you navigate to the channel by clicking. Regardless, the end result is the same. You are given a graphical environment as opposed to a grid to help you make your video entertainment choices.

Networked Navigation Terms

- **Button** – a graphical button on the screen or a physical button on the remote control

- **Cursor** – a graphic, blinking bar or arrow that indicates screen position

- **EPG** – electronic program guide

- **Focus** – highlighting an area of the screen with the cursor

- **Frame** – a specific rectangular area on a screen

- **Grid or Grid Guide** – the classic interactive programming grid

- **GUI** – graphical user interface, a graphical way to interface with a system

- **IPG** – interactive program guide

- **L** – The "L" shape of a screen with a vertical bar on one side of the screen and a horizontal bar on the bottom or top

- **Lower Third** – The lower third portion of the screen, usually used for text and graphics

- **Mosaic** – a screen filled with tiles showing available entertainment options

- **Mouse** – a computer mouse

- **Navbar** – an area of the screen with navigation graphics

- **RFI** – request for information, a form that can be pre-populated to enable users to get additional information about a given offering

- **Scroll** – a linear scrolling grid guide that is not interactive

- **Select/Enter** – remote control button used to make a selection from the interactive user interface

- **Tile** – a small area of the screen, typically filled with video

- **UI** – any user interface

Mosaics are a nice alternative to grid guides, but they come with their own unique problems. For example, because the mosaic becomes new "real estate" for the system operator to sell, it has the ability to offend the promotional sensibilities of networks that don't want you thinking about programming choices from competitive networks.

The Future of Navigation

Is there a better way to navigate 500 or 1,000 channels? If there is, no one has found it yet. And what of on-demand? Not to make your brain hurt, but if we cannot navigate 500 channels, how are we going to navigate 10,000 individual shows in a networked environment? The answer is most probably a version of branded search and there is some evidence to support the concept. Most "best practices" television research firms, including Nielsen, agree that despite the fact that they can chose from over 500 channels, on average viewers regularly watch less than 15 channels. Over 90 percent of viewers are watching affiliates of the major networks — ABC, CBS, NBC, Fox, etc. — and the top ten cable channels, and the kicker: Even when viewers use PPV, VOD, the new-fashioned DVR or the old-fashioned VCR, they still are watching the same shows.

The problem is that we have so many choices that, in order to take control of our media world, we seek the comfort and familiarity of favorite brands. That being said, the statistics are often misinterpreted; mostly because people mistake unbranded networks for brands and branded networks for brands. Let's take a moment to explore the concept of television brands.

Branded Vs. Unbranded Networks

Great products make great brands, – not the other way around. A brand is only as good as its last successful product and to the level that it stands for something. Brands enable business to engender consumer trust, enjoy consumer permissions and thereby increase consumer spending (on their brand).

Want to kill a brand? Just put out some bad products — it won't take long for your brand to give up the ghost.

So how is it possible for broadcast networks to put out so many failed products and still maintain their brands? It isn't. Broadcast networks such as NBC, ABC, CBS and FOX are not consumer brands; they are trade (or business-to-business) brands.

Consumers watch shows, they don't watch broadcast networks and, for the most part, they don't watch stations either. "CSI" is the brand, not CBS; "ER" is the brand, not NBC; "Desperate Housewives" is the brand, not ABC, etc. People watch shows.

One of the hard and fast rules of television promotion is the mandatory "time and tune-in" information at the top and bottom of each spot. "Tonight on ABC, blah, blah, blah, that's tonight at 9, 8-central, only on ABC." Unbranded networks use their call letters because they can't use their actual channel locations with one-to-many broadcasting technology. Unbranded broadcast network television signals are propagated throughout the United States by affiliated local stations – each with their own channel and call letters.

Local Brands

If you live in New York, you may think that the ABC television network and WABC are the same thing, but they aren't. ABC is the network and WABC-TV is the locally owned and operated station for the New York metro. If you live in Manchester, Vermont, you watch ABC on WTEN-TV, Albany and they call themselves NEWS10. Why don't they proudly call themselves ABC and help their biggest revenue source become a national brand? Firstly, the broadcast network is not their biggest revenue source. Secondly, there is no such thing as ABC, the consumer brand.

Nobody goes home to watch ABC at night; they go home to watch "Desperate Housewives" or "Lost." The shows are the brands, not the networks.

What the local affiliates with news departments are trying to do is take their best asset — local news — and brand it. NEWS10 accomplishes a great deal of branding with this six-character logo. It says that they are a news station and that they can be found on channel 10. You may be familiar with other types of local station branding efforts like "Newschannel 10," "Eyewitness News 10," or the ever-popular, "News Center 10." There are many variations of this theme, each with a consumer value proposition, a consumer promise and specific positioning in their local markets. Stations try to brand themselves and their news product because it is, more than likely, their top revenue producing asset and they own it.

How does this work if a local station is known for its top-rated prime-time line up? Interesting question. It works because people don't watch stations or networks, they watch shows. Stations that produce local news usually produce several shows daily: a morning show (pre-network morning show circa 5-7 a.m.), a noon news show, a 5 p.m. soft news, a 6 p.m. hard news and 10 p.m. news break and an 11 p.m. late news. Independents or stations without a full primetime lineup will have a 10 p.m. hour-long news offering.

Times and durations of these shows vary by market and time zone, but an average local news station can produce as much as four hours of original news programming daily. The idea behind NEWS10 is to brand their news product, not their station call letters or their affiliated network (which are unbrandable). We only need one example of this disassociated station branding attempt to prove our point. It is repeated in every market, by almost every local station with a news department nationwide.

Switch Campaigns

Over the past few decades, a number of local stations have, for various reasons, switched network affiliations. One counterintuitive result of these switches was that the audience did not seem to follow their networks or their shows; they stayed with their local stations. Much proprietary research was done in an attempt to understand this phenomenon. Some studies suggest that people become "friends" with their local news anchors and do not feel comfortable leaving them. Other studies suggest that people are creatures of habit and that once you are in the habit of tuning in a particular channel, you are unlikely to change the behavior unless highly motivated.

Television executives will tell you that the numbers don't lie. However, all of this research was done using sample-based metrics and diaries and it is just as likely that people had switched the channels to find the shows they liked and simply misreported their behaviors. Interpreted one way, the numbers foretell a bleak future for VOD and networked television. However, interpreted another way, they support the thesis that local stations are predominantly branded by their news products and that strong brands can hold an audience.

National Network Brands

Many cable networks (which are also available on satellite and IP systems) are branded. MTV is music television, ESPN is sports, FoodTV is food, Golf is, well ... golf, etc. They are brands because they market themselves as brands. ESPN makes a promise to consumers that they provide sporting events and sports news. They keep that promise and they have come to stand for excellence in sports.

There are several branded shows on DIY, but most people can't name them. The network is about "do it yourself" projects, and consumers have a reasonable expectation of finding a show about doing something yourself. The network is the brand. This is also true of HGTV, Fine Living, Golf, FoodTV (with the exception of their biggest stars like Emeril, who is his own brand), FitTV, Jazz, Ovation, The HistoryChannel, etc.

Obviously, Headline News is about news headlines and most viewers don't care who is sitting at the anchor desk if they want quick overview of the day's headline news stories. That being said, people still watch "Modern Marvels" on The History Channel and "Pimp My Ride" on MTV. These shows are real brands like their broadcast counterparts.

Networks, Stations or Shows?

This not so subtle, semantic argument has been the subject of much intellectual curiosity and debate for years and it might continue but for the advent of VOD and DVR technology. In a time-shifted, on-demand world, broadcast networks cease to have relevance. Nobody goes home to watch NBC or CBS; they go home to watch their favorite shows, making the transition to this new distribution methodology especially difficult for the unbranded broadcasters. In truth, you will not even have to be "home" to watch. But, back to the present issue.

You won't pick a broadcast network name from a list in your DVR or your VOD system, you'll pick a show name or show genre to explore. This will bode well for a branded network environment like Discovery or Disney, but it may be absolutely devastating (from a consumer branding perspective) for broadcast networks. The primetime entertainment divisions don't have the brand power to make the transition.

Oddly enough, most broadcast network news and sports divisions have strong brands and will probably do just fine. Brands like CBS Sports and Fox Sports, etc. stand for excellence in sports coverage and brands like ABC News, NBC News and Fox News stand for excellence in news coverage. The broadcast network sports and news brands could easily be VOD or DVR picks for their exclusive coverage of big brand sports like NFL, MLB, NBA, etc.

Will the big sports franchises continue to work with the big broadcast networks on an exclusive basis? As part of the fight for survival, for now and into the future, you will see extraordinary dollars being poured into exclusive relationships with live events (like sports) and emergent news. These are the top two genres on a very short list that are well served by massive broadcast distribution.

Casual and Directed Viewers

Casual viewers are media consumers who are in the habit of watching television. They may have favorite shows or they might just grab a soft drink, a bag of chips, the remote control and plop themselves down on the couch. Casual viewers may watch much more television than directed viewers; the big difference is that casual viewers let the medium take them wherever it takes them.

On the other side of the coin is the directed viewer. This type of viewer takes a proactive role in their television viewing experience. They plan what they are going to watch and, if they are linear television customers, they plan when they are going to watch. They use the grid guides, the printed TV guide and even the Internet guides to help them make choices about how they will spend their viewing time.

The perfect navigation system would effortlessly metamorphose between lean-backward (casual) and lean-forward (directed) mindsets.

Every viewer in America falls somewhere between these two extremes; the problem is that most people are both casual and directed viewers – just not at the same time.

Combining Both Viewer Mindsets

The biggest opportunities for networked television lie in the servicing of these two mind-sets: a system that can feed you a relevant, informative, enlightening and entertaining experience when you are in a casual mood but can instantly metamorphose into an accurate search environment when you are in a directed mood.

Obviously, many companies are working on "intelligence layers" for television navigation, and we will see many attempts at a graphical user interface that both emotionally and intellectually satisfies consumers' needs.

Branded Search Solution

One probable future of this technology is the concept of branded search. In this environment, a network might still have meaning, since consumers are at least minimally aware that certain network logos stand for quality. If NBC was my "television portal" in a semi-random access world, what would I expect to find there? That is a question most media executives are going to be asking for the foreseeable future.

You can (and should) ask the same question about high traffic Web sites like Google, Yahoo!, MSN, Amazon, eBay, and of course, about every existing broadcast and cable network. A trip to the video section of the Apple Music Store through iTunes is a very interesting experience, particularly when you see how the interface handles show branding vs. network branding.

Social Search Solution

Another probable future is Tim Halle's vision of a "social search," a recommendation system that will emerge from social networking sites. Of course, the biggest social networking sites like friendster.com or myspace.com are also big brands, so this may be just another permutation of branded search. (See "Folksonomy" in Chapter 6.)

The Myth of the Media Center – the Fight for the Living Room

Media center computers are personal computers that include television tuner cards and special software that enables them to act like a television set with a DVR and associated feature sets. Most media center computers also include functionality that allows the user to aggregate video, audio and digital photos into one centralized user interface. The interesting thing about media center computers is that they come with remote controls and are supposed to be hooked up to a television monitor 12 feet away. However, they can also be used like a regular computer with a mouse and keyboard.

The most popular version of this type of computer is the Windows XP Media Center Edition which, many people say, only exists because of an off-hand remark made by Bill Gates. This tale is usually evoked when someone schooled in the art of media and entertainment queries a Microsofty about why anyone would ever use a Windows XP Media Center Edition computer as configured and designed. It is also mentioned when you ask how many people use the computer in "12-foot" mode as a replacement for a television set.

In truth, there is nothing wrong with combining all of these features into one box. Any combination of hardware and software that helps you organize your media is probably better than trying to do it yourself. But, in this case, we are not discussing loosely connecting a bunch of well organized individual computers into a household network; we're talking about the "media center" as central media hub for a household of non-technical, average consumers. The present issue challenges the assumptions that the average American family has a living room to put a media center in and that an all-in-one device solves a problem or offers a demonstrable benefit.

Centralized or Distributed Entertainment?

Do we live in a world of centralized or distributed entertainment? This fundamental question did not exist in the past when everyone gathered around the big color television set in the living room to watch a primetime show. Those days are long gone. A typical modern family (if there is such a thing) has its media distributed throughout the household with dedicated technology.

There are portable music players, portable video players, video game consoles, television sets, DVD players, computers, personal digital assistants and mobile phones, all over the house. The list is not endless, but it is vast. Do families gather together to watch programs together? Sometimes. Is it the way they consume media on a daily basis? No.

As it turns out, there really is no living room to fight for. The real fight is for the appropriate way to aggregate the various media in the household and make it available for distribution to the various devices that the family owns. This type of "busy work" is best done on a computer in "2 foot" mode. But that has not stopped the consumer electronics and computer industries from trying to figure out how to solve this problem from 12 feet away.

I Saw Auntie @#$%^& Santa Claus

With his newly minted NY learner's permit, Ethan, a 16-year-old junior was driving his mother, Barbara, a 49-year-old lawyer, up to their home in Vermont for winter break. Paying homage to the ironclad rule that "he who drives picks the radio station," the duo was treated to a playlist that Ethan loves and trusts: "RAW," XM Satellite Radio's uncensored Hip Hop Channel.

This is a four-hour trip the pair were used to taking weekly, but this was the first time the Ethan got to drive – and therefore, the first time he got to be the program director for the entire car. To say that this particular playlist would not be Barbara's first entertainment choice would be to understate the obvious. So they settled back to some 50 Cent and Kanye West and headed north. Everything was going as well as could be expected until a particular parody song started to play. Since RAW is completely uncensored, the lyrics can be quite graphic. In this case, the lyrics were about performing a particular sex act and, just before it got to the "good" part, both mother and son were reaching for the power button simultaneously.

When asked why she reached for the power button at that particular moment, Barbara said, "I was fine with the material, it was funny, but there are some things I just don't want to share with my son." When asked why he reached for the power button, Ethan said almost exactly the same thing, "Yo man, my mom was sitting right there."

For the previous 11 years of round trips to Vermont, Ethan has sat in the back seat listening to his MP3 player (or more recently, watching a video) with earphones on, minding his own business while Barbara and her husband sat up front and listened to their own musical choices over the car's stereo system. However, that technical solution does not work with the 16-year-old at the wheel. Should Barbara get an iPod?

One of the biggest obstacles to media center life is the overwhelmingly personal nature of our media choices. Sure, you can have personal directories, personal remotes, personal access to a centralized system – but it is truly just as convenient (maybe even more convenient) to have a bunch of dedicated systems that are the personal property of the users.

The Future of the Living Room

Are we likely to see all-singing-all-dancing media center set-top devices that bring our entire world of media together in one place? It's doubtful that such a box would have a big market. Who would get to use it? Would Dad take control of the remote? Would the teenagers be willing to put their photos or videos in a place where Mom or Dad could easily search them? Is there a family in America where a mother and daughter have identical music playlists? No, no and no. There is no living room to put this box in.

To be fair, there are systems by Motorola, Scientific Atlanta, Microsoft and many others that address the problem of "who gets to hold the remote." Though technologically impressive, they offer imperfect sociological solutions. If there is a need for a central server or local area network in the home with password-protected client software for household members, consumers have not yet warmed up to it.

To reach critical mass, these systems will have to be as simple to use as dialing a telephone. Perhaps we will see a friendlier version of network software evolve over time to meet this need. However, the content companies will weigh in against this concept. Not that a household area network violates any copyright laws; it doesn't. But the content companies are used to selling — or more accurately, licensing — content to users for consumption in a specific form factor.

A central location and easy access to files will take a big bite out of their business models, so they won't be at the forefront of the proponents of this type of mass-mediated household. For now, and in the foreseeable future, we are likely to find our media completely distributed in very clumsy ways throughout the house.

MISS – Make It Simple, Stupid!

When will consumers actually be able to hook up their own networking equipment? Some businesses are trying to exploit the overwhelming complexity of hooking up home networking components. The "barrier to entry" posed by seemingly incompatible technologies like: routers, WiFi access points, switches, hubs, wireless or wired, feels like an insurmountable obstacle.

Who will win the battle for media dominance in the home? It will come down to simplicity or truck rolls. If the CE manufacturers cannot make technology which "wakes up" knowing where it is and how to hook itself up, the winner will be the group that has the best customer service. Whichever company can roll the most trucks to the most houses and leave a branded, user-friendly, satisfaction-guaranteed mark on the consumer will have a fantastic competitive advantage. Will it be the consumer electronics retailers, telcos, cablers or some OEM service? This issue may be the ultimate key to the future potential of networked living.

Key Takeaways

- People who consume the most media care the most about how that media is delivered to them and what devices they consume it on.

- You can create very useful planning tools by overlaying demographic and geographic data with the AMCI.

- With regard to media consumption, there is no evidence to support the idea that everyone wants "anything, any place, any time." People easily toggle between "casual" and "directed" media consumption.

- Innovation in media navigation and media search tools are extremely important. Practically everyone in the business is trying to create a user interface that can adapt to the way people actually consume media.

- People watch shows, not networks.

- Media consumption is highly individualized and portable; personal media technology and decentralized access to media may render the battle for the living room moot.

9 Digital Rights Management and Copyright Laws

The content business in the United States is very large, and the intellectual property it represents is an exceptional store of economic value. Protecting that value is the full-time job of a virtual army of corporate executives, lawyers and even a few politicians. Copy protection is so important to the health and well-being of the media industry that it is responsible for an entirely new, and very controversial, industry: digital rights management (DRM). The controversy is directly related to new technology and the concept of the "final" form factor. Digital content can be transformed into any kind of physical copy or converted to any other type of file. More importantly, it can be easily distributed over the public Internet at the touch of a button – in many cases without the knowledge or consent of the rights holder.

History of Intellectual Property

Throughout history we have stored our intellectual property in form factors. The first was our memories. For thousands of years, the history of humanity was passed verbally from one generation to the other. There were several flaws with this methodology, but for most of history, it was all we had. Some primitive cultures used iconography to assist their memories. One tribal group still uses intricate lanyards and knots to keep the institutional memory. The advent of the written word eventually led to certain stories being carved in stone.

Print

But mass media really begins with the printing press. You could argue that the most pirated work in history is the Bible,[1] although the Church doesn't seem to mind. It has used the intellectual property stored in that book to create one of the largest institutions in the world. Yet, surprisingly, they don't charge publishing houses for the right to print and sell the book. This may not be a fair example of the store of economic value contained in an average piece of intellectual property (IP), but it is always fun to bring it up!

Once on the Internet, unencrypted computer files are free for anyone who wants them.

Prior to 1995, the biggest barrier to piracy was copying fidelity. It was very hard to make a book that looked like a book and felt like a book without literally millions of dollars worth of equipment and the trained manpower to use it. This could be said for almost every physical form factor that content assumed.

However, personal computers put an end to these economic barriers and the Internet has ended the need for physical distribution channels. As we have stated several times, a file is a file is a file. Computer files can be very well protected – right up until the time that the media is used, seen or heard. At that point, it is virtually unprotectable. Once on the Internet, unencrypted computer files are free for anyone who wants them.

Media Form Factors Through the Ages

Audio

Wax recordings
Lacquer records
Vinyl records
Open-reel tapes
Audio cassettes
8-track tapes
Digital audio cassettes
DAT tapes
.wav files, SDII files (professional computer file formats)
Compact discs
.mp3 files, .aac files (consumer audio file formats)   CONTINUED ▶

---

1. The Bible (both Old and New Testaments) is public domain. But any unique interpretation, translation or annotated version could be copyrighted under current U.S. copyright law. In this example, I am using "pirating" to mean any copy made without the knowledge or consent of the rightsholder.

CONTINUED ▶

Video

Film
Television
Kinescope
2" quad video tape
¾" U-matic professional videocassettes
1" type C open-reel professional videotape
½" consumer open-reel video tape
½" VHS (and Betamax) consumer videocassettes
LaserDisc
Betacam professional videocassettes
Hi-8 videocassettes
MiniDV videocassettes
.wmv, .avi, .mpg video file formats
DVD
HD-DVD & Blueray HD DVD
.mp4, .m4p, 4K video file formats

Music

Since the 1920s, recorded music companies have been repackaging audio as often as the technology allows. People bought albums on vinyl, then either taped them themselves (onto audio cassettes) or bought factory releases of the same albums on audio cassette. Then, they bought the compact disc set, then ripped the CDs to MP3 files.

Some people actually even purchase a song or two from legal downloading services. Once the song is a file and the file is on the Internet, it is pretty hard to resell it, since it can be downloaded for free. Yes, there are lots of people who will never download a song or a video, but the top 20 percent of media consumers are the ones who download 80 percent of the available files.

Television

Since this book is about television, let's look at a quick history of video form factors: Live television broadcasts, Kinescopes of the televised performances, the advent of commercial video tape, consumer video tape (VHS and the short lived Betamax), optical discs, DVDs, .avi, .mov and other video file formats. As with audio, the final form factor is a computer file and the computer really doesn't differentiate between file types. To a computer, it's all ones and zeros.

File Transfers of Intellectual Property Today

You transfer files every day. You send e-mail attachments, you send reports over your corporate local area network (LAN), or you save a PowerPoint presentation to a Jump Drive. Everyone uploads and downloads files all day long and music and video files are no exceptions.

It was relatively easy to protect a vinyl record from piracy. Yes, there were people who owned record pressing plants that broke the law and made illegal copies of vinyl LPs. When found, they were put in jail. But the average person did not have the capacity to copy an LP in its original form factor. You could make an audio cassette and share it with your friends, but copying was real time and there was a cost associated with the process. You may have made a mix tape or two in your day, but it wasn't something you probably made a habit of.

Limitations of DRM

The human senses of sight and sound are analog. We cannot interpret digital data without technological help. At some point in the chain from rightsholder to rights purchaser, there has to be a digital to analog conversion because human beings cannot enjoy media in any other form. You must see the picture, hear the audio or both.

DRM cannot and will not stop file sharing. If you can hear it, you can copy it. If you can see it, you can copy it. No matter what digital format you use. No matter how you encrypt a file, it must be decrypted or decoded to be played back.

What this means is that even if you have the most ironclad copyright protection schema ever conceived, you still have to remove all of it for a human being to experience the content. At the point that the audio is audible and the video is visible, it can be copied by anyone who has even a casual interest in doing so. Once copied, it is just a few mouse clicks to worldwide distribution.

This technology is in the hands of absolutely everyone one who wants it. There is absolutely no practical financial barrier to entry. This type of copyright infringement can

If you happen to completely control the playback system, both hardware and software, you could marginally limit video piracy, but not audio. There are no completely closed hardware and software systems for the full bandwidth playback of audio and video with mass deployment in the United States.

be accomplished by a 10-year-old using a $200 used computer with an average broadband connection. It is even possible on a dial-up connection, but it would take much longer. More to the point, a college student with virtually unlimited bandwidth, a modern computer and a desire to share his or her creative preferences with the known universe can effortlessly accomplish his or her goal.

Why DRM Is Used

So how is it possible that DRM is even a topic of conversation? As it turns out, not everyone in the world is a born pirate. In fact, most people are honest and, even though that's true, we tend to lock our doors each evening. DRM and all versions of current vintage encryption are the equivalent of putting consumer-grade door locks on glass front doors. Real criminals could just break the glass and enter the house. But ordinary, honest people would not. In fact, very few people would even test to see if the door was locked. So a lock on a glass door is pretty effective in our culture. We have learned to respect the boundaries of privacy and we have police to help us enforce these boundaries.

On the other hand, we also have legal ways to enter a house. You can call ahead, knock on the glass door and gain entry lawfully with relative ease. Unbelievably, you could not legally purchase a piece of major label commercial music until about 1999 when Peter Gabriel's OD2.com came online. Early legal download services included

Rightsholders gave honest people no choice but to be criminals for the better part of the history of this technology. Given no choice, people made their own rules. Sadly, we now have an entire generation of digital natives who honestly believe that music and video downloads should be free.

listen.com, musicnet.com and pressplay.com. However, it was not until Apple created the Apple Music Store in April 2003, and coupled it with its iTunes interface, that legal music downloading hit the mainstream. More astonishingly, you could not purchase a video of a broadcast television show online until Apple (again through its music store and iTunes) launched the service in October 2005.

This unintentional training of an entire generation of computer users will have a huge impact on the future of networked television. In fact, it is this training that will actually create it. As the digital natives get the next generation of console video games, desktops and portable media technologies, they are going to do what they have been trained to do: download.

This is more than a probable future of television, it is a guarantee. Downloaded files have no geographic or temporal restrictions and they cannot be protected by rightsholders. DRM is a myth for the 20 percent of the downloaders that will do 80 percent of the downloading. The old business models will pick up what's left. Does this mean that the media business is in danger of losing 80 percent of its top-line revenues? No. Because not everyone downloads every media offering, nor do they do it all of the time. However, a meaningful drop in gross sales of physical copies and a very, very slow growth curve for digital form factors over the next decade would not be unreasonable to assume. After all, why buy it if you can download the exact same file for free?

DRM that Might Matter

There are some concepts in DRM that do make sense. The fact that a file is a file is a file is actually a positive. So too is the fact that you are probably on some kind of a network if you are downloading a file from someone else's computer or server. This means that the file or the software used to download it can do certain things. For example, one benign type of DRM simply "phones home" when a file is downloaded and tells the serving computer that someone has copied it. This may not sound useful, but in actuality, it is probably the most useful aspect of any downloading schema.

Knowing how many people downloaded a file is a census-based metric that can be used by marketers to determine the success of any given piece of content. As technology evolves, it will be possible to know how many people used the files and how often. This stands in stark contrast to the waste model that is the cornerstone of traditional television and radio. Advertisers would much rather know how many people actually took the time to download something than get some estimated metric from Nielsen about a gross rating point.

There are also slightly more sophisticated DRM schemas that use two other technologies to help rights-holders understand the medium: digital watermarking and digital fingerprinting. With digital watermarking, a "watermark" is added to a file. This invisible electronic marker is easily identified by specific computer software but is completely transparent to the users. There are both audio and video versions of digital watermarking and it can be a very effective way of creating accurate census or sample-based metric reports.

The other technology is digital fingerprinting. This can also be done with audio or video. The concept is that several samples are taken of the file at various predetermined points. Because audio and video files are very complex, a multi-point match has a mathematical probability of correctly identifying any particular piece of work that has been previously fingerprinted. It is not as exact a science as watermarking, but it has the feature of not have to be done during the initial encoding of a master. You can take the digital fingerprint of any file at any time and add it to the database. Digital watermarks have to be encoded into the master file before it is distributed.

In the mean time, big media will continue to use casual copy protection, walled gardens and physical form factors which (although weakened) have worked as copy protection schemas since the beginning of the audio and video businesses. Nobody has a meaningful strategy to thwart file sharing completely, but by disabling certain outputs of cable and satellite set top boxes and adding creative packaging, big media companies will squeeze the last drop of money out of the public until they no longer have a way to do so.

DRM from an Industry Perspective

Everyone involved with the DRM process is trying to find a solution that will fulfill consumer needs, be within manufacturing capabilities, meet legal requirements and most importantly, offer protection to rightsholders. This would almost be an impossible task if the technology actually existed to accomplish the stated goals (which it does not).

It will be instructive for us to take a very brief look at some of the work that is being done. The issue of DRM is never going to go away. Actually, it is going to become a much more intense problem as the technological arms race heats up. At some point, there will have to be significant changes in the way that protected content is packaged and distributed. Without such a change, the content industry will be forced to adapt to a new financial model, which would ultimately be quite unfortunate for almost everyone.

DTCP 1.0 Specification

In February 1999, a group called the "5C" (Hitachi, Intel, Matsushita, Sony and Toshiba) published their 1.0 specification for DTCP (Digital Transmission Content Protection over Internet Protocol), a digital rights management system that governs content transferred over home networks using Internet protocols. They were trying to deal with the five different threat levels to copy protection:

- **Casual copier** – will press the record button on back-to-back devices
- **Hobbyist** – will download circumvention software or purchase a "black box" to make copies
- **Hacker** – develops circumvention techniques

CONTINUED ▶

CONTINUED ▶

- **Small-Scale Pirate** – operates a bank of recording devices
- **Professional Pirate** – well-funded and well-equipped

They had a stated requirement: "Keep honest people honest."

They also had specific requirements:

- Authentication and key exchange
- Copy control information (CCI)
- Content encryption
- Device renewability
- Licensable components (like patents)
- Robust device implementation

DTCP specifies the conditions under which copyrighted content can be copied. CCI is embedded in the content and an Encryption Mode Indicator (EMI) provides a "protected" mechanism for identifying the copy protection status of the content. There are four modes of copy protection under DTCP.

- Copy free
- Copy once
- Copy no more
- Copy never

From a rightsholder's perspective, high value content must be protected from unauthorized copying. The DTCP specification attempts to do this through a combination of technical, legal and policy means. So, it does not matter for our purposes whether DTCP is universally adopted, is ultimately the best version of DRM, or evolves into something else entirely. The features and benefits of DTCP will have to be incorporated into any successful DRM schema.

Copyright Laws May No Longer Apply

We learn by mimicking. In fact, human beings are the most successful mimics on the planet. "Watch Mommy!" or "Daddy will show you how to do it," or "Repeat after me" are all phrases we have heard all of our lives. You will learn about advanced media by mimicking the words, acronyms and concepts found in the pages of this book – that's why you are reading it!

Art vs. Craft

Interestingly enough, artists are among the best mimics. They are experts at copying the techniques that allow them to practice their art. We think of someone as a great artist when they can communicate an idea that is familiar to us but feels somehow new and exciting. Although there are many ways to describe art (and by art, we are discussing fine art, music, videography, film making, writing, etc.) let us use a simple description we can all agree upon: "Art cannot be ignored."

This is opposed to "craft" which is pure technique and which we can easily ignore. In the distant past, the line between a creative artist and an expert technician was clearly visible to people schooled in the art. A good technician could fool most or all consumers of art into thinking that they had artistic talent, but to a professional, the differences would be quite clear.

In the more recent past, say since the 1960s, it has become much more difficult to make such declarative statements. One reason is that the proverbial "bar" has been raised to unimaginable levels. In order to become a modern, world-class professional in any discipline (athlete, musician, singer, dancer, fine artist, concert performer, entertainer) you literally have to spend all of your waking hours pursuing that goal from early childhood.

Notwithstanding, there is another side to this coin – and quite a dark one indeed. Remember the old cliché, "Success is 1 percent inspiration and 99 percent perspiration?" This holds true only where the competitive talent pool is extremely shallow or where the 1 percent inspired person actually has the necessary amount of talent to be the best. The bar for mediocrity has also been raised by zealous parents who over-schedule their children and live vicariously through them. Uniformed, organized, travel-team after school sports with professional coaches and referees are just the tip of the iceberg.

As it does in many aspects of the human endeavor, the law of unintended consequences here too plays a mischievous role. Due to the immense amount of training required to just be average, it is extremely hard for lay persons to appreciate the level of technique and technical achievement that most professional artists have today. But, do not be fooled by the fact that you do not understand — or can't relate to — the content that new, young artists are producing. A young adult entering the arts today, with a hope of being successful, will have blinding, extraordinary technique. So much so that the average person would mistake it for artistic talent.

This is such an important concept, it needs to be repeated. Today, most people who are not schooled in the art cannot tell the difference between someone with true artistic talent and someone with extraordinary technique. In fact, the time, dedication and perseverance required for world-class technical achievement is so respected in our culture, that some truly talented professionals laud lesser talents because of their technique.

Current Laws and Artistic Expression

With respect to our current intellectual property and copyright laws, the consequences of this reality are dire. To demonstrate this point, we shall look at three examples of modern artistic expression: the written word, music and video.

Written Word

It is well known that the personal computer created the desktop publishing business. Programs like Microsoft Word and PowerPoint, Adobe Photoshop, Illustrator and Pagemaker, and even Quark have put the power to create professional-looking written work product into the hands of anyone who wants them. Anyone with rudimentary computer skills can select (Ctrl-a), copy (Ctrl-c), cut (Ctrl-x) and paste (Ctrl-v) any letter, word, sentence, paragraph or entire document. With a few seconds of additional training, you can be taught to make text **bold** (Ctrl-b), *italic* (Ctrl-i) or underlined (Ctrl-u). These techniques are so simple and common, we almost never think about them.

Using a personal computer, the Internet, a Web browser and a search engine, we can go out into cyberspace and collect any number of pages of text on any topic that interests us. For this example we'll just grab all of the information we can find out about copyright law in America. In 0.32 seconds, Google returned 407,000,000 pages of text on the topic. A few clicks and I have more information at my fingertips than I could read, write or copy in a lifetime.

With just a few hours of copying and pasting text from this Google search, I can generate 350 pages of text. I have entitled my work, "Comments and Commentary on the Intent to Infringe" and I'm ready to publish. Off I go to one of the wonderful vanity publishing Web sites, and for a few dollars per book, they will make me as many copies (hardcover, perfect-bound or saddle-stitched paperback) as I care to order. All that remains is to purchase an ISBN (International Standard Book Number) number and the book is ready for sale to any major bookseller, including Amazon.com.

Is it? Of course not. This is plagiarism and it is illegal under the current copyright laws. The words are not only copied, they are literally cut and pasted directly from other peoples' works. Anyone can see that the text is identical to previously created, protected work. The resulting tome can not be called an original work. Even with proper attributions, it would be hard to mount a "fair use" defense. Of course, if you just made a few copies and shared them with your family and close circle of friends, you would not have any legal troubles at all.

Is there a legal way to realize this work? Of course there is. Study and understand the topic, read all of the available writings on the subject, collect them in a bibliography, write your own original thoughts, properly cite the passages you have taken from others and you probably have a winning "fair use" defense. It may read like a scholarly work, but you will have a document you can legally call your own. Can you have an original thought about a subject that you learned about through books and articles? We'll address that in a moment.

Music

Moving on, let's try the same trick with music. But let's turn the clock back before 1986. Prior to that time all musicians who learned to play musical instruments did so by trying to copy (as exactly as possible) the way their music teachers played. That's right — they listened to a note and did everything in their power to copy it exactly. Intonation, quality, volume, attack, decay, sustain and release — every aspect of every note played was to be copied as exactly as possible. If you could put some notes together in a sequence, you could play a song. If not, you went out for a sports team.

As it turns out, everyone on Earth is unique. Although we all have many, many similar attributes, we – each of us – are uniquely gifted with some level of intellectual and physical skills. No, we are not stating the obvious. Unknown to most, acoustical musical instruments do not automatically play in tune. This is not the time or the place to explain a well-tempered Western musical scale, but suffice it to say that the physics of acoustic musical instruments actually prevent the design and manufacture of any wind or stringed instrument that can inherently play in tune.

Every acoustic musical instrument has several inherent physical barriers that must be overcome to master it. These include use of your embouchure (how you use your mouth on a woodwind or brass instrument), motor memory (how you use your fingers to manipulate the instrument) and a complex set of mental skills (including hearing) which are not well understood. How a musician overcomes these obstacles is unique to the individual and it has a name: musical style.

This is why, prior to April 1986, performance skills were among the most respected on Earth. Great acoustic musicians and singers are truly prodigies of nature and (to this day), are very, very rare.

Now, there is another aspect to the creation of music … notes to play. Where do they come from? In our Western culture, the basic building blocks of music are the notes of the well-tempered chromatic scale. There are 11 unique notes to this scale. The physical limitations of constructing and playing a musical instrument have limited the practical range (low notes to high notes) of all acoustic musical instruments to roughly that of the acoustic piano. The piano has 88 keys which span the frequency range 27.5 Hz (A0) to 4186 Hz

(C8). However, as you press every key on the piano keyboard starting from the bottom, you will notice that every twelfth piano key plays a note that is exactly twice the frequency of the note played by pressing the key 12 keys below it. This interval is called an octave and the name of every twelfth note is a repeat of the note 12 piano keys below or above it – only the frequency of the wave changes. So, in practice, there are only 11 unique notes. In theory, after you learn to play all of them across the entire range of your instrument, you can play anything that has ever been written.

One could easily argue that no living musician has ever played an original combination of notes, regardless of their level of technique or their isolation from other musicians. Why? Because in order to learn to play, you must copy someone else's work product.

What does this have to do with musical composition? Everything! Putting notes together in combinations is also a learned behavior. We learn to play a song exactly the same way we learn to play a single note – by listening and copying. When you pen your first musical composition, you are paying homage to the work of every composer and every musician you have ever heard. The nature of musical composition and performance is that it is the highest form of mimicry. No one could ever become a world-class musician or composer without playing or writing things they had heard before.

So now, let's talk about a sixth grader in 1986 who has been taking music lessons in school since the fourth grade. She can play many familiar songs and communicate with her musical instrument and her relatively newly acquired skill of mimicking other musicians. If she is being trained as a classical musician, she is judged by how exactly she can play what has been written more than two centuries ago. If she is learning to play popular music, she is judged by how much she sounds like the original artists she is copying. No matter how we judge her musical ability, it is in the context of her personal ability to copy (as closely as possible) work that already exists.

Now, let's say that this young lady is truly extraordinary. Let's imagine that she is musically mature beyond her years and can already combine some of the notes and musical phrases she has heard and mastered into new groups of notes and musical phrases. If this is accomplished seemingly at will, she is said to be able to improvise. If this is done by writing the notes and musical phrases down for others to play, she is said to be a composer. Regardless of her skill level, she can share her interpretation of the work she has learned to copy by playing it for you live or teaching it to other musicians so they can play it for you.

Sixth graders who demonstrate this type of musical acumen are lauded and paraded around as child prodigies and their work is protected by the current copyright laws as written. Under these laws, she is prohibited from selling, distributing or reproducing an exact copy of someone else's work and calling it her own. But, if she creates a work that is "inspired by" as opposed to "ripped off from" music she's heard, no one is going to bother her. To be sure, there is a certain amount of craft required to communicate the "feel" of a song without copying it note for note. But to a trained composer/producer/musician (even one in training), it's all in a day's work.

Fast forward past April 1986 – that's the month that the first commercial tapeless (random access, hard-disk-based) recording studio, Creative Audio Recording Services (CARS), went online in midtown Manhattan. It was the practical turning point in the creation of music, as it ushered in the era of consumer digital sampling.

Two decades later, things have radically changed. Let's look at the way new technology has impacted this creative process. A sixth grader in 2006 does not have to spend any time learning to master the physical limitations of acoustic musical instruments. Programs like Garage Band, Logic Pro, Digital Performer, Acid Pro, Ableton Live and Reason are all within the budget of absolutely anyone who wants them. In many cases, purchasing one of these programs is less expensive than renting an acoustic musical instrument.

These programs make music. People can control them, but the programmers and engineers who created the computer programs endowed the software with the ability to reproduce absolutely any sound that can be heard. These programs are not synthesizers that create synthetic sounds of acoustical musical instruments, these programs are computer-controlled digital audio recorders that make exact duplicates of other sound recordings and allow the user to manipulate them. It is a new generation of computer-based musical instruments that present no physical limitations for users to overcome, although there are still those pesky intellectual limitations (including hearing) that have a dramatic impact on the outcome of the work product.

The sixth grader who opens and starts to use one of these new computer-based musical instruments makes music exactly the same way her compatriot made music 20 years earlier – with one notable exception. Instead of trying to copy the notes that she hears or trying to copy the musical phrases, she simply takes the existing recording of the work and imports it into her computer. Using the program, she manipulates the recording into a new work, by adding her own unique signal processing, other sounds and maybe even a few well placed original notes to the new work. It's called a remix or a mash-up, but it should not need a new name; it is a unique, creative musical work – the musician is simply using more modern tools to create with.

There is, however, a profound difference in the way our existing copyright laws view this new work. It is not considered original – and there is no practical way for it to ever be so considered. As long as our sixth grader plays this work for her family or close circle of friends, she's fine. But, far from being considered a prodigy, she is instantly considered a plagiarist and a thief and there is no commercial future for her work.

Creative Commons

Creative Commons is a group of future-thinking individuals who have tried to tackle this very difficult issue. The following describes each of the six main licenses offered when you choose to publish your work with a Creative Commons license.

1. Attribution Non-Commercial No Derivatives (by-nc-nd)

This license is the most restrictive of the six main licenses, only allowing redistribution. This license is often called the "free advertising" license because it allows others to download your works and share them with others as long as they mention you and link back to you, but they can't change them in any way or use them commercially.

2. Attribution Non-Commercial Share Alike (by-nc-sa)

This license lets others remix, tweak, and build upon your work non-commercially, as long as they credit you and license their new creations under the identical terms. Others can download and redistribute your work just like the by-nc-nd license, but they can also translate, make remixes, and produce new stories based on your work. All new work based on yours will carry the same license, so any derivatives will also be non-commercial in nature.

3. Attribution Non-Commercial (by-nc)

This license lets others remix, tweak and build upon your work non-commercially, and although their new works must also acknowledge you and be non-commercial, they don't have to license their derivative works on the same terms.

4. Attribution No Derivatives (by-nd)

This license allows for redistribution, commercial and non-commercial, as long as it is passed along unchanged and in whole, with credit to you.

5. Attribution Share Alike (by-sa)

This license lets others remix, tweak and build upon your work even for commercial reasons, as long as they credit you and license their new creations under the identical terms. This license is often compared to open source software licenses. All new works based on yours will carry the same license, so any derivatives will also allow commercial use.

CONTINUED ▶

CONTINUED ▶

6. Attribution (by)

This license lets others distribute, remix, tweak, and build upon your work, even commercially, as long as they credit you for the original creation. This is the most accommodating of licenses offered, in terms of what others can do with your works licensed under attribution.

Other licenses

Creative Commons also offers a set of other licenses for more specialized applications. Sampling licenses allow for snippets (not whole work) to be remixed into new works, even commercially. Their Public Domain Dedication license lets you free works from copyright completely, and their Founders Copyright lets you do the same, but after 14 or 28 years. Musicians looking to share their work with fans might want to look at the Music Sharing license. The Developing Nations license lets you offer less restrictive terms to countries that aren't considered high income by the World Bank, and finally, for those licensing software, they offer the GNU GPL and GNU LGPL licenses.

This is one possible solution, but at its core, it is a bandage on a chronic problem that needs to be solved by rethinking and rewriting the Intellectual Property laws of the United States. For more information, please visit www.creativecommons.com

Video

Since this is a book about television, let's use a video example to fully establish the disconnect between the existing copyright laws and the evolution of technology. This same sixth grader who creates digital music also has a wealth of video editing software at her fingertips. Final Cut Pro, Avid Express, Video Vegas, Adobe Premiere, iMovie; the list of software tools is long. More importantly, the feature sets of all of these desktop video editing programs rival the capabilities of a major motion picture studio of just a few years ago.

Should our modern-day sixth grader decide to take a bunch of video from her collection, some video output from her Xbox or Playstation and mash it all together with some music and add a comedy voice over, her friends would call her a genius. She could post her work on her Web site or upload it free to Google Video or AOL – then she would be a criminal. This type of video mash-up violates the rights of so many stakeholders, it's hard to cite them all. The music rights, unions and guilds, and rightsholders of all kinds would all have a claim to this as a derivative work. It would be practically unclearable under our current laws.

So, not only do we have a problem with the recorded music and video industries' lack of vision with regard to having a legal way to upload and download their work products, we have a much bigger problem in that the same laws practically prohibit new, creative talent from exploring and growing their art.

Many people will disagree with the logic of this argument; I submit that none of them have ever learned to play an instrument or made a living from doing so. I also submit that you can not have it both ways. We have given our children new tools to create wonderful new art with, so we must rewrite the copyright laws to allow them to thrive and prosper from their work.

Author's Note

The United States of America is not a democracy; it is a republic. We elect politicians to represent us. They vote on the issues on our behalf. No matter which side of the copyright debate you are on, your vote only counts if your elected officials know where you stand. Please visit www.televisiondisrupted.com/gov to find contact information for all of your elected officials. Please write to them and tell them what you want them to do.

Key Takeaways

- Unless you completely control the hardware and software used for distribution and playback, true digital rights management is not possible.

- DRM techniques can be used very effectively for measurement purposes.

- Copyright laws in the United States are woefully inadequate for the technological times in which we live and must be rewritten as soon as possible.

10 The Evolution of Advertising and Audience Measurement

If television content has value to consumers, it has been quantified for the past 50 years by the amount of money advertisers have been willing to pay to affiliate themselves with it. Like any vital business system, the mechanism and marketplace that has evolved is both loved and hated by everyone involved with the buying and selling of television commercials. That being said, for better or for worse, when a major advertiser wants to launch a new product, television still figures prominently in the media mix. How soon will this change? To help us make an informed guess about how vulnerable the current marketplace is to the onslaught of networked technology, let's start by reviewing the current infrastructure.

As we have described, each broadcast network may have a broadcast affiliated station in a local market. This station will likely be retransmitted on its assigned channel location (although it may not be) by the local system operator. There may be multiple broadcast affiliated stations in a market. Sometimes, there are two stations that overlap in the cable footprint, but not in the DMA; you could possibly have two affiliates from the same network on a local cable system. None of this should surprise you unless you are totally unfamiliar with television in the United States.

However, it may surprise you to know that practically every channel offered on an average system operator has a different revenue model or multiple revenue models. The economic forces that govern these disparate business models will have a powerful effect on the probable futures of the industry. Understanding them will help us think about how the business of television may evolve.

The TV is on about 60 hours per week in a household that gets television from a systems operator. It's on about 40 hours per week for a broadcast only (antenna) household. By any measure, that's a lot of television.

Although they make money in many varied and different ways, systems operators have two basic revenue streams: subscriptions and advertising. Broadcast networks have multiple revenue streams, but their two major sources are advertising and affiliates. Local, sectional and regional subsets of these sales verticals can be found in almost all of the big media companies.

Show Me the Money!

It is possible to pick up a telephone and purchase commercial time on a broadcast television network in prime time. If you have a few hundred thousand dollars and you are pretty sure that everyone that could possibly be watching the show is a potential customer of yours, it might be a good idea. But it probably isn't. Most products are sold to targeted audiences who have very specific viewing and leisure time habits. To reach the right audience, you need professional media planning help. This is not a book about media planning and execution, but I should mention that it is both an art and a science. And the science is complicated.

Economics? Supply and Demand. That's it.

Broadcast networks are available to approximately 99 percent of total U.S. households; at best, cable and satellite combined are available to about 88 percent of U.S. households. But these national numbers are averages; the actual figures vary wildly from market to market. For example, in Springfield, Mo., the majority of households watch television on satellite systems, not cable systems. So a spot cable commercial running in that market will reach fewer than half of Springfield's multi-channel television viewers.

Now for the fun part: The 15 percent of the households that are "broadcast only" always over-deliver broadcast ratings. So a 4 rating for a broadcast network show might actually deliver something like a 6 or a 7 rating in the 15 percent of the households that use antennas to watch television and only a 2 or 3 rating in a household served by a system operator. Media planners will tell you that "broadcast only" households are demographically less desirable for most advertisers as they are usually occupied by lower income families with commensurately lower purchasing power. So throwing more media dollars at broadcast television based upon ratings alone is not a very good idea. Like I said, the media business is complicated.

When you are watching a program on a broadcast television network, why does 30 seconds of your time sell for two to three times as much as it does when you are watching a rerun of that show on a cable network? Ask a television sales executive and you'll get one answer; ask a cable sales executive and you'll get another. The actual answer was brilliantly given in a classic sketch from *Saturday Night Live*. Father Guido Sarducci (Don Novello) gave an economics class in his Five-Minute University. "Economics? Supply and demand. That's it." Although he didn't know it, he was talking about the media business too. For example: to reach the same size audience as you can with one :30 second spot in the Super Bowl you would need to run that spot more than 100 times on a top-rated cable network show. But that is an exceptional situation. If you are buying a broadcast show averaging a 4 rating and you are buying a cable show averaging a 1.5, the ratio is much, much closer.

The reason cable advertising (on average) costs less than broadcast advertising is the legacy perception that cable is a "disadvantaged" distribution system. When cable only had 20 percent penetration, it could not truly offer "national" distribution even though it was (as an industry) still bigger than any individual television market. Legacy prejudices, simple lack of knowledge and supply and demand (there are more cable spots available than broadcast spots) keep the pricing out of whack.

Could the Marketplace Be More Efficient?

For years there has been talk about making the broadcast media marketplace more efficient. There have been suggestions about creating an electronic marketplace that would let supply and demand set the price for any given moment of media time. There are any number of reasons for the reluctance of the industry to attempt to evolve the system into a more efficient one – but the number one reason is government regulation. Setting up an electronic marketplace for media would require all kinds of oversight from all kinds of regulatory agencies and interested parties. And, to quote Barry Fischer, EVP Market Strategy, Turner Broadcasting System, "The media marketplace is a self-adjusting, self-regulating system that works pretty well." Of course, the title of this book suggests otherwise, so we might see some movement towards a more efficient media marketplace sooner rather than later.

Back to local broadcast television: Each station has a sales department that is responsible for local advertiser sales. The local affiliated station is most probably owned by a station group, which will also have a sales department. All of the local station sales managers and the local cable operator's sales managers will compete for local business. If there is a station group involved, the operator and the group will probably compete for regional business as well. If the local affiliate carries a primetime feed, they will have some spots to sell in primetime right next to spots that are sold by the network's national sales department. And, it is possible for the local station to belong to several unwired networks or be represented by a third-party sales organization for certain types of transactions.

And, as you know, there are many national branded networks that accept advertising like TNT, TBS, Bravo, Lifetime, WE, CNN, Fox News Channel, etc. These networks are sold by national sales departments and spots can also be purchased from the local system operator as well. These commercials, called "spot cable," are said to be fairly inefficient to buy because of the business rules employed by media buyers, but to consumers they are indistinguishable from their nationally sold counterparts. So, it is quite commonplace to see a commercial that costs one advertiser $300,000 running directly before or after a spot that cost a different advertiser $500. But it is important to note that the $300,000 commercial will reach a national audience and the $500 spot will be geographically targeted to a local market. That's the beauty of the existing media marketplace. It is precisely the idea that a consumer cannot tell the difference between a national spot and a spot running just on their local cable system that makes the current system work. Welcome to the TV biz!

The First Television Commercial

Commercial broadcasting was authorized by the FCC to start on July 1, 1941. NBC began with a 10-second Bulova watch commercial. This first commercial, which simply showed the face of a watch, gave the network a profit of $7.00. CBS and others started commercials in the fall of that year.

Now, these first few paragraphs don't sound like an argument foretelling the disruption of a broken system. As presented, the marketplace sounds healthy and certainly the industry, as a whole, is making money. All true. But, just as this system evolved over time from a $7 time buy to the $66 billion industry it is today, there are new markets emerging that also offer "aggregated eyeballs" for sale.

Your Attention, Please

Richard Dawkins, the famous evolutionary biologist, coined the term "meme" in his Pulitzer prize-winning book, "The Shellfish Gene" (Oxford: University Press, 1976). A meme (rhymes with gene) is a non-biological life form. It is born, it replicates, it mutates, it dies, and eventually it goes extinct. Memes are everywhere. Jesus and Christianity are extremely successful memes. "Ring around the collar" was successful in its day, but now is almost extinct. The hook from Beethoven's Fifth Symphony ("da-da-da-

daaaaa," the part everyone remembers and can sing) is a successful meme. There are literally billions of memes and they all enjoy relative levels of success, from obscurity to omnipresence.

Media professionals design special types of memes, called shows and movies, specifically to get and keep your attention. But the truth is, all of the content ever created is competing for your attention. How will it get it?

In the media business, you see commercials promoting goods and services. (Actually, the largest advertiser on television is television itself — about 25 percent of all television commercials are promos for upcoming shows or branding campaigns about the channel you are watching.) All of this content exists only for one reason: to get your attention.

Obviously, there are other ways to package content for propagating Memes: product placement, event marketing, print, contests, word-of-mouth — if you think about it for a minute you'll come up with literally dozens of ways that people (and nature) try to get your attention.

Human Instinct

Human beings are born with more instincts than any other animal on Earth, among them are two fears: fear of falling and fear of loud noises. Apparently, when a doctor slaps a newborn to get it to breath, it is the sound of the slap, not the pain of the slap that startles the infant. Its pain centers are not developed at the ripe age of a few seconds old; however, it can hear perfectly. The same study suggests that the doctor could hold the child up and drop it a foot or two, which would scare the hell out of it and cause it to gasp its first breath. Oddly enough, we never lose either of those two fears, so sound pressure (commonly called volume), remains a valuable tool for getting someone's attention.

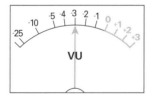

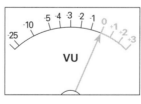

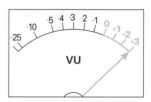

1. Production company sets level at -3VU and marks the box 0VU which is the industry standard.

2. Television station engineer set the level to 0VU as the box is marked in the industry standard way.

3. You hear the commercial at +3VU which is about twice as loud as the audio from the preceding television program.

FIGURE 10.1 *Why commercials are so loud.*

Think about how many times you've been watching television and had to turn down the volume when the commercials came on, only to turn it back up again when the show started. This is because producers of advertising have known for decades that you can trick the television engineers by reducing the level of the test tones that they use to calibrate volume when preparing a spot for broadcast. The engineers at the broadcast center assume that the test tones were recorded correctly, because that's standard procedure. When the spot plays out, it can be up to three volume units (+3 VU) louder. That's perceived as twice as loud by your ears at home (see Figure 10.1).

Why do advertisers do it? Because as soon as the relative volume changes (louder startles you, softer makes you curious) you are going to look up to see what caused it. During that instant, it's up to the visuals to get (and keep) your attention. But volume has done its job. You're looking up.

You would think that someone on the broadcast side would have caught on by now. Of course, the most Machiavellian of us would assume that the broadcasters tolerate this trick because they know it makes the advertising pods more effective. If you enjoy conspiracy theories, this one would be a good candidate.

Want to do a quick test? Next time you are in a small gathering (like a cocktail party or conference room), scream one word really loudly. I promise you'll get everyone's attention in the room.

Attention Is Finite

There are libraries filled with books about how to get someone's attention. From brand advertising to the formation of religious cults, the techniques are the same. This is because people are mostly wired the same way. If you are interested in the concept of memes and their propagation, I strongly suggest an overview of evolutionary biology. If you are interested in getting someone's attention (and you know you are), you need only look at the way it is handled in your immediate world.

Attention flows in two directions. You are vying for the attention of others and they are vying for yours. Obviously, there is only a finite amount of attention to go around, so some of us live in a world of severe attention deficits.[1] We'll define attention as simply the amount of time you have in your day and the realistic expectation of what you can pay attention to.

We must also look at the reverse: how much attention you need from the people around you and how much they can give you. For our purposes, there is a gigantic disconnect between how many people want to get your attention and how much

---

1. Thomas H. Davenport, John C. Beck, *The Attention Economy* (Boston: Harvard Business School Press, 2001)

attention you have to give. This becomes extremely important in a world where information is a form of currency and in our culture they are equivalent.

So how good is television at getting and keeping someone's attention? For over 50 years, the boob tube has been the central focus for over half the living spaces in America. Television is our window to the world and it has done a pretty spectacular job of getting and keeping our attention. But now, there are other media opportunities for us and everything is competing for our attention. It is no longer about making a great show or a clever commercial, it's about creating a meme that transcends any one form factor and sticks to its target.

Information = Currency

Imagine a cab driver on West 38th Street in midtown Manhattan driving aimlessly and looking for a fare. If he had a device in his cab that told him that there was a fare waiting on 38th and Lex, he could almost immediately turn that information into currency. If several cabs had that information, it would be less valuable. If every cab had that information, it would simply be a business methodology with only commodity value.

Any Wall Streeter will tell you that information (especially exclusive information) is currency. But a housewife living in the suburbs with knowledge of a sale at a local store or with an electronic promotional offering can turn information into currency just as easily.

Everyone can use information and it is the information's job to get your attention: "share of mind = share of wallet."

Share of mind is simply another way to say that you have someone's attention or, in contemporary parlance, that you or your product are "relevant" to the target. Share of wallet is self-explanatory. To sum this up: the better you are at getting people's attention, the more money you are going to make. The longer you can keep someone's attention, the greater the store of economic value.

Waste Models

Although professional media planners will do their very best to incorporate techniques such as demographic targeting, geographic targeting and behavioral targeting into their media plans, there is always a significant amount of advertising dollars wasted on people who have absolutely no interest in (or ability to consume) a given product. Some professionals refer to this type of media plan as a "waste model," which simply means that advertisers purchase air time based upon a "best guess" of who is watching, rather than on an actual census of who is watching. Media planners use a common currency to develop their media plans and, for the most part, the numbers that they slice and dice come from Nielsen Media Research. Here's how Nielsen explains its sample-based measurement system (from www.nielsenmedia.com/whatratingsmean/)

How do you make sure that a sample is representative of the population?

If every member of the population has an equally good chance of being in the sample, then this makes it a representative sample. Through statistical theory (and many years of practical experience which is consistent with that theory), we know that fairly drawn (or random) samples vary in usually small ways from the population. Over time these small differences tend to average out.

We check our samples in various ways. Where we do know something about the characteristics of the entire population (thanks to U.S. Census Bureau data), we compare our sample to the population. We find that although the samples aren't identical to the population, they are about as close to it as statistical theory predicts. The most important thing to check in our samples is the television viewing information. Although no one has measured the viewing of the entire population, we do have ways to cross check against other samples and other methods of measurement. We regularly compare our National People Meter audience data to the combined information from the diaries all across the 200+ local markets we measure.

Occasionally, we do special studies called telephone coincidentals. In these tests, we call thousands of randomly selected telephone numbers and ask people if their TV sets are on and who is watching. This research provides a completely independent check on the amount of TV usage and viewing, and when we have found some differences, it has helped us zero in on ways to improve our ongoing measurement systems.

How can Nielsen Media Research tell if people are really watching TV?

This is really one of the most difficult questions we face. Some of the information we measure is possible to check by independent means. Programs are carried by stations and we can observe that when it happens. TV sets are tuned to particular stations and not to others, and we can measure that when it happens.

The only person who knows when viewing occurs is the viewer. Viewing is not necessarily looking at a TV; it is not necessarily being in the room with a TV; it is something that only the viewer can define. This is why we use the diary and the people meter, so viewers can tell us what they do.

Nielsen Ratings have been the *lingua franca* of the television advertising business for decades. While they were the only way to measure audiences, the industry was more or less happy to use their sample-based ratings system as a common currency. This is changing rapidly.

Census-Based Metrics

With the advent of DVRs and digital cable set-top boxes, census-based metrics similar to the exact numbers reported by Web sites for click-throughs started to appear. System operators retrieve and analyze data from set-top boxes that tells them what is being watched, when the channel is changed, when the set is on, and can even predict (with moderate accuracy) if there is anyone in the room watching.

DVRs have the added benefit of reporting viewing preferences and time-shifting habits. Why doesn't the whole industry just use them? There are privacy issues. People would have to opt-in to these systems as they would tell the reporting company an unbelievable amount about the habits and behaviors of the individuals being monitored. Then, there is the problem of explosive amounts of data. Where would you store thousands of terabytes of data each day? How would you parse it? Who would have the time to analyze it? Additionally, they would be cable-centric, since satellite homes do not really have the capacity to report usage without dialing back over a telephone line and antenna households have no technology for this type of reporting. And, lastly, the mechanism to collect these data are owned by the system operators, not the networks, producers or the ratings companies.

Census-based metrics seem unimaginably scary to those who make their livings from the status quo. They should not. Metrics alone do not tell the story of advertising efficacy. Questions like who clicked, who else was in the room, and why did they click are not answered by metrics alone. Then there are important components to the advertising efficacy equation like "decay value," which is absolutely unaddressed by metrics methodology of any kind. If you are of a "certain" age and I ask you to associate a product with "Mean Joe Green" you will say "Coke." That commercial aired 25 years ago. If I start singing, "I'd like to teach the world to sing, in perfect harmony ..." and you are of a slightly more wizened "certain" age, you would also say "Coke." That jingle campaign ran 30 years ago. One must be careful to appreciate the subtleties of the advertising business before positing that a "better mousetrap" will change everything. ROI is a complex calculation with industry-specific terms. Networked technology has the power to alter only some of the terms of the equation, not all of them.

Commercial Skipping

There are many things that make DVRs important. First and foremost is the feature that consumers and industry executives understand very well — if you record a show, you can easily skip through commercials when you play it back. Although this is the most talked about feature of DVR technology, the act of commercial avoidance

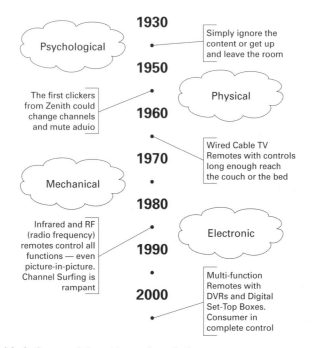

FIGURE 10.2 *Commercial avoidance through the ages.*

is as old as the technology of television. There are four main types of commercial avoidance: psychological, physical, mechanical and electronic (see Figure 10.2).

Psychological Avoidance

On Dec. 7, 1930, W1XAV Boston did a video simulcast of a CBS radio program, "The Fox Trappers." It was a concert sponsored by I. J. Fox Furriers and the broadcast included what some people call the first television commercial. (Back then, commercial announcements were prohibited by law. Wait a minute – simulcasts, pirated video and banned content in 1930 ... are we sure this book is about the future?) Anyway, from that point on all you had to do to avoid a commercial was to ignore it. Let's call this psychological avoidance.

Physical Avoidance

A popular commercial avoidance technique also goes back as far as the technology itself – walking away. Let's call this physical avoidance. Physical avoidance is fairly well documented by a large portion of the TV viewing public. We've all been trained to use the rest room or grab a snack during commercial breaks.

The Toilet Flush Syndrome

Pundits often refer to the undocumented, "I Love Lucy Toilet Flush Syndrome." This is a charming myth about the dangerous drop in water pressure during the commercial breaks of "I Love Lucy" back when there were only three networks and any show could enjoy a monstrous rating just by being good.

However, just before Super Bowl XXII, Harvey Schultz, commissioner of the New York City Department of Environmental Protection, issued a "Bowl Warning"[2] (pun intended). He asked New York City Super Bowl viewers (especially beer drinkers) to please stagger their trips to the bathroom during commercials to reduce strain on the city's water mains. This was a good-natured joke done to get the commissioner's name in the news, nothing more.

There was actually a television event that did have an effect on water pressure levels in NYC: the last episode of M*A*S*H. The two-and-a-half-hour episode aired in 1983 and enjoyed a 60 rating (percentage of TV households) and a 77 share (percentage of houses using television). That makes it one of the biggest television audiences in history and, according to the Commissioner's office, both big water mains were affected during the commercial breaks.

Mechanical Avoidance

From the very beginning you could psychologically or physically avoid commercial announcements. Wired remote controls appeared in the early 1950s, but consumers didn't like the bulky cables so they really didn't take. The first practical mechanical avoidance occurred during the Golden Age of Television. In 1955, Zenith introduced the "Zenith Space Command." It was immediately nicknamed "the clicker" because when you pressed the button it made a distinctive clicking sound as the device generated its ultrasonic signal. (The Zenith Space Command is considered to be the first practical wireless remote control).

Electronic Avoidance

To be fair, the ratio of commercials skipped to commercials watched was not truly felt until battery-operated, electronic remote controls became standard features of television sets and cable boxes in the late 1970s and early 1980s. By 1985, "channel surfing"

---

2. Cecil Adams, *The Straight Dope*, "Did New York water pressure drop due to toilet flushing after the Super Bowl?" February 13, 1987, www.straightdope.com/classics/a2_371.html

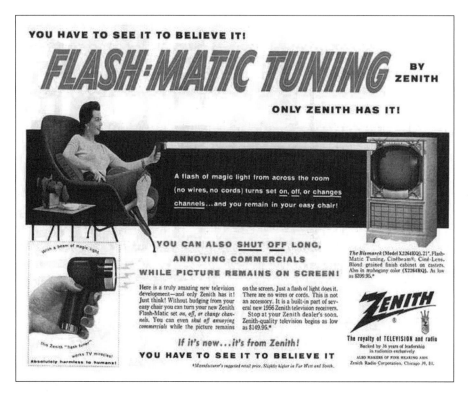

FIGURE 10.3 *This 1955 ad features the ability to shut off long, annoying commercials while the picture remains on the screen, but this "flashlight-based" technology was not a hit with consumers.*

was the biggest problem facing television, and advertising execs and the industry started to do everything it could to minimize it.

In the mid-80s, television and cable channels were basically competing with each other for advertising revenue, which was based upon selling aggregated eyeballs. Back then, cable did not have a very big advertising business, so they were more focused on getting viewers to subscribe to their systems. Remember, this is a full 10 years before the Internet existed and although there was an explosive business in video games, they were still the bastion of teen-aged boys.

A great deal can be learned about how people will use television by examining how local stations and networks dealt with channel surfing. One of the first things they noticed was that people started to surf during the commercial breaks. Audience research showed that the problem was at its worst on the half hour and hour, when shows began and ended. Several techniques were tested to deal with channel surfing.

Credit Squeeze

The most effective was the credit squeeze, which took the long, boring 30 to 60 seconds of end credits and squeezed them to one side of the screen. The end title music was cut short and in three-quarters of the screen, you were treated to promotional announcements for upcoming shows. The credit squeeze/promo fix cut channel surfing significantly during the credits and preserved lead-in/lead-out ratings for a while.

Cold Open, Hot Switch

Another weapon used to reduce channel surfing was the "cold open," which is sometimes referred to as a "hot switch." Instead of going to a commercial pod at the end of a show, the programmers would launch from a credit squeeze directly into the opening act of the next show. This "cold open" did not leave any time between shows for you to go the bathroom or change the channel. After the cold open, you would see the show's opening title sequence, then a commercial break, then a bumper back into the first act of the show.

This opening sequence technique ultimately evolved into what we see on commercial network television today: Most credits are squeezed, most opens are cold, and opening sequences and their title songs are as short as possible.

The problem was handled a little differently for news programming. To quash as much channel surfing as possible, news programs completely dumped their long, elaborate openings and started their programs with a five second graphic, a musical flourish (or hook) and a 45-second to two-minute teaser promoting the day's top stories. After the tease, they would do a short seven- to 10- second opening sequence and jump right into the day's top story.

These techniques, which survive to this day, are in place to reduce channel surfing. Obviously, they have no (or very limited effect) on commercial avoidance.

Do People Really Skip More Commercials Today?

This is one of the most serious financial issues facing television executives today. However, it's rhetorical because the answer doesn't matter. DVRs may be the cause of this particular panic, but they are not to blame. If anything, it is modern measurement capabilities that have created this critical climate. Add to this the enhanced (though still imperfect) measurement system and the fact that the biggest, most powerful retailers all employ exceptional computer-based, just-in-time inventory and distribution systems. You may think that these issues are unrelated, but if you run a "call to action" television spot with the sole purpose of increasing sales, you will know quickly and dispassionately if consumers responded. This does not apply to all advertising, but the damage to television advertising budgets has already been done.

Nielsen Measurement

For years, television advertising was sold based on ratings estimates from Nielsen Media Research. You purchased a spot in a particular show because it was going to be viewed by a certain number of people who fit a particular set of demographic requirements. The shows were rated, not the commercial breaks. So you were paying for the number of people who were supposed to be watching the show, not the people who were supposed to be watching your commercial. Now, Nielsen measures everything that it can possibly measure: TVs, programs, commercials and people. Because they can now measure with more accuracy, they can report what happens during commercial breaks, and the news is not good!

Perhaps there is a better question to ask: "Can you still make an effective :30 second television commercial?" For the time being, television continues to be the most efficient geographically and demographically targeted and measured system for the delivery of sight, sound and motion. This is changing, but not nearly as fast as some would have you believe. What is changing (and much quicker than anyone in the business could have imagined) is how advertisers value audiences and how much weight they are putting on factors such as engagement, interests and behaviors.

Networked Advertising

We have often heard that time-shifting is very unfriendly to advertisers because the technology also enables easy fast-forwarding or skipping of commercials. But DVRs are not unfriendly to advertisers; they are unfriendly to networks. And, they are specifically unfriendly to highly interruptive, five-minute commercial pods in the middle of the content that someone wants to watch.

The Short-Term Economics vs. Long-Term Benefits of DVRs

There is a short-term, narrow area where DVR technology is advertiser-unfriendly (as opposed to network-unfriendly, which DVRs always are). CONTINUED ▶

> CONTINUED ▶   As measurable commercial skipping through pre-recorded content reduces the amount of salable commercial time, the scarcity of the resource will cause the price for air time to increase. In the long-term, this may be offset by the value of additional consumer engagement, spots with higher relevance or the two-way interactivity that the technology will ultimately enable. But in the foreseeable future, the laws of supply and demand say that advertisers will have to pay more for less.

The advent of networked television is going to spawn some new types of advertising. Since it is easily skipped through, the traditional :30 second spot is not well suited for use in on-demand systems or in a DVR environment. Many professional trade groups have been toying around with names for the new advertising forms and their functions. Here are some very brief descriptions of the most popular concepts:

- **Telescopes.** A short advertisement or graphic in program content directs the user to press a button to "telescope" into additional content.

- **Showcases.** These are specific menus of enhanced content, user bookmarks, chaptered content or a "trailer" or "promo" that all lead to an enhanced user experience.

- **Pause Trigger.** When a user presses the pause button, an ad message appears. This technique can also prompt the user to press another button to telescope the ad.

- **Speed Bumps.** When a user presses fast forward, a logo or other still frame is overlaid on the screen.

- **Navigation.** Banners in the GUI lead to advanced media functions.

These functions can be incorporated into DVRs and VOD systems and they open up a whole new world of advertising possibilities. The problem, of course, is not the technology; it's the consumers. This kind of interaction requires a behavioral change and has a learning curve associated with it. Is there a compelling value proposition for consumers here? "Press this button and you'll get a better widget." These are all good concepts; we'll have to see if consumers choose to use them.

Engagement Index

An engagement index is used to assign value to quality and quantity of time spent paying attention to specific content. It could be a scale of total time spent or time spent singularly engaged. The concepts are not new, but the technology to collect and analyze the data is emergent. In a networked television environment, engagement is very easy to quantify. If someone is pushing buttons, reacting to or transacting with your television show or commercial, you have a census of their exact behaviors.

The more someone pays attention to your offering, the more likely you are to sell them something. On networked television, this can easily be measured and used in place of frequency in a response calculation: Reach + Engagement = Response. When planning for IP video or any on-demand service, this is a workable model.

On the traditional network side of the business, media planners have come up with their own version of an engagement index. When thinking about a traditional network media sale, engagement is not one specific thing. Planners must consider the size of the advertising unit. After all, in a network television environment, a :30 second spot usually out-performs a spot of shorter duration. Clutter is a big factor: the more units in a given pod, the less likely viewers are to respond to it. Environment and situation are very important. How many people are in the room, is this a personal video experience, is there a party going on next door, etc. And, lastly, relevance: if the commercial is not relevant to a viewer, response will be much lower. Relevance is so important that many network and networked salespeople have developed metrics solely based on how viewers respond to topical relevance. Traditional marketers would equate relevance to branding – I would not disagree. In both cases, the goal of an engagement index is the same; to create a more accountable television metric.

Nielsen Is not Totally Asleep at the Wheel

Nielsen Media Research is the data source and the *de facto* currency that the television industry uses for the "doing of business." Do not be fooled by rhetoric or techno-babble into believing that big advertisers, big media and Nielsen are "out of touch" with reality. They are not. There is a frighteningly large amount of money that changes hands daily in this business and the people responsible for "watching the store" do so with a keen eye. Yes, there are things that are going to change and new technology will be a key driver of that change. We will see very big improvements in the way media is measured and accounted for in the coming years and a certain amount of confusion caused by the introduction of disparate "currencies" into a previously homogenous ecosystem. But, in the end, sample-based and census-based measurement systems will co-exist and be incorporated into the optimization schemas that enable and empower the media marketplace.

Key Takeaways

- There may be dozens of sales organizations competing to sell very similar airtime – even within the same companies. To consumers, however, there is little differentiation between a spot sold by a local affiliate or system operator and one sold by a media conglomerate.

- Traditional commercials are priced based upon a sample-based, waste model that relies on a "best guess" of who is watching at that time.

- People began skipping commercials long before the advent of the remote control or the DVR, but these developments have created an even bleaker picture for network television advertisers.

- Many television trade groups are working to develop new advertising models for the new reality of on-demand, time-shifted viewing.

- As new technologies and advertising models develop, additional ways to calculate ROI will have to be developed, such as engagement indices which measure the quality and quantity of time spent viewing specific content.

11 Emerging Advertising Technologies

Often when thinking about the interactive nature of networked television, people gravitate toward the concept of user-initiated interaction. A viewer will pick up a remote control and press a button. Maybe it's as simple as changing a channel or maybe it's more complicated and requires a sequence of buttons to be pressed. User-initiated interactivity is built into networked television, but some of the most important interactive features may actually occur in the background. It is the inherent two-way nature of the system that makes it so valuable. Let's look at some of the ways that networked television advertising is evolving.

Dynamic Ads

There are several versions of dynamic advertisements. You've seen them for years during sporting events. At the stadiums, you can see the ads change (usually on rollers) during the course of a game. Many signs and billboards are now at least partially electronic and can be changed from a remote location over wired or wireless connections. Their broadcast counterparts have been around for a while as well. During the average televised sporting event, the television audience may see banners and billboards that are different from the ones seen by fans at the stadium. They can be superimposed over the existing stadium graphics by the broadcaster. This is the same technology that paints the blue line of scrimmage and yellow first down line on a televised football game. In some cases, there is an area painted Ultimatte Green or Chromakey Blue that the broadcaster uses to key in dynamic broadcast-only graphics (people in the stadium see a green or blue painted area).

The technique has found its way into live and online versions of console videogames and many other places you might not expect them. Then, there is the more recent technology that allows television commercials or broadband video to be dynamically generated during delivery. This dynamic property allows the spots to be "custom built" for the viewer.

Creating Dynamic Ads

Dynamicism might be used to generate ads that read the seller's automated inventory levels and change out products "on the fly." The value here is that the seller or sponsor never runs out of merchandise. Alternatively, the same technique could be used to "push" a product that is not selling as well as it should be. Dynamically tying television commercials to indexes is a primary use for the technology. Dynamicism transforms television into a reactive "call to action" medium. Where traditional television spots take about three days to make the journey from traffic control to master control and onto the air, a dynamic television spot can be changed just minutes before airing. This technology gives television advertising a dramatic speed-to-market advantage over radio or newspaper advertising.

There are several technologies and methods that are commonly used to create dynamic video. For IP Video, the most common approach is colloquially referred to as the "brute force" method. Since hard disk space is relatively cheap, it is possible to create every viewable version of a spot and store it as a complete file on a server. If a user satisfies a specific set of predetermined rules, a specific version will play for that user. It's called brute force because this method has no intelligence on the production side. The system simply creates every possible version of the video, stores them for possible use and delivers the appropriate version on demand.

Seth Haberman's Visible World technology uses a similar system to deliver dynamic commercials through broadcast and cable systems. The unique attribute of Visible World dynamic ads is that only one commercial is actually produced. It includes all of the scenes that could possibly be combined to make every version of the commercial, but television viewers only see the spot that conforms to the rules set up for them by the advertiser. This technology allows a promotional announcement to be easily and inexpensively customized for each market ("tagged and bagged") with time and tune in information. Or, commercials can be created that include different offers at different times of the day, or even if the stock market is up or down. Dynamic advertising offers video broadcasters a near live, reactive tool to communicate with consumers.

Addressable Dynamic Ads

Aside from yield managing manufacturing or retail capacity in real time, dynamic ads can also be used to customize content based upon viewer location, behaviors or preferences. When all of these attributes are combined, the system is said to have addressability. Many people confuse addressability and dynamicism, but they are different functions.

As we have discussed, dynamic ads change based upon business rules. Addressable ads are ads that can be addressed to a specific set-top box, computer, person, household, neighborhood, town, city, DMA, region, time zone or any combination thereof. Addressable ads are not necessarily dynamic and dynamic ads need not be addressable.

Dynamic addressable television commercials are the most powerful tool available to the current broadcast and cable infrastructure for creating relevant content.

When you put the two technologies together, you get a powerful combination of communication tools: custom spots sent to specific marketing targets. This technique empowers advertisers to create relevant messages and get them to the right people. In theory, the more relevant something is, the more likely you are to pay attention to it.

The clear benefit of this technology is its ability to prolong the life of the :30 second commercial form factor.

Addressability

Printing presses have been around for well over a thousand years. And, although scholars identify the "Diamond Sutra" (circa 868 A.D.), as the earliest printed book, the art of printing most likely predates this work. In 1041, movable clay type was first invented in China and, more known to western culture, Johannes Gutenberg invented his famous movable type printing press in 1436.

By 1450, Gutenberg was printing up a storm and, if asked, he would not have had a problem creating a personalized, printed letter addressed to every land owner in Germany's Rhine Valley. The cost — a day's wages for a master and an apprentice for several years — would not have been a practical use of time or money.

Junk mail was not invented until the beginning of the 20th century when Mr. Sears created his first "direct mail" campaign. The cost of personalization was still out of reach. Your name was "occupant" and, if you were greeted with a letter, you were "Dear Friend" or "Dear Customer."   CONTINUED ▶

CONTINUED ▶

It was not until the advent of the high-speed laser printer (circa 1977) that serious personalization became so inexpensive that there was no reason not to treat every piece of printed matter as if it were a personal, one-to-one communication.

Television content (programming and commercials) has been a one-to-many medium for more than 50 years. Technology now exists to customize every aspect of the television experience. The companies that provide dynamic and addressable content for traditional broadcast or digital cable television are offering an interim technology. In a networked, IP-based world, every communication can be customized. It is this transfer of control and the potential interactivity that makes the inherent two-way nature of IP-provisioned distribution so exciting.

Behavioral Targeting

Behavioral targeting is a catch-all phrase. In general, it describes the idea of delivering ads to audiences that have demonstrated a specific behavior, such as clicked on an ad, surfed the Web in a specific way, searched for certain types of things, made a purchase, visited a store, watched a program on their DVR, etc.

In an IP-provisioned world, you can customize every communication ... but should you? Depending on who you ask, advertising executives will tell you that it is just one of many marketing techniques or that it is the Holy Grail. Like dynamic ads and addressability, behavioral targeting helps deliver relevant messages to consumers. The danger with all of these techniques is that you can get so granular with your message that the law of diminishing returns creates a real marginal cost/marginal gain problem.

There are two issues that need to be considered when creating campaigns that utilize behavioral, dynamic/addressable or other advanced technology targeting techniques — one is on the consumer side, the other is on the business side.

Business-Side Issues

On the business side, it is important to make sure that you have the business rules in place to interpret and financially analyze the data generated from advanced targeting. ROI models that have been created to utilize "waste advertising metrics" are not usually built to report the efficacy of a targeted campaign. More to the point, (excluding direct response-specific products) the marketing data that most brands aggregate does not paint a picture that can easily be applied as granularly as the technology allows.

This disconnect falls under the category of "setting up to fail" rather than to succeed. The reason is simple: if you don't have a properly defined or reportable goal, you won't have a way to demonstrate success. This issue has caused many companies to dismiss interactive advertising and advanced targeting technologies as a parlor trick as opposed to the paradigm shift that some of them truly are.

Consumer-Side Issues

On the consumer side, there is always the danger of getting too granular or, worse, misusing or misinterpreting the aggregated data and creating offers that are actually less effective than their untargeted counterparts.

Back in the mid 1990s, one of the biggest discount retailers was approached by one of the highest technology direct mail marketing companies of the day. Because this retailer had a database approaching 25 million customers, which included a complete sales history of each customer, this retailer was uniquely positioned to take advantage of a very sophisticated direct mail/customer loyalty campaign. The idea was simple: send a personalized letter to each consumer within a few days of their purchase thanking them for making the purchase. In the letter, include an offer that was specifically targeted to that consumer's profile and the respective purchase. For example: if a customer bought a VCR, the letter would include an offer to purchase a 10-pack of videotapes at a deep discount. This sounded like a good idea to everyone.

As a control, they decided to test the letter two different ways. One with a percentage discount at various rates ("Save 30% on a 10-pack of videocassettes") and one with a dollar amount ("Save $5.00 on a 10-pack of videocassettes").

If you know anything about direct marketing, you know that this test was doomed from the start. As it turns out, a representative from their regular advertising agency suggested one more group of letters be sent with the test group. It was a very low technology, untargeted coupon that simply said, "Thank you for your recent purchase. To show our appreciation, we'd like to offer you $10 off your next purchase of $100 or more."

You can see where this is going. The $10 coupon out-pulled the targeted, granular marketing letter about 20 to 1. Why? Because everyone knows what $10 is and not everyone who buys a VCR needs or wants 10 blank videocassettes. Information is not knowledge and technology by itself can be extremely dangerous.

The Civil War – Strategy Disrupted

Often described as "the first modern war," the Civil War was also the bloodiest in our country's history. More men died in the first major battle, Shiloh, than had died in all other American wars up to April 1862. And, quite sadly, more Americans died in this war than the total of American casualties in all other wars combined.

A technological transition is universally cited as the cause of the 620,000 casualties and 50,000 amputee survivors. These grim statistics speak directly to the disconnect between technology, strategy and tactics. During this technological transition, Armies and Navies were still using tactics developed at a time when you needed to see your enemy to kill them. Unfortunately, the generals of the day did not fully understand the power and accuracy of the newer weapons they were using.

The Model 1861 Springfield Musket was one of the shoulder arms of choice for the Civil War foot soldier. It had a rifled bore, interchangeable parts, percussion cap ignition and it was extremely accurate and dependable. Weighing just 9.25 lbs, this 58.5 inch workhorse came with a particularly nasty, triangular 21-inch socket bayonet. The unique attribute of this most lethal weapon was the .58 calibre conical minie ball that it fired at a remarkable 950 feet per second.

This weapon was deadly accurate at 800 yards and passably accurate at 1,000 yards. Put in human terms, a marksman of average 1860s skill could kill or maim a man standing half a mile away. However, that's not where the projectile stopped, so you could be standing up to a mile away from the battleground and still be critically injured. Add the lack of medical and surgical knowledge to this situation and you've got a recipe for disaster – which is exactly what happened.

You may consider this sidebar "over the top" or simply inappropriate as an example of what happens when technology outpaces rules of engagement. And it is not my intention to dishonor or trivialize these brave souls who gave their lives to our posterity. Business is not war, but business competition mimics the structure of war and, though graphic, it is instructive to see just how important it is to match technology, strategy and tactics.

Key Takeaways

- User interaction does not need to be active or conscious; networked television advertising can take advantage of user behavior and advertiser goals.

- Dynamic and addressable advertising can extend the useful life of traditional advertising and create a completely new genre of relevant networked advertising.

- The value of targeting is directly related to an advertiser's ability to properly define and measure its success.

- Technology is often very far ahead of business rules, strategy and tactics. The resulting tension is the most powerful engine for change.

12 Television Disrupted

It is important to point out that no form factor is likely to completely wipe out a previous form factor in the media business. Photography did not put an end to painting, recordings did not replace concerts, web sites did not render newspapers obsolete, home videos did not destroy the movie business and networked television will not destroy network television. However, more and more households are becoming networked everyday. When the transition reaches critical mass, the impact will be significant.

In the media business, content is the product and technology enables it to be realized and distributed. Eight-track tapes might be hard to find, but the songs are still available in literally a dozen other form factors that are currently in use. Will CDs go away? Someday. But the songs will live on as files and continue to be monetized. Will network television cease to exist? Not as long as it is the most efficient way to reach the massive audiences needed for emergent events like live entertainment, news and sports.

As a practical matter, the public Internet could not be used instead of the Fox Television Network to watch an NFL football game on a typical Sunday afternoon. Were millions of viewers to attempt to watch it streamed live or even delayed a few minutes so it could be progressively downloaded, the public Internet would go "tilt." That being said, networked television has the opportunity and the available technology to substantially disintermediate entire distribution verticals.

161

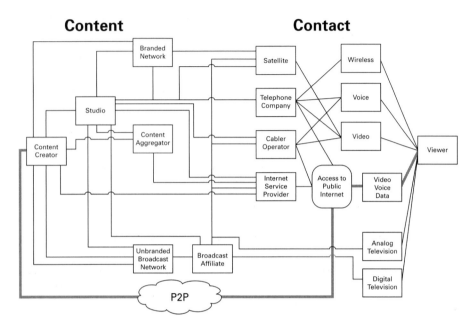

FIGURE 12.1 *Consumer Media Choices in the Networked Television Era.*

Consumer Media Choices Revisited

Now that we've looked far enough into the past to think about the probable futures of the industry, let's examine a revised version of our consumer media choices diagram. As you can see, all of the media choices are still represented in Figure 12.1. Voice, video and data are the primary media categories and we have broadcast television (both analog and digital) and wireless communication indicated as well. Let's leave two-way wireless communication out of this mix for a moment as it plays an enormous role and will be covered later in this section.

The most striking difference between Figure 1.11 in Chapter 1 and Figure 12.1 is the addition of the peer-to-peer (P2P) network and broadband access to the public Internet. Figure 12.1 is simplified as much as possible to illustrate a conundrum for cable companies and telcos: access to the public Internet.

No matter how "walled" your video, voice and wireless walled gardens are, you have to provide open access to the Internet or people will find a provider who will. Hence the conundrum.

Walled Gardens

As we have previously discussed, cable television systems and telephone company television systems are walled gardens. Whether they use QAMs and DOCSIS or QAMs and IPTV or are pure IPTV networks, they are all closed systems. This allows for a quality of service guarantee and as much DRM as can be accomplished. Walled gardens have proven to be extremely profitable. Sadly, for every provider of access to the public Internet (the data portion of the holy trinity: video, voice and data) the public Internet is, by definition, public.

As you know, almost everything you have ever seen or wanted to see, heard or wanted to hear, watched or wanted to watch is available somewhere on a P2P network. To be sure, there are reasons you would not go looking for them, but they are there.

Personal Networked Television

One probable future is the advent of a GUI that will enable viewers to easily search for content and automatically create adaptive playlists that relate to personal preferences or behaviors. An interface like this would create the equivalent of personal television networks for each individual viewer. It would combine VOD, DVR, search, P2P and high-speed Internet access to significantly disintermediate the existing cable, telephone and satellite infrastructure.

Controlling Access by Limiting Bandwidth

To combat this probable future, systems operators who offer Internet access may try to limit bandwidth outside the walled gardens. Limiting bandwidth can have an impact on certain types of P2P networks. However, it is much less of an issue with torrent files. In this arms race, the prey (file-sharing networks) will always be just a little ahead of the predators (systems operators).

You need about 30 Mbps down to receive a modest combination of HDTV signals, SDTV signals and VoIP services. But, in reality, you don't need more than 3 Mbps down and 1.5 Mbps up to have a very satisfying experience on the public Internet. By creating a tiered service, operators (like telcos or any other organization that owns an Internet pipeline) could potentially use their high-capacity broadband pipes for themselves and deny access to their competitors. This would also allow them to price consumer services in "regular" and "premium" tiers and ultimately help them control unwanted (and possibly illegal) traffic. They are already lobbying Congress to allow them to provide tiered Internet services (although not for this specific purpose).

Of course, this kind of bandwidth limiting would also create a more competitive marketplace for pure Internet service providers, who would be able to offer bundled services like VoIP and data at super-high speeds without the burden of content fees.

Regardless of how this eventually plays out, to legitimately use the "best efforts" public Internet for the distribution of HDTV or SDTV or full screen, nice-looking, emotionally satisfying IP video, you are going to need a big pipe. Will the phone companies and cable companies have to sell it to you? Will the fact that there are several paths to the public Internet available inspire enough competition so that someone will offer 50 to 70 Mbps down and 30 to 50 Mbps up for a reasonable monthly fee? You can almost bet on it. At the end of the day, attempts to limit service probably won't be a good defense strategy for anyone. But, then again, with the government involved, it is hard to make a reasonable prediction about the outcome.

The Art of War

Since we are now going to look at some industry conflicts, it might be fun to pay homage to a favorite author of mine. "The Art of War" is considered by many to be the definitive treatise on military strategy. It was written during the 6th Century BC by a Chinese general named Sun Tzu. My favorite passage from the book describes the five things a general should absolutely know before going into battle.

"The art of war is governed by five factors, to be taken into account when seeking the field of battle: The Tao, The Heaven, The Earth, The Commander and The Troops.

- The Tao causes the people to be in complete accord with their ruler, so that they will follow him regardless of their lives, undismayed by any danger.

- The Heaven signifies night and day, cold and heat, times and seasons.

- The Earth comprises distances, great and small; danger and security; open ground and narrow passes; the chances of life and death.

- The Commander stands for the virtues of wisdom, sincerity, benevolence, courage and strictness.

- The Troops are the army in its proper subdivisions, the graduations of rank among the officers, the maintenance of roads by which supplies may reach the army, and the control of military expenditure.

These five factors should be familiar to every general: he who knows them will be victorious; he who knows them not will fail."

Personally, I do not believe that Sun Tzu wrote the "Art of War" as a business book. And, I am certain that people whose lives are in danger react very differently than people who simply have a few dollars at risk. However, there is a CONTINUED ▶

CONTINUED ► zeitgeist to the way that Sun Tzu instructs his readers to think. We can learn some important lessons from the text if we redefine his terms to fit our needs.

The five factors we must consider in the following pages are: Consumer permissions, economic climate, distribution, messaging and execution.

- The Tao stands for consumer permissions – the willingness of consumers to accept your standing to sell them your product. MTV really can't sell you designer clothing, you won't let them. They don't have your permission.

- The Heaven signifies economic climate – this doesn't need much of an explanation. When the economy is good, people are willing to spend more money than when the economy is bad.

- The Earth comprises distribution – whether physical or electronic, wide, cost-effective distribution must be in place for a product or service to reach its consumers.

- The Commander stands for messaging – a clear and concise marketing message that can be quickly and easily communicated is essential in a cluttered, mass-mediated world.

- The Troops represent execution – do you have the organization to get it done? As is often said (though not often enough), God is in the details.

These five factors should be familiar to every manager: he or she (since we are updating) who knows them will be victorious; he or she who knows them not will fail.

Disruptees vs. Disruptors

We shall conclude our journey though the probable futures of television by having a think about which technologies or organizations or industries represent the disruptees and which represent the disruptors. It is not important to pick sides or to pick a winner (although the exercise is great fun and makes for an excellent office pool). What is important is to think about where you and your organization might position yourselves to take advantage of the various conflicts that are in progress and on the horizon. If you need a little help with these thought experiments, perhaps you can start by thinking about which organizations have all of Sun Tzu's five factors going for (or against) them.

Content vs. Contact

Channing Dawson, senior vice president at Scripps Networks, offers up a concept that makes excellent sense. He asked, "When will my media find me?" What he was really asking was, "When will media be smart enough to know that I need it and make itself available to me for consumption?" This is, of course, the job of all media; it is just outside the realm of current technology. It will not be for long.

Google is one of the most interesting success stories of the dot-com era. Much has been written about this company and how they have captured the minds and wallets of advertisers, small and large all over the world. *Contact is king!* There is a very profound lesson for the television and media business to be learned here: "Contact is King." How can your media find you? It needs to know you need it. Is that via search or via behavioral targeting? It doesn't matter. We are quickly approaching a time when media will do more than self-assemble; it will make itself available to consumers in highly relevant ways.

This may start on the PC side of the business with broadband or IP Video offerings. It may be an automated version of "myYahoo for video" that plays in your RSS reader or home page whenever you log on. The media may be fed to your portable device through your local area network, via WiFi or other wireless means. It may be a logical extension of the clipcasting services, which up to now have been solutions waiting for problems.

What will be first? Most likely news, weather and sports. These emergent media are most valuable when they are specific to the viewer's personal preferences, the time of day and the viewer's location. Mobile phones have 911 chips that can tell the carriers where the user is during an emergency. The same technology can tell the system where you are for advertising purposes. Is there a localized "Google Ad-sense for video" coming soon? Of course!

Your media is being empowered to find you every day, and this is much more than a trend — it is an important business strategy. In order to maintain a competitive advantage, media providers are going to have to offer the benefit of "intelligent" media or consumers will switch to providers who can more adequately service their needs.

However, there is a group of companies that don't need to be told anything about the value of content, the long tail or how a power law might relate to consumer needs — the contact providers.

Contact Providers

Contact providers are not just search engines. Certainly Google enjoys an extraordinary market cap for a company that does not create any original content. (In practice, they do create some content, but the bulk of their business and most of their profit comes from enabling people to search and, more importantly, find stuff that other people create) but the entire genus of companies that create communities-of-interest falls into the category of "contact provider."

Is there truly an upcoming battle between content providers and contact providers? Actually, it is going to be more like a war. The fundamental principles upon which each type of company is based, as well as the value chains from which they profit, are at extreme odds with one another.

Content providers want you to find their content. Contact providers want your content to find you. Sound like a semantic argument? Google's market cap is bigger than the total commercial television advertising business - content is not king, contact is king! Are we likely to see an industry death match with marquee billing like "The entire television industry vs. the contact providers?" It is inevitable. The acknowledged Holy Grail of the networked media business is what you want, when you want, where you want it. There is no way that the existing television infrastructure can achieve this goal. Only a networked television infrastructure, which includes elements from the contact provider community, can ever hope to realize it.

When? Parts of the networked television future are here now. The more important issues are how significant the networked television future will be and how much market share and gross revenue it will bleed from the existing system.

There are no easy answers to these questions. But it may be instructive to examine the total penetration of digital set-top boxes in use today. Of the 73 million cable households, only about 40 percent have digital set-top boxes and very, very few of those have a digital set-top box on every television in the house. This may mean that we will have to wait a very long time to feel the impact of the contact industry on the content industry. On the other hand, it is possible that multiple client-side playback devices (rather than converged single hybrid computer/television/media centers) will utilize the contact network while the more traditional household technologies like television sets and flat-screen monitors continue to use the content networks. As we have said, these networks will undoubtedly coexist. Unfortunately, the contact network value chain is extremely unfriendly to the way that content providers like to monetize their content.

One very probable future is the evolution of a new value chain for video content that closely mimics the Vickrey auctions made popular by search engine advertising. It can't truly happen until the traditional media business reinvents they way television media is bought and sold.

Will the content providers compete with the contact providers by creating a truly modern, computerized marketplace for media? One that resembles "best practices" electronic exchanges like the NASDAQ, as opposed to the existing media marketplace — which most closely resembles a fifteenth-century textile bazaar? Remember, media planners and media buyers are people too. They behave just like ordinary consumers in that they will shop and buy where it is easiest and most convenient to do so.

Cable vs. Satellite

The turf war between cable television and satellite television is truly old news. The fight is ongoing and the battle lines are drawn. Cable offers VOD, DVR, local programming and interactivity. Cable offers the triple play (video, voice and data) and in some cases the quadruple play (video, voice, data and wireless). Satellite offers all-digital service everywhere, DVR, some exclusive programming, and a lower price. For years the cable industry has viewed the satellite industry as the enemy and nothing is likely to change that perception (although many things should).

Cable vs. Telephone Companies

This is a relatively new, ferocious battle. The ferocity comes from the fact that in the foreseeable future it will be much easier for a cable company to offer competitively priced telephone services than it will be for telephone companies to offer cable television services. This is because enabling cable subscribers to use VoIP telephone services over their existing cable networks requires only a minimal investment for the cablers.

On the other hand, for telcos to offer all of the services that cable offers, they need to build a new, expensive network. The fiber optic/IP-provisioned infrastructure requires an investment of several thousand dollars per household from the telco. This fiber-optic telephone network will be several times more powerful and efficient than most existing cable networks, and it will allow the telco to sell-in a slightly differentiated triple-play bundle. However, it is not possible to estimate the short-term threat that telcos pose to cable. Firstly, they have to build the network. Telco executives estimate they can pass about 3 million homes per year. They won't bring fiber-to-the-home to every household in America, but to reach 60 million households (a good competitive number), we're still talking about 20 years. Homes passed has absolutely nothing to do with subscribers. It simply means that the telco has the ability to turn on the service if you decide to subscribe.

No matter how you look at it, this is a multi-billion dollar gamble, but in their minds, the telephone companies simply don't have a choice. The cable companies are taking access lines away from them at an alarming rate. VoIP is a very easy service for cable companies to provide. It is cost-effective and profitable. As you might imagine, the most vulnerable telephone companies are the smaller Independent Local Exchange Carriers (ILECs). Imagine having a universe of 2,500,000 access lines and losing 150,000 of them to cable each year.

Even if it levels out at a 40 percent loss of gross revenue (as many telco analysts predict), the reduction in cash flows may be fatal. To fight back, the telcos are going to try to get into the television business. For some reason, telephone companies think that they can get enough market share in the television business to get a respectable ROI. Pundits say they might hit 20 percent market share; telcos hope to take 26 percent of the market ... time will tell.

There are some very smart people who think that the telephone companies are delusional in thinking that they should be in the content business. Others believe that it is the only way for the telcos to survive. By 2020, we'll have an answer. Perhaps, if the telcos do survive until then, the cablers will be scrambling to build new infrastructure to compete with their hyper-efficient fiber networks.

MVNOS – Private Label Mobile Phones

If the satellite and telephone companies continue to gain market share, the only place they can take it from is cable. So, cable will work hard to fend them off. Some cable systems are even creating their own MVNOs (Mobile Virtual Network Operators) to bring their customers wireless telephone services — just like the telcos.

Yes, the cable companies are buying these services from their newest competitors. But, as we have seen so often, business makes strange bedfellows.

An MVNO is a cellular telephone network that is sold "wholesale" to anyone who can afford to purchase minutes in bulk. If you can commit to a couple of hundred million anytime minutes, your plan could include your own MVNO. Sprint is the biggest telco provider of these services. If your mobile telephone comes from Virgin Mobile, you are a customer of an MVNO.

The upside for the consumer is that smaller, service-oriented organizations with very specific consumer value propositions will often offer higher quality customer service than traditional telephone companies. Virgin "owns the customer experience" from the handset through to the customer service call center. You can expect to see several attempts at "affinity" or "branded" mobile phone services using this MVNO concept. Industry experts say that after it shakes out, the business can truly only support a handful a major players. In the meantime, expect to see wireless phones from cable companies giving them a quadruple play so they can compete "apples to apples" with the telcos.

Cable, Telco and Satellite vs. Churn

Enemy number one for all of the current system operators is subscriber defection or "churn." When someone churns out of cable, they are most likely going to satellite; when someone churns out of satellite, they are most likely going to cable. As soon as telcos achieve anything close critical mass, consumers will have three competitive television services to churn between.

The conventional wisdom on churn reduction revolves around the concept of "multiple service offerings" or "bundled services." It is believed (and backed up by research and experience) that the more services a customer is subscribed to, the less likely they are to churn. You hear statements like, "The triple play (video, voice and data) reduces churn by up to 40 percent." This makes some sense, as the thought of changing over your video, voice and data connections all on the same day probably sends shivers down your spine. And, to quote Rick Mandler, vice president and general manager of ABC's Enhanced Television, "America is the land of the all-you-can-eat buffet." People just seem to love "all-inclusive" pricing models.

There are several arguments that also seem to make sense when thinking about the downside of the triple play. One is that most people are paid bi-weekly and a triple play bill — or worse, a quadruple play bill — will be three or four times the size of a single play bill. One has to wonder in which pay period a consumer would like to receive such an invoice.

Another cogent argument against this concept is that if you have a dispute with your vendor, you are at risk of losing all of your services over the billing dispute. And, along the same lines, when one services goes out, so do all of the others, leaving you with no video, voice or data as they attempt to fix the problem.

For all of these issues, the full focus of systems operators in the battle against churn is the service bundle. You can expect to see every kind of marketing push to get consumers to "bundle up" for years to come.

Regular vs. Premium Internet

Some major telcos have started lobbying our elected officials for the right to create a two-tiered Internet with "regular" and "premium" service. Not only would the telcos get to charge everyone more for the faster service, they'd also get to deny the faster service to competitors.

As you can imagine, the prospect of a two-tiered Internet with proprietary super-high-speed broadband service has absolutely everyone's attention. The debate is fierce (at least in the blogosphere). In November 2005, the House held hearings on a preliminary draft by two Republican Congressmen, Joe Barton of Texas and Fred Upton of Michigan, which would allow the telecom companies to establish premium broadband services. Much angst has ensued.

It is unclear how this will play out in Congress. There are powerful lobbyists on both sides. But this proposed legislation should be viewed as a bold statement from the telcos: they're ready for a fight and they'll do whatever it takes to survive. This conflict may last for years. It will make many lawyers and lobbyists rich, but most of all, it will cause millions of passionate Internet users to take up arms. If nothing else, it is sure to be interesting.

TiVo (the DVR) vs. Advertising

We've discussed commercial skipping at length in Chapter 10; here we must look at the more disruptive feature of the DVR and other on-demand technologies — the pause button.

In a current value chain, the advertiser is paying a network to air a spot. The distributor is paying the network per subscriber to carry the network, selling some commercial time and, most importantly, billing the customer monthly. In our hypothetical distribution channel, the content flows like this: producer, network, local station, cable operator, consumer.

Consider this: The consumer presses the pause button (or fast forward) on the remote control and a graphical advertisement is superimposed on the screen. (These are called "pause triggers" and "speed bumps" respectively. See Chapter 10 for more information.) Who gets to sell that ad? Is it the cable company? After all, they own the billing relationship with the customer. Or is it the local station? They own the billing relationship with the local and regional advertisers whose ads you are skipping. Or, is it the network? They own the billing relationship with the national advertisers whose ads you are skipping. What if you are skipping an ad for Coke and the graphic is for Pepsi? What if the show is produced by an advertiser as branded entertainment and a competing brand buys all of the DVR-based inventory around it? What if it is a virtual, dynamic, addressable ad from a "Google Ad Sense-type" system drawing data from the operator, the Internet, public and private databases and combining the sources to serve the ad?

There is no clear copyright solution and no clear moral rights solution. However, there is a very simple, very real business solution: "He who owns the billing relationship owns the customer." As you can probably guess, the company that is closest to the consumer (or point of sale) has the most power.

This becomes extremely important as we redefine the concept of "transactional" television. If you were watching a national commercial for a movie and were given an option to press a button to purchase a movie ticket at your local theater, who gets paid? This might sound like an easy question, but it isn't. The movie company is a wholesaler, the movie theater chain is the retailer, the network that runs the ad is a wholesaler, the local cable operator is the retailer – you would have to work out a deal with all parties. Now add an option to purchase the DVD or a first run PPV of the same movie – it's a billing nightmare. It is also a commission nightmare. Does the DVR middleware provider take a transaction fee for processing the transaction? How about customer service? Who will the consumer call if there is a problem with the order? These are just a few of the myriad issues the transition from network to networked television will bring to light.

Sony vs. Microsoft

Although there are many places where these two corporations face off, one of the most important for our purposes is Playstation vs. Xbox. We covered the game consoles feature sets in earlier chapters, so let's just ponder the goal of each organization. Both companies want to sell as many boxes as possible. Ideally, they'd like to make these sales in the shortest possible time. Both companies have adopted the "give 'em the razor – sell 'em the blades" mentality with regard to console sales vs. game sales. The lion's share of the money comes from the royalty they charge developers for each game disc sold.

How many game consoles can we expect? It would not be unreasonable to assume that there will be 25 to 30 million full-featured, third-generation game consoles attached to the Internet by 2009. That would make this particular interactively connected community of interest bigger than Comcast's entire footprint. There is a battle between Sony and Microsoft to win the hearts and minds of video game enthusiasts worldwide. But this battle may largely be fought by the video game developers, with market share being decided by which exclusive game is the flavor of the month. The real winners are likely to be consumers who, by default, end up with extremely powerful media centers without actually thinking about buying or using one.

Game Consoles vs. Cable, Satellite & Telco

Before third-generation game consoles reach critical mass, the concept of system operator-bypass or the disintermediation of the traditional television infrastructure is going to take center stage. If a few percent influx of DVRs caused a panic amongst networks and advertisers, the concept of systems operator bypass (also called IP-bypass) is going to cause a meltdown. No one in the television business wants to imagine a world where consumers would select and prefer to watch their entertainment content on a third-generation game console running software that exploited the P2P, BitTorrent, grid and IP video world — but it is a very probable future. For technical reasons, this system may not work well for emergent, live media in the near term. But for evergreen, pre-recorded entertainment and relevant personal playlists, it is practically unbeatable.

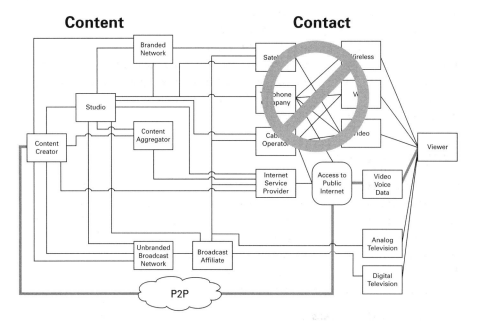

FIGURE 12.2 *Mesh and P2P networks have an opportunity to bypass the system operators and go straight to the consumer.*

This will be good for the gaming industry. These new boxes will offer interactive, dynamic, addressable advertising and sponsorship opportunities to advertisers and the technology will allow them to favorably compete with the television industry. Many cable, satellite and telco executives have quietly, in a straw-man kind of way, suggested that their biggest competition is not each other, but the unrecoverable churn out to the public Internet. This is a future you can count on.

Telephone companies are planning to deploy as many IPTV television systems as they possibly can in the shortest possible timeframe. To do this, they are spending a literal fortune bringing fiber-optic broadband connections to as many households as possible. These broadband connections have significantly higher bandwidth than was previously available at mass-market consumer pricing. Consumers will need capacity in excess of 30 Mbps down with increased upwards capacity to allow for IPTV, VoIP and traditional Internet surfing. The telcos must offer a differentiated product to favorably compete with cable operators. Big broadband pipelines to the home are required to effectively market these services. They may not have to sell this premium speed band-width to their competitors, but they will need to sell it to their customers.

The cable companies will not just watch this happen. They will compete as hard as they can to preserve their market share. To do this, they will offer their own version of IP-provisioned services over broadband. They already have a pretty big cable going into the house; they just need to change some hardware — and they will. Part of this competitive offering will include very high bandwidth connections because they will want to provide every service that consumers could possibly get from a competitor.

As we have previously discussed, when you take a new-generation game console and attach it to a very fast (30 Mbps – 60 Mbps) Internet connection, you get the closest thing imaginable to a fully converged, media center computer attached to a television set. In fact, that's exactly what it is. It doesn't take much to imagine a game DVD or software download that is actually a GUI into a video search engine, or simply a file-sharing client. Here you will have the perfect storm: a very large Internet connection into a box that is basically built to take advantage of it. This is one of the most graphic and disruptive versions of the law of unintended consequences one could ever imagine — but you don't have to imagine it — it's happening right now ... everywhere.

Game console statistics are compelling

Let's take a quick look at some statistics that portend another serious disintermediating force: Sony® PS2® deployment. According to well sourced estimates on www.broadq.com, there are over 28 million PS2® consoles installed in the US. That's about 25% of television households and over 35% of those households are broadband enabled. Approximately 57% use the game box to watch DVDs so they've got them connected to their television sets and they know how to use them. If you add Microsoft's Xbox® statistics to this already impressive number, there are more "network enabled" game consoles than DVRs deployed in the US. When a substantial portion of these devices become "network attached", big dollars are going to follow them.

What this will mean in practice is unclear. Certainly, there are countermeasures that will be taken by the television industry, the gamers, the cablers, the telcos and the content owners. Band-aids on this heart attack may include attempts to limit upload capacity; the theory is that if it takes too long to upload, you are a less valuable member of your P2P network. This might work for a while, but consumer advocates are going to have a field day with the policy. Others will try various types of file encryption and DRM. This won't work at all, but it will make it possible for executives everywhere to look their shareholders straight in the eyes and say that they are doing everything possible to combat illegal file sharing. It is possible that we might see some real movement in the legislative branch of government. Our copyright laws are woefully inadequate for the technological time in which we live. This may get some politicians to take notice, but I wouldn't hold my breath.

Metcalfe's law: "The power of the network increases exponentially by the number of computers connected to it. Therefore, every computer added to the network both uses it as a resource while adding resources in a spiral of increasing value and choice."

What's the answer? Maybe it won't happen. But if it does, it will deliver several millions of 13- to 32-year-old males who are unbelievably valuable to advertisers. We will certainly notice the paradigm shift, but it should be quite gradual. The reason it will feel slow is that these systems can only roll out a few markets at a time. As you know, for the impact of this technology to be truly felt by the television industry, millions of households will have to be enabled for very high speed broadband. There are a certain number of truck rolls associated with this infrastructure upgrade and there are only a certain number of trucks. Add to this the idea that not everyone is going to think that more is more. After all, just being available is not going to be enough; these services are going to have to be heavily marketed. And, at this writing, the telephone companies do not have a cohesive consumer value proposition for their television services nor do they offer a big price advantage.

So what will drive consumer demand? If DVR deployment is any indication, consumers are not going to understand why they need an IPTV system instead of their regular digital cable package. The telcos unique selling principle can't be "the lowest price, always." They have real costs against this build-out. They can't discount the network offerings because they must pay content owners on a per-subscriber basis — just like cable and satellite. Suffice it to say, the telcos will have a real uphill battle with their quadruple play of wireless, IPTV, VoIP and the Internet.

That being said, this wealth of commoditized bandwidth is going to have a huge impact on the way the future unfolds — especially for content on mesh networks. Remember Metcalfe's law, "The power of the network increases exponentially by the number of computers connected to it. Therefore, every computer added to the network both uses it as a resource while adding resources in a spiral of increasing value and choice."

Sony vs. Apple

Sir Howard Stringer said, "IPod is a great device, but it doesn't sell us a helluva lot of content. What we didn't do well, that Steve Jobs did, was iTunes. We have excellent hardware and content, but we need to improve our client software and have better integration between our services and our device portfolio."

Once you get over the fact that the electronics company that invented the miniaturized personal music business (transistor radio, Sony Walkman, etc.) has been dethroned by a computer company, the rest of the battle is easier to understand. Both companies are thinking about how to become your entertainment company and, unlike the other companies mentioned in these pages, they are offering integrated hardware and software as a vertical solution. At this writing, Apple is ahead and Sony is struggling – this may not be the case forever.

These companies represent the battleground between ecosystem solutions and evolving individual technologies that make up an ecosystem. The benefits to distributing your creative with Apple are instant unified standards for CRM, DRM, payment schemas, warrantee service, etc. It is in this holistic arena that Sony and Apple compete. But all of their compatriots will try to work their way into this battle by partnering and benefiting from the adoption of open standards. The obvious downside of these particular types of battles for consumer relevance is that, like the software or content businesses, a "hit" is very hard to predict. How many personal media devices will never capture the imagination of consumers? Most. This is much more than a technological arms race — it is a battle for the hearts and minds of consumers.

Consumer Electronics vs. Television

If you look on the back of a modern flat-screen television set, you will see an impressive array of analog and digital audio/video inputs and outputs. Many people are intimidated by all of the sockets and receptacles, but a few minutes with the manual and even the most technologically inept person can easily hook up a contemporary television monitor. If you look very closely on the back of a modern flat-screen you are likely to find a connector that is usually not associated with television or video at all – an RJ45 socket for an Ethernet connection (suitable for broadband Internet or LAN connections). So, the sets are as Internet-ready as they are cable-ready. Which begs the questions: why and when?

At the Digital Media Conference on June 17, 2005, in McLean, Virginia, John I. Taylor, vice president, Public Affairs, LG Electronics USA, was asked when we might see a walled garden or at least a start-up splash page from LG. Taylor said that both walled gardens and start pages are in the plans, but he cautioned that it could take as long as three to five years before you will see them. He was wrong! LG introduced a full line of flat screen television sets at CES 2006 (less than six months later) that automatically connect to a Web site powered by Gemstar (TV Guide) when you turn them on.

The scary thing (from the system operator's point of view) is how incredibly disintermediating a television monitor with a built-in or manufacturer-provided GUI might be.

The sets have hard drives and DVR technology built in, so think of them as TV-centric media centers.

Wow ... televisions that wake up displaying a start page that looks like television (but are actually dynamically generated from the Internet) with features like local news, traffic and weather, e-mail, Web access and all of the downloadable files in the universe at your fingertips. It sort of takes content to a different place, doesn't it?

We are seeing the advent of CE devices that know what they are, where they are, and who they belong to. This might sound a little strange, but don't let the anthropomorphic description distract you. These devices do not even need an intelligence layer to completely change the way their owners consume media and entertainment. If you add wireless technology such as Bluetooth, WiFi or UWB to them, they create an ecosystem of media devices that have the power to seamlessly interact with one another.

The scary thing (from the system operator's point of view) is how incredibly disintermediating a television monitor with a built-in or manufacturer-provided GUI might be. The EPG is the core of the system operators offering. It is the system operator's primary real estate; they would always want it to be the first (and only) place you go to look for content. A manufacturer's portal, no matter how simple, puts another layer of advertising and media choices between you and them ... food for thought.

Point of Deployment (POD) Cards

The Digital Video Subcommittee of the Society of Cable Telecommunications Engineers (SCTE) published SCTE 105 2005, which specifies a Uni-Directional Receiving Device Standard for Digital Cable. Known as POD cards or, more commonly, CableLabs, trademarked CableCARD™, these devices have not enjoyed wide consumer acceptance. The idea was to offload the systems operator's set-top box costs to the consumer by allowing them to purchase an inexpensive card that "unlocked" the encrypted television signals. The main reason cited for the failure of this CE product is the lack of competitive features offered to users. For example: Time Warner Cable customers using CableCARD™ cannot get PPV, two-way programming and services, including IPG, on demand, season sports packages or interactive and enhanced TV services. Consumers have all but ignored this technology.

However, there is a two-way POD module specification in the works and, should that become a CE product, it would add an interesting twist to the interplay between the systems operators and CE manufacturers. The availability of hardware and software that can decrypt service offerings from a systems operator brings several questions to mind: Will there be "software only" solutions that can be CONTINUED ▶

CONTINUED ▶   downloaded which might enable a new level of hacking and theft-of-services issues for the operators? Will CE manufacturers allow for more than one POD card, thereby enabling the decryption of a distant cable service over IP? If so, you might be able to use a POD card in a remote location to view the encrypted services you purchase at home. To follow the progress POD technology, visit www.cablelabs.com

Placeshifting vs. System Operators

There is one emergent technology that is likely to get everyone's attention as broadband and EVDO and other high-speed wireless networks become ubiquitously available: placeshifting. The earliest deployed CE example of placeshifting technology is brought to you by a company called Sling Media. Their product, the Slingbox, enables you to watch your TV programming from wherever you are by turning virtually any Internet-connected PC into your personal TV. Whether you're in another room or in another country, you'll always have access to your television. More interestingly, the technology also works with certain mobile phones and portable media devices over wireless networks. Scientific Atlanta offers placeshifting technology and has demonstrated a "set-top box-centric" version that also works with mobile devices.

Imagine accessing your DVR from your mobile device in another city and watching a local program both time and "place" shifted. This is not a future technology – you can go to Best Buy and get a Slingbox today. When this technology achieves anything like critical mass, it will have a demonstrable financial impact on subscription revenues since you will only need to purchase a piece of content once for use wherever you are.

Record Industry vs. Consumers

When the history of the recording industry is written, they will cite the RIAA's lawsuits against their customers as their darkest hour. There are some executives and industry pundits that believe that this approach to thwarting piracy was a good idea. They will wax poetic about the effectiveness of the "speed limit" approach to keeping honest people honest. When we look back, it may be that they are correct, but most people think of it as winning the battle and losing the war.

> ## File Sharing Speed Limit
>
> In an effort to reduce the amount of illegal file sharing on the Internet, the RIAA has taken to suing its customers. Why would they sue the people they want to sell to?
>
> The concept is often referred to as the "speed limit." The national speed limit for automobiles is 55 mph. If you are going 64 mph or under in a 55 mph zone, there is very little chance that you will be pulled over and issued a summons. However, if you are going 75 mph in a 55 mph zone, you run a much higher risk of getting a ticket and, of course, if you are doing 95 mph in a 55 mph zone, you are very likely to get a ticket and several points put on your license. (You can also get killed doing 95 mph in a 55 mph zone and to date, no one has died from file sharing, so this is an imperfect analogy).
>
> The idea behind the lawsuits is that minor offenders are basically left alone and that major offenders are sued. Although it seems to be superficially working, most people outside the industry think it is a terrible approach to solving the problem.

The recording industry is now an enemy of the public and this is truly sad. Consumers love the artists and hate the unbranded, faceless, nameless distributors that keep them from accessing what they now believe should be totally free. Of all of the battles caused by the transition to networked media, the most bloodied and most devastated industry will be recorded music.

The missed opportunity to understand the consumer and the unwillingness to adjust its thinking almost pale by comparison to the cultural and societal damage that the industry's collective "head in the sand" position has caused. Not only are people now trained to find what they want and get it for free, there is a "cool factor" to piracy that will never go away. The younger the audience, the more empowering the concept of doing something a little bit taboo. It is a business nightmare from which the industry will not awake.

After the shakeout, we will most likely see a completely new distribution model emerge. This may take a decade or it might happen sooner, but at the end of the day, music distribution is the most broken model and it is under the most pressure to evolve.

Movie Industry vs. P2P

If file sharing over P2P has hurt the record business, its impact on the movie industry is yet unknown. The reason for the lack of actual knowledge is the form factor of motion pictures. There is a true emotional satisfaction to being in a movie theater and watching a movie on a big screen. Movies can also be enjoyed in a home theater environment (big flat screen or a good old-fashioned television set). In other settings, like on a PC or a portable media device, the experience is compromised. This is not to say that if you have no other choice, you won't watch a movie on a 2" screen. It's just not as much fun as seeing it on a big screen.

Up until very recently, people thought of streaming video or downloadable video as low-quality, postage-stamp-sized, low-resolution visual experiences. There was no reason to believe that such a sub-optimal experience would have much of an effect on box office receipts or any of the sales windows that the movie industry has traditionally enjoyed. In a networked P2P world, file size becomes meaningless. Real-time downloading may still be out of reach for most households, but with even a marginal broadband connection, if you are willing to wait (usually overnight), you can download absolutely anything — and, the quality can be HD or higher!

The advent of BitTorrent and similar P2P technologies are to the movie business what file sharing was to the recorded music business. This particular battle will be very interesting. It is unclear just how many people have or will have the technological wherewithal to take advantage of the vast number of movies already available for illegal downloading. In practice, it may end up being an extremely small percentage. Or, it may become so simple and ubiquitous that the movie industry finds itself in the nightmare scenario extremely soon. The MPAA is doing everything it can to restrict the distribution of movies in digitizable formats (which is basically any format at all these days) before the movies are theatrically released. But, as we have discussed in detail, a file is a file is a file and once a DVD or tape is available, almost anyone can upload it for the world to download.

Census-Based Metrics vs. Sample-Based Metrics

Census-based metrics are exact measurements taken on an individual basis. It is a popular form of reporting for ads on the Web. Reports may include information about how many unique users visited a site, how many of those users interacted, a time stamp and other data that is specific to the user like who they are, where they live, their credit card information, etc. This type of reporting is called census-based because it is an aggregation of every single user of the media being measured. Sample-based metrics are created by taking a representative sample of a group of media users, aggregating the data, and using a mathematical formula to estimate the size and actual behaviors of an audience. (See the section on Nielsen Ratings in Chapter 10.)

What if you had an Internet-style, census-based, accurate-to-the-click metric associated with the media consumption habits of your television audience: what they watch; when they watch; who's in the room; how long they watch; and how the spots affected lift, purchase intent and brand awareness. Imagine the report broken down by device and form factor, and accurate to the second. Or, more simply, what if you had an accurate census of the exact amount of consumer engagement (however you define it) for any given media event? Would everyone involved in the valuation of the media time be equally served by the advent of this technology?

At best, the science of measurement is a double-edged sword. Some people responsible for media P&L's dream of a day when they will be able to accurately measure consumption of their media messaging against their respective investment criterion. On the other hand, there are people responsible for selling one-to-many or gross impression advertising who would truly not benefit from an accurate measurement technology.

It's easy to make a prediction that portends a day when technology will enable all of us to measure media consumption accurately and that the current "waste model" of sampled metrics provided by companies like Nielsen Media Research and Arbitron will go quietly into the night. But this type of gross oversimplification of a hugely complex issue is precisely what we are trying to avoid.

Consider the box that Zeus gave to Pandora. Her husband, the titan Epimetheus, told her never to open it. One day, sadly for us, Pandora's curiosity got the better of her and she opened the box, releasing all the misfortunes of mankind (plague, sorrow, poverty, crime, etc.). Realizing what she had done, even more sadly for us, she shut the box just in time to keep hope trapped inside. The world remained extremely bleak for some time. One day, Pandora happened by the box and opened it again — hope fluttered out. Thus, mankind always has hope in times of evil, but hope has a great deal of catching up to do.

There's nothing like a good creation myth to help you get right to an underlying issue. So, what's in our "census-based metrics" version of Pandora's Box? Well, there are deployed and soon-to-be deployed products that accurately monitor and analyze operations and performance data from millions of digital-enabled subscribers for real-time analytics, historical reporting, and on-demand advertising. Soon, the box will be full, but should we open it?

Just how many 30-second spots will I want to purchase when I find out exactly how many people actually watch them? How will accurate measurement affect the disconnect between value of a cable viewer vs. a prime time broadcast viewer? Would the lack of big audiences create scarcity and drive spot prices up? What kind of per-subscriber bargains would a cable operator drive if they knew, with frame accuracy, how many people actually watched a specific network? Would product placement be worth more on premium cable than it is on a broadcast network? Is it possible that nobody ever bought a Buick after watching the Buick Open on television?

A common currency and common unit size make intelligent negotiations possible.

The *lingua franca* of the television media business is Nielsen Ratings, but if the box is opened, that will immediately change. Good, bad, or indifferent, a common currency and common unit sizes make intelligent negotiations possible. How will the world of media look when every media buy has a census-based, quantitative measurement attached to it?

Many executives find the census-based metrics box almost irresistible. The battle between people who want accurate measurement and responsible reporting vs. those who make their living using the common currency of sample-based estimated metrics is ongoing. Sometime in the very near future, the census-based camp may get their wish.

HDTV vs. Multiplexed SD

When the FCC allocated digital television spectrum to local television stations the only thing they mandated was that it be used for digital terrestrial television transmissions. The stations were left to decide how they wanted to use the bandwidth. Left up to their own devices, they may opt to broadcast any combination of HDTV and SD signals. They may also use this bandwidth for datacasting or they may resell it or sub-lease it to other commercial operations.

How many broadcast channels are we likely to see in any given market? Who will watch them? Will they all be "free" over-the-air channels? Will every station offer HDTV? The answers to these and other questions will evolve with the marketplace and the technology. It is still possible to purchase an SD television set. Within a few years, all sets will be HD/SD sets (similar to AM/FM radios). In this day and age, it's pretty hard to find a radio that only plays AM stations. So it will be with television receivers.

Are people likely to make the switch to broadcast DTT and actually watch HDTV with an antenna? The bigger question is when will the network and advanced media "sticker shock" hit America? Since the government is not printing any more money and the economy is only growing at a moderate pace, where does the media industry expect consumers to get the extra money to pay for advanced media services? What is the maximum dollar tolerance of the average American family for television services? Is it $1,000 per year, $1,500, $2,000? At some point, the food bill, health care costs and energy prices will have to come first. When deployed innovation exceeds the consumer's ability to pay, we will see if there is a need for a free or lower-priced digital alternative.

This is not a guaranteed future of television. If history teaches us anything, it's that people will find a way to pay for things they want – especially entertainment and especially when times are tough.

Networks vs. Affiliates

Back in 1946, the "big three" television networks — ABC, CBS and NBC — started continuously broadcasting over a network that evolved to include approximately 200 local affiliated stations each. At that time, you needed to have local affiliates because the technology to reach the entire country without them did not exist. More to the point, the FCC licensed transmitters, the frequencies on which they could transmit and the maximum power (wattage) of each local transmitter. This divided the country into broadcast coverage areas for television that survive to this day. (See Chapter 1.)

The deals between broadcast networks and their affiliated stations usually include an agreement to carry some amount of morning, daytime, news, sports, primetime and late-night programming. There is cash compensation paid as well as advertising units pledged and bartered between the parties. As we have discussed, local stations often do not fully associate themselves with their affiliated networks preferring to be branded by their local news departments. But many affiliates are known by and promote themselves as part of the larger whole. Stations tag lines like: "ABC5" or "FOX5" are quite commonplace.

Some of these alliances date back more than a half-century, so it is no wonder that the business rules that evolved to accommodate mid-20th century technology are coming into question in the post-Internet era.

Do local stations have the right to retransmit network programming over the Internet? Should they? How about making the material available for download? Can it be streamed in real time if restricted to the local DMA? How will affiliate relationships change now that networks are taking programming that was traditionally or contractually supposed to be distributed through local affiliates and putting it on the Internet? Who will have the rights to distribute this programming directly to consumers using local cable or telco VOD systems?

Sometime soon, the broadcast affiliates and the networks are going to have to deal with the reality that the old network model is no longer the only way to do business. In truth, it may never be more efficient to distribute an emergent news event to the largest possible audience than it is through a broadcast network and its affiliates. But, it is also quite possible that the need to serve massive audiences is diminished by the availability of niche, relevant content and consumer relationship marketing. In any event, the financial glue that holds the traditional broadcast networks together is getting dry and cracking. One of the very probable futures of television is the inevitable re-engineering of this technology and the business rules that govern it.

Wireless vs. Wired

When we think of wired and wireless competition in the television business, we are usually thinking about the old broadcast model (transmitters and antennas) vs. the cable/telco/satellite television distributors (cables to and around the household). This makes perfect sense, but there is a new wireless television on the horizon and it is the enemy of all the established distribution networks.

There is a concerted effort being put forth by consumers, municipalities and commercial enterprises to create a nationwide two-way wireless network capable of transporting data using TCP/IP (Transfer Control Protocol/Internet Protocol), the language of the Internet. The goal of these organizations is to create an environment where all of your wireless devices are connected all of the time. They will use spectrum licensed from the FCC, possibly some of the old analog television spectrum being auctioned off during the analog to digital television transition.

As this battle unfolds, you are going to see fierce legal fights between all of the companies that have existing infrastructure and all of the companies and municipalities that want to obviate or disintermediate these old distribution platforms in favor of the new, cheaper, more efficient, inherently two-way wireless systems. The consumer benefits of the new wireless world will be explosive.

What will they do with the spectrum? Other than the squatters and speculators, the people who decide to build networks will put up radio towers all over the country. They will create digital two-way wireless networks suitable for broadband Internet or any other desired wireless protocol. Some companies will create "me too" products that offer familiar products at reduced prices or with some value-added features, or we may see inexpensive wireless broadband connections over WiMax and the like. Some will use the networks for business-to-business applications like tracking packages or terrestrial positioning systems.

Others, however, will try to change the world by creating vast two-way wireless networks that are built to disintermediate the existing telephone company and cable company infrastructures. This will take billions of dollars, but it can be built in far less time than anyone can imagine. We could see wireless broadband connections with up to 60 Mbps of bandwidth (enough for simultaneous HDTV, VoIP and super-fast Internet usage) by the early part of the next decade.

The Biggest WiFi Cloud in America

As of November 2005, the biggest WiFi cloud in the United States was centered on the city of Hermiston, Oregon. This 700-square-mile "hot spot" extends across four counties and into the state of Washington. The brainchild of Fred Ziari, CEO of EZ Wireless, the cloud is supported by many local government organizations and businesses. To cover this vast area, the network uses meshed repeaters, so it is self-healing. Local uses for the cloud include wireless surveillance cameras, Internet access, farm machine automation and anything else you can do with WiFi. Want to see the future? A visit to Hermiston will give you a close-up and personal view.

This type of network would truly change everything. It would actually impact the way we live our lives. For example, in a wireless broadband, high-bandwidth city, with a mesh network overlay, you would know the location of your children by looking at the screen on your handheld device. Your news, weather and traffic media would be personalized and delivered to you with constant updates that were triggered by your movements or specific environmental, temporal or spatial needs. No matter what the business category, there is a need for inexpensive, ubiquitous two-way wireless connectivity: medical, education, automotive, telecom, media, entertainment, manufacturing, retail.

This type of network would feel more like living in an episode of Star Trek than anything else. Imagine retail packaging that not only knew when you picked it up, but knew when you put it down. The concept of check-out counters disappears. There is no longer a need for wireline telephones; all of your voice communication is wireless (like VoIP, only everywhere). No more cell phones, no more wired Internet connections — every device you own can access the network all of the time. When your PDA is on, it is in sync with your desktop; when you download a piece of content, you can access it from anywhere on anything you own that can read it or play it. You can carry an electronic wallet, links to all of your medical records and every movie and song you could ever want in a wireless handheld device that is no bigger than a PDA.

This type of network would spawn industries that we cannot even conceive of. New types of aggregators, search engines, intermediaries, payment processors, and criminals — the change will be even more profound than the industrial revolution or the space age. This will take the information age to a place no one today can understand. But it is not 10 years away.

When you add the power of utility-based grid computing to this type of super-powerful wireless mesh network, you simply change the world. Will the telephone companies and the cable companies be able to compete? Not with their current infrastructures. This type of wireless network would render their plants and equipment completely obsolete. However, it is very possible that these will be the very companies at the forefront of this communications revolution. Other obvious players are Google, Microsoft, Intel, the big electronics companies and big media.

How probable a future is this SuperNet? There are so many smart people and organizations with means and motive thinking about this that it is unlikely that anything can stop it.

Deployed Innovation vs. Consumer Aspiration

One of the hardest concepts for technocrats to deal with is the "solution in search of a problem" parable. Engineers like to engineer their way out of situations, and that can create a "just because you can, doesn't mean you should" scenario. We see many different technologies brought to market everyday, but very few actually capture the imagination of consumers. More accurately, very few technologies capture the imaginations of enough consumers to justify the research, development, manufacturing and distribution costs of bringing the technology to market. This is due to the fairly large disconnect between deployed innovation and consumer aspiration.

When is the right time to bring a new technology to market? When is the right time to offer a new pricing package for your services? When is the right time to bundle an offer with a unique selling principle that cannot be articulated in a sound bite? These questions fall more into the metaphysical realm of marketing climate and social readiness than they do into the practical world of design and manufacturing.

Television is being disrupted by new, interesting, powerful technologies, but — after the hype is over, what will the true financial impact be?

DVRs truly change the way people experience television. This is an undeniable fact. The vast majority of the people who have a DVR no longer enjoy watching television without it. Adepts of DVR technology have all of the attributes of a religious cult. Unfortunately, these consumers also fall into a very high slot on the Advanced Media Consumption Index and that means they have a demonstrable preference for the form factors that their media choices take. (See Chapter 8 for more information.)

Will we see half of the U.S. television households (approximately 55 million homes) with DVRs any time soon? What's stopping this technology from enhancing everyone's experience? Among the many factors, one stands out as paramount: there is not enough consumer aspiration for this deployed innovation (at least, not yet). The other factors preventing DVRs from taking the television world "by storm" include price, learning curve, availability, and lack of understanding what it is or why they need it. Consumer aspiration is a subtle art form; there is very little science involved.

This very issue is the seminal point of this writing. Television is being disrupted by new, interesting, powerful technologies, but — after the hype is over, what will the true financial impact be? (Many believe that because almost every major media company is publicly traded that the impact of hype cannot be discounted. Hype is often reflected in the market, which renders the idea that "hype is just hype" moot. After all, if hype changes your stock price, it is a real as it gets.)

You often hear people talk about the "killer app" — an application for a new technology that will quickly take it to critical mass. This is always a bad thing to say out loud and an even worse thing to wait for. It is the same as saying, "What we really need is a hit." Yes, we all know we need it, but if it's not obvious to anyone in your group, it is unlikely to just happen out of thin air. Sure, sometimes somebody comes up with something truly wonderful out of the blue, but not too often. Another red flag should go up when you hear an engineer say, "The creatives in Hollywood will do something great with it." This is always a very bad sign.

Very often, you will not have the skill set or personal knowledge to make an accurate assessment of a new technology. That's OK. The introduction of this book cites several examples of important inventions that were created to solve specific problems but ultimately enjoyed success being used for other purposes. That being said, we live in a world with lots of smart people. If nobody around the table can see how a technology will change the world, it probably won't.

The Vice President of Electricity

While doing research and fact-checking for this book I happened upon a reference to an interesting corporate title: vice president of electricity. It was a senior-level management position that existed at many major corporations during the early years of the industrial revolution. Back then, if you needed industrial quantities of electricity, the best (and possibly only) way to get it was to generate it yourself. Next to the vice president of engineering, there was no executive at any of these companies with more technical skill and training than the VP of electricity.

As we all know, within a few decades, this position was replaced by a line item on the P&L that simply said, "Electricity." Complex generators and the technologists to run them were replaced by off-premises companies that provided all of the required electricity through a utility grid. On premises, the only skill required was the ability to plug a machine or appliance into a wall socket.

We can think about the demise of the VP of electricity in a few different ways. First is the concept that his position was equivalent to our current IT executives. If you follow that logic and spend any time thinking about the next generation of utility-grade grid computing schemas, you could posit that we are all headed for a day when every computer in America or possibly the world will be part of a massive computer grid and that there will be companies that harness, license and provide access to this grid for others to use. Grid computing is not new, but the reality of a utility-grid for computer power, if realized, would change the world into an unrecognizable place. Access to that much computing power has never been in reach for average individuals. It may be the most exciting transition in the offing.

The other way to think about the demise of the VP of electricity is to understand that it was not the advent or existence of utility electrical grids that ended his career, it was simplicity. As soon as there was a simple, easy alternative to a complex problem, everyone jumped on it. That is the lesson we should learn here. We are the architects of the future and, as industry professionals, it is up to us to shape the business the way we want it to be shaped. The sooner we make technology so complex that it disappears, the sooner everyone will enjoy the benefits.

Glossary of Terms

.aac	Audio File Type – Advanced audio coder. An audio-encoding standard for MPEG-2 that is not backward-compatible with MPEG-1 audio.
.aif	Audio File Type – Apple's Audio Interchange Format.
.avi	Audio/Video File Type — Microsoft Window's Audio Video Interleave Format
.doc	Document File Type — Microsoft Word files.
.gif	Graphics File Type — Graphics Interchange Format or Graphic Image File format, a widely supported image-storage format promoted by CompuServe that gained early wide-spread use on online services and the Internet. Resolution is limited to 8-bits, or 256 colours. GIF89a is a more recent format that supports interlacing.
.jpg	Graphics File Type — Joint Photographic Experts Group. A compression technique used for saving images and photo-graphs. This compression method reduced the file size of the images without reducing its quality. Widely used on the World Wide Web.
.m4p	Video File Type — Motion Picture Experts Group (MPEG) — Apple's iPod Video Format

.mov	Video File Type — Apple Quicktime Format
.mp3	Audio File Type — MPEG-1 Audio Layer-3. Compression scheme used to transfer audio files via the Internet and store in portable players and digital audio servers.
.mpg	Video File Type — Motion Picture Experts Group MPEG file format
.pdf	Document File Type — Portable Document File, the Adobe Acrobat file format.
.ppt	Document File Type — Microsoft PowerPoint
.raw	Graphics File Type - Photo Format — The RAW image format is the data as it comes directly off the CCD, with no in-camera processing is performed.
.swf	Video File Type — Shockwave Flash file (.swf). Can be referred to as a "swiff." This is the file format of a rendered Macromedia Flash file.
.tif	Graphics File Type — Raster Graphic Image Format — The Tagged Image File format is a lossless format for storing image data. TIFF is a popular output format for scanners and other similar devices.
.wav	Audio File Type — Waveform Audio - A digitized sound file format for Microsoft Windows, which has ".wav" as the file name extension. Most pre-mastering software ill extract CD (CD-audio) tracks and write them to the hard disk as a Wav file. Wav files can have various qualities of sound depending on how they are created or saved, but the most common is 44,100 Hz, 16 bit, stereo (equivalent to audio track on CD).
3G	Third Generation—the next generation of wireless technology beyond personal communications services. The World Administrative Radio Conference assigned 230 megahertz of spectrum at 2 GHz for multimedia 3G networks.
4K	Industry slang for a digital video file with 4,096 by 2,160-pixel resolution. For most major movie studios it is the preferred digital intermediate file format.

5.1 (Surround Sound) Dolby Digital is the trademarked marketing name for Dolby Laboratories' "lossy" AC-3 codec. The common version contains six total channels of sound, with 5 channels for normal-range speakers (Right front, Center, Left Front, Right Rear and Left Rear) and one channel for the LFE, or subwoofer. The Dolby Digital format supports Mono and Stereo usages as well.

A&E   The A&E Network is a cable and satellite television network based in New York, New York. The channel, which focuses programming on biographies, documentaries, and drama series, reaches more than 85 million homes in the United States. A&E is a joint venture of the Hearst Corporation 37.5%, ABC, Inc., 37.5%; and NBC, 25%. The A&E channel is the flagship of the A&E Television Networks group, which also includes the The History Channel and the The Biography Channel.

A/B Switch   enables a user to determine which of two different sources (ie: cable feed or antenna feed) will be displayed on a single television monitor.

ABC   The American Broadcasting Company is a television and radio network in the United States. It is owned by The Walt Disney Company, and the company name is ABC, Inc.

ADS   Alternate Delivery System, see MVPD.

ADSL   Asymmetrical Digital Subscriber Line. ADSL is type of DSL that provides T1 rates or higher in the downstream (towards the customer) direction and 64 KBPS or higher in the upstream direction.

Advanced Television Enhancement Forum (ATVEF)   ATVEF (pronounced "at-fef,") representatives developed a technology specification that enables broadcasters to send data (based on Internet standards) through the "Vertical Blanking Interval." If the viewer's set-top box has the proper software to receive and interpret ATVEF data, whatever was designed and sent will show up on the TV screen. That data might appear as raw data or complex interactive interfaces.

AMCI	Advanced Media Consumption Index ranging from 1-10 is a useful tool for any type of forecasting by helping understand how different people consume media differently depending on where on the AMCI they can be found. See AMCI at http://www.amvgllc.com
Analog Television	A video standard established by the United States (RCA/NBC) and adopted by numerous other countries. This is a 525-line video with 3.58-MHz chroma subcarrier and 60 cycles per second. Frames are displayed at 30 fps.
AOL	America Online — owned by Time Warner Inc.
ATM	Asynchronous transfer mode. A high speed data transmission and switching technique that uses fixed size cells to transmit voice, data, video which greatly increases the capacity of transmission paths, both wired and wireless.
Backbone	Large networks that inter-connect with each others and have individual ISPs as clients.
Backchannel	Term commonly used to describe the action of sending data back to a host server.
Bandwidth	A measure of the capacity of a communications channel. The higher a channel's bandwidth, the more information it can carry.
Banner	Slang for banner advertisement — a specific size and format of type of web advertisement. See http://www.iab.org
Behavioral Targeting	the idea of delivering ads to audiences that have demonstrated a specific behavior such as: clicked on an ad, surfed the web in a specific way, searched for certain types of things, made a purchase, visited a store, watched a program on their DVR, etc.
Billboard	Slang for billboard advertisement — a specific size and format of type of web advertisement. See http://www.iab.org
Bit	Bit is short for binary digit. It's the smallest unit of data in a digital system, with a value of either 0 or 1. A group of bits, such as 8-bits or 16-bits, compose a byte.

BitTorrent	is both the protocol and the name of the peer-to-peer (P2P) file distribution application created by programmer Bram Cohen that makes it possible to massively distribute files without incurring the corresponding massive consumption in server and bandwidth resources. The original BitTorrent application is written in Python and its source code has been released under the BitTorrent Open Source License (a modified version of the Jabber Open Source License), as of version 4.0. The name "BitTorrent" refers to the distribution protocol, the original client application, and the .torrent file type.
Blockbuster	a national retail video rental chain.
Blog	A short form for weblog, a frequent and chronological publication of comments and thoughts on the web.
Bloomberg Terminal	Bloomberg Terminals provide real-time and historical pricing, indicative and fundamental data, customized analytics, print and multimedia news and electronic communications on-demand 24 hours a day.
Blueray	Sony's High Definition DVD format
BPL	Broadband over Power Lines — a way to use ordinary electrical wiring as a computer network.
Broadband	Broadband comes from the words "broad bandwidth" and is used to describe a high-capacity, two-way link between an end user and access network suppliers capable of supporting full-motion, interactive video applications.
Broadband Content	A colloquial term for rich media assets or audio and video content that is best delivered to consumers over a fast Internet or "broadband" connection.
Broadcast	Transmission to a number of receiving locations simultaneously.
BtoB (B2B)	(Business-to-Business) — businesses whose customers are other businesses

Bundled Services   A colloquial term that describes combining two or more services for sale to consumers. For example: when video, voice and data are sold together in a package they are said to be "bundled."

Cable Modem   a modem (modulator/demodulator) that uses part of the capacity of the local cable system to transmit data rather than TV channels to the home.

Cable Operator   See Multi-Systems Operator.

Cable Over-Builder   In the late 1990s, the FCC ended the practice of licensing sole cable TV operators in a given market. To increase competition, they allowed additional cable systems to come into existence. The companies that were formed to exploit this ruling were known as "overbuilders."

Cable Plant   Term which refers to the central equipment and broadcasting headquarters of a cable operator.

Cable Television   A broadband distribution network, using coaxial or fiber-optic transmission technology, which carries multiple television channels to domestic and business subscribers within a franchise area. Cable television networks can also carry telephony and information services.

Cable Television Laboratories (CABLELABS)   A non-profit research and development organization for cable operators in North and South America. CableLabs organizes member meetings and develops standards for all manner of cable equipment and software.

CATV   Community Access Television

C-Band   the band between 4 and 8 GHz with the 6 and 4 GHz band being used for satellite communications. Specifically, the 3.7 to 4.2 GHz satellite communication band is used as the down link frequencies in tandem with the 5.925 to 6,425 GHz band that serves as the uplink.

CBS   The Columbia Broadcasting System, or CBS, is a major radio and television network in the United States. CBS was one of the three commercial television networks that dominated broadcasting in the United States before the rise of cable television. In the days of radio, it grew to acquire one of its original founders, Columbia Records, which it sold many years later. Viacom, itself founded by CBS, owns the network today.

CD	Compact Disc, a high density storage media based on a 4.75" reflective optical disc. Can hold up to 650,000,000 bytes of data, that is equivalent to 12,000 images or 200,000 pages of text. CDs may all look the same, but there are numerous standards for different applications.
CDMA	(Code Division Multiple Access): A technology for digital transmission of radio signals between, for example, a mobile telephone and a radio base station. In CDMA, a frequency is divided into a number of codes.
CDN	A Content Delivery Network (CDN) provides fee-for-service delivery of streaming content via the Internet. Their network consists of linked "edge" servers throughout the Internet that help reduce network congestion and server overload for content delivered to many users.
CES	Consumer Electronics Show — the industy's largest trade show held in Las Vegas each January.
Churn	Losing customers to competitive services..
CLEC	Competitive Local Exchange Carrier. A company that creates and operates communication networks and provides customers with an alternative to the local telephone company.
Client/server	A client is defined as a requester of services and a server is defined as the provider of services. A single machine can be both a client and a server depending on the software configuration.
Clipcast	A short video clip that is sent over a network to a receiving device.
CNN	Cable News Network, owned by Time Warner.
COFDM	(Coded Orthogonal Frequency Division Multiplexing) a modulation scheme for digital television broadcasting which competes with 8VSB.
Compuserve	One of the original online services.

Conditional Access Technology Technology embedded on the set-top box and satellite receiver that enables the cable or satellite broadcaster to filter out content the subscriber has not paid for or provide them with movies or special programs they have purchased on a pay-per-use system.

Content A term-of-art used to describe any type of intellectual property that can be packaged and sold.

Content Aggregators Organizations that collect content and repackage it for sale or distribution.

Convergence The coming together of two or more disparate disciplines or technologies

Coverage area A geographical area which defines the transmission coverage of a particular system.

CRT Cathode Ray Tube. In this context it is referring to the picture tube of a traditional NTSC television set.

DA Digital to Analog Converter (also DAC)

Delphi One of the original online services.

Demographics Classifications of populations according to sex, age, race, ethnicity, income, etc.

Designated Market Areas A C. Nielsen's geographic market designation which defines each television market exclusive of others based on measurable viewing patterns. Every county or split county in the United States is assigned exclusively to one DMA.

Destination Television A marketing term that usually refers to scheduled, linear broadcast programming that people must watch at a certain time.

Digital a method of storing, processing and transmitting information through the use of distinct electronic or optical pulses that represent the binary digits 0 and 1. Digital transmission/switching technologies employ a sequence of discrete, distinct pulses to represent information, as opposed to the continuously variable analog signal.

Digital Broadcast Satellite (DBS) An alternative to cable and analog satellite reception initially utilizing a fixed 18-inch dish focused on one or more geostationary satellites. DBS units are able to receive multiple channels of multiplexed video and audio signals as well as programming information, Email, and related data. DBS typically uses MPEG-2 encoding and COFDM transmission. Also known as digital satellite system (DSS). Also known as direct-to-home (DTH) satellite.

Digital Cable A service provided by a cable operator that employs digital technology. Because they use bandwidth more efficiently, these systems typically offer more channels, interactive services and better picture quality than their analog predecessors.

Digital Fingerprinting This can be done with audio or video. The concept is that several samples are taken of the file at various pre-determined sample points. Because audio and video files are very complex, a multi-point match has a mathematical probability of correctly identifying any particular piece of work that has been previously fingerprinted. It is not as exact a science as watermarking, but it has the feature of not have to be done during the initial encoding of a master.

Digital Natives People who were born during the early to mid 1990s or later who have always lived in a digital media world.

Digital Rights Management A technology that allows content owners to determine and control how users can view content.

Digital Subscriber Line (DSL) A family of digital telecommunications protocols designed to allow high speed data communication over the existing copper telephone lines between end-users and telephone companies.

Digital Television (DTV) A term that broadly describes digital television transmission formats designated by the Advanced Television Systems Committee (ATSC) to replace the traditional National Television Standards Committee (NTSC) system.

Digital Terrestrial Television (DTT) Digital terrestrial television. (DTT) The term used to describe the broadcast of digital television services using terrestrial antennas.

Digital Video Broadcasting (DVB)   A digital television standards development body with its primary influence in Europe. Standards developed include digital broadcasting for cable, satellite, and digital terrestrial.

Digital Video Broadcasting Mutimedia Home Platform (DVB-MHP)   See Digital Video Broadcasting. DVB-MHP is a standards based software layer developed by members of the DVB that allow ITV producers to develop applications that will run on all DVB-compliant set-top boxes.

Digital Video Recorder (DVR)   A high capacity hard drive that is embedded in a set-top box, which records video programming from a television set. These DVRs are operated by personal video recording software, which enables the viewer to pause, fast forward, and manage all sorts of other functions and special applications. TiVo® is the most popular commercial DVR. The functionality is also incorporated into several set-top boxes available from cable, satellite and IPTV providers. Software-only applications are designed to run on properly equipped personal computers and video game consoles. Also known as a Personal Video Recorder (PVR)

Digital Video Server   A robust, dedicated computer at a central location that receives command requests from the television viewer through a video-on-demand application.

Digital Watermaking   A pattern of bits inserted into a digital image, audio or video file that identifies the file's copyright information (author, rights, etc.)

Digitize   To capture an analog video signal and save it to a digital video format.

Direct-To Home (DTH)   Term used to describe satellite broadcasting to the home to 18" dishes. (See Direct Broadcast Satellite).

DirectTV   DirecTV is a direct broadcast satellite (DBS) service that broadcasts digital satellite television and audio to households in the United States and the rest of the Americas. DirecTV is owned by DirecTV Group, a subsidiary of News Corporation's Fox Entertainment Group.

DOCSIS	Data Over Cable Service Interface Specification. The governing body, which certifies cable modem vendors, is called CableLabs®. The DOCSIS standard and close derivatives are also being adopted in other countries around the world.
Downlink	The action of transmitting analog or digital signal to a satellite dish receiver on earth via a transponder on a satellite.
Downstream	To send information from the network to the user.
DRM	Digital Rights Management, a technology used to protect digital products from copyright infringement.
DSL	See Digital Subscriber Line.
DSS	See Direct Broadcast Satellite.
DTH	Direct to Home — see Direct Broadcast Satellite
DVD	Digital Video Disc
DVR	See Digital Video Recorder
Dynamic ads	any audio, video or graphic advertisement that can be dynamically changed, updated or customized automatically.
Electronic Programming Guide (EPG)	A application that allows the viewer to interactively select their television programming. Also referred to as a graphical user interface (GUI) pronounced "goo-ee."
Encode	Encoding is the process of converting one digital format to another, applying known algorithms to either obscure the content of the file, or to compress or convert it to another format.
Enhanced Television	Term used for certain digital on-air programming that includes additional resources for viewers. Viewers can simultaneously watch an enhanced TV production and interact with the content via their remote control or, in a two-screen application, use a personal computer or mobile phone.
ESPN	Entertainment Sports Programming Network, owned by The Walt Disney Company.

Ethernet (IEEE 802.3) A type of high-speed network for interconnecting computing devices. Ethernet can be either 10 or 100 Mbps (Fast Ethernet). Ethernet is a trademark of Xerox Corporation, Inc

EVDO Evolution Data Only, Evolution Data Optimized, often abbreviated as EVDO, EV-DO, EvDO, 1xEV-DO or 1xEvDO is a wireless radio broadband data protocol being adopted by many CDMA mobile phone providers in Japan, Korea, Israel, the United States, and Canada as part of the CDMA2000 standard. Pronounced as separate letters, "EE-VEE-DEE-OH"

Extensible Markup Language (XML) A language which acts as a "meta-language," XML allows programmers to create their own markup languages for specific uses. It is written in Standard Generalized Markup Language (SMGL).

FCC Federal Communications Commission. The government agency responsible for regulating telecommunications in the United States.

Fiber Optic refers to the medium and the technology associated with the transmission of information as light pulses along a glass or plastic wire or fiber.

Flash Flash is a vector-based animation technology from Macromedia.

Flash Downloading The ability to automatically send software upgrades to a set-top box network. It comes from the computer industry's term for "flashing" or burning new computer programs into an Erasable Programmable Read Only Memory (EPROM) chip.

Focus Moving a cursor over an area of the screen to highlight it.

Folksonomy Folksonomy is a neologism for a practice of collaborative categorization using freely chosen keywords.

FoodTV Food Network is a unique lifestyle network and web site that strives to surprise and engage its viewers with likable hosts, personalities, and the variety of things they do with food. The E. W. Scripps Company is the manager and general partner.

Footprint	A term used to define a logistical area in a region covered by a cable or satellite operator, though not necessarily served directly by them. This term is also used to define the amount of space a particular piece of software or hardware takes up inside a set-top box.
Form factor	The tangible form of an object.
Fox	The Fox Networked, owned by News Corporation
Frequency (Hz)	Frequency is the measurement of the number of times that a repeated event occurs per unit time. To calculate the frequency, one fixes a time interval, counts the number of occurrences of the event within that interval, and then divides this count by the length of the time interval. Measured in Hertz (Hz). One Hertz is one cycle per second.
FTTH	Fiber to the Home — Fiber optic service to a node located inside an individual home.
FTTP	Fiber to the Pillow — Fiber optic service to a node located inside an individual home to specific locations, like a bedroom — more complicated and time consuming than just bringing the connection inside the house.
GPRS	General Packet Radio Service. A GSM data transmission technique that does not set up a continuous channel from a portable terminal for the transmission and reception of data, but transmits and receives data in packets. It makes very efficient use of available radio spectrum.
Grid/Grid Guide	See Electronic Programming Guide
Gross Rating Point	GRP represents the percentage of the target audience reached by a television advertisement. If the advertisement is aired more than once, the GRP figure represents the sum of each individual GRP. Therefore, a commercial aired 5 times reaching 50% of the target audience would have 250 GRP = 5 x 50%.
GSM	Global System for Mobile communication. A European digital standard for mobile or cellular telephony
GUI	Graphical User Interface — A interface, such as Windows or OSX, that is based on graphics instead of text.

Hard Drive/Hard Disc   The primary storage unit on PCs, consisting of one or more magnetic media platters on which digital data can be written and erased magnetically.

HBO   Home Box Office, owned by Time Warner

HD-DVD   High Definition DVD format (see Blueray)

HDTV: High Definition Television   The 1,125-, 1,080 and 1,035-line interlace and 720 and 1,080-line progressive formats in a 16:9 aspect ratio. Officially a format is high definition if it has at least twice the horizontal and vertical resolution of the standard signal being used.

Headend   The electronic control center of a cable television system. The Headend takes incoming signals and amplifies, converts, processes, and combines them into a common coaxial or optical cable for transmission to cable subscribers.

High Bit Rate Digital Subscriber Line (HDSL)   HDSL is a type of DSL that Transmits 2 Mbps bi-directional signals over one or two twisted copper pairs.

Host   Any computer on a network that offers services or connectivity to other computers on the network. A host has an IP address associated with it.

HTML   Hyper Text Mark-Up Language (HTML), a subset of Standard Generalized Mark-Up Language (SGML) for electronic publishing, the specific standard used for the World Wide Web.

HTTP   The Hypertext Transfer Protocol is the set of rules for exchanging files (text, graphic images, sound, video, and other multimedia files) on the World Wide Web.

Hybrid Fiber-Coaxial (HFC)   A local cable TV or telephone distribution network. An HFC consists of fiber optic trunks ending at neighborhood nodes, with coaxial cable feeders and drop lines downstream of the nodes.

Hybrid subscription   A business model where subscribers pay for content but also see commercial advertising messages.

Hyperlink   a hypertext link or link in a graphic or text string which, when clicked, opens a new web page or jumps to a new location in the current page.

Hypertext   Any text within a document that is linked to another object in another location. See Hyperlink, HTML and HTTP.

IE   Microsoft's Internet Explorer — the most popular web browsing software in the world.

Intellectual Property A creation of the intellect that has commercial value, including copyrighted property such as literary or artistic works, and ideational property, such as patents, appellations of origin, business methods, and industrial processes.

Interactive Television A combination of television with interactive content and enhancements. Interactive television provides better, richer entertainment and information, blending traditional TV-watching with the interactivity of a personal computer. Programming can include richer graphics, one-click access to Web sites through TV Crossover Links, electronic mail and chats, and online commerce through a back channel.

Interface   A set of textual or graphical symbols that allow a computer user to communicate to underlying software. Computer Interfaces work in many ways. Some are text-based and communicate only in letters, numbers, and other keyboard symbols. Others are graphical and require the use of a mouse. Still others are touchscreen. See GUI and EPG.

Interlaced Scanning   The rectangular area of the TV screen is scanned by an electronic beam (raster) as it is deflected horizontally and vertically and creates an interlaced video display we see as the TV picture. Referred to as interlaced scanning because the raster skips every second line on the first pass and then fills in those lines on a second pass. The interlaced scanning system may result in a screen flicker.

Internet Protocol (IP) A protocol telling the network how packets are addressed and routed.

Internet Service Provider (ISP)   An organization that provides access to the Internet.

IP Address   An identifier for a computer or device on a TCP/IP network.

IP Bypass   the disintermediation of the traditional systems operators (cable, satellite, broadcast, telco) infrastructure.

IP Video Internet Protocol or Internet Provisioned video distribution. This is the preferred term to describe streaming video or broadband video. Not to be confused with IPTV (Internet Protocol Television) which is television using Internet Protocol.

IPG Interactive Programming Guide — see EPG.

IP-provisioned Internet Protocol Provisioned — a system that uses some version of TCP/IP (transfer control protocol/Internet protocol) to package, transmit and receive data.

IPTV (Internet Protocol TV, Internet Protocol Television) Television using Internet Protocol - a method of transporting data using Internet Protocol (usually over a private network). Not to be confused with IP Video, Broadband Video or Streaming Media.

Java An object-oriented programming language for portable interpretive code that supports interaction among remote objects. Java was developed and specified by Sun Microsystems, Inc.

JavaTV Sun invented this application programming interface (API) called JavaTV, which enables the development of more complex functionality and interfaces to launch from the set-top box if this Java layer is embedded in the device.

Key Slang for Chroma Key — A chroma key is the removal of a color (or small color range) from one image to reveal another "behind" it. The removed color becomes transparent. This technique is also referred to as color keying, colour separation overlay, greenscreen and bluescreen. It is typically used for weather forecasts. The presenter appears to be standing in front of a large map, but in the studio it is actually a large blue or green background.

Keywords Single terms or short phrases that best define the main points of a topic. Keywords are used for searching catalogs and databases.

Ku-band The frequency range 10.7-18 GHz, used today for the transmission to and from existing broadcast satellites.

LAN (local-area network) (Local Area Network) is a collection of computers linked together by an enclosed network.

Lean backward	Industry slang for casual viewing of television — leaning back on a chair or couch from 10-12' away.
Lean forward	Industry slang for using a computer leaning forward in your chair from about 2' away.
Linear Channels	Traditional television channels that broadcast one signal 24 hrs. a day.
Long Tail	The phrase The Long Tail (as a proper noun with capitalized letters) was first coined by Chris Anderson in a 2004 Wired Magazine article to describe a power law known as a Zipf's Distribution.
Master File	A database file, often created manually as needed, that contains static records used to identify items, customers, vendors, bills of material, work centers, etc. as opposed to files used to track the dynamic status of orders and inventory balances.
Mb or MEGABIT	106 bits of information (usually used to express a data transfer rate; as in, 1 megabit/second = 1Mbps).
Mbps	Megabit - 1 million bits per second (notice the small "b")
MBps	Megabyte - 1 million bytes per second (notice the big "B")
Media Center	A computer, set-top box or game console that in equipped to display television programming as well as video, audio, pictures and other media from its local storage devices or network attached devices or from the Internet or a private network. Media Centers usually include software specifically designed to make all of these functions easy for users to control.
MediaFLO®	A brand name of a dual tuner mobile phone technology from Qualcomm that allows the multiplexing of linear television signals to be broadcast to a mobile phone handset.

Meme	As defined by Richard Dawkins in The Selfish Gene (1976): "a unit of cultural transmission, or a unit of imitation." "Examples of memes are tunes, ideas, catch-phrases, clothes fashions, ways of making pots or of building arches. Just as genes propagate themselves in the gene pool by leaping from body to body via sperms or eggs, so memes propagate themselves in the meme pool by leaping from brain to brain via a process which, in the broad sense, can be called imitation.
Metadata	Data that describes other data.
Metatag	A word or short phrase that describes an object.
MHz-Megahertz	One million Hertz, or one million cycles per second.
Microsoft	Microsoft Corporation, headquartered in Redmond, Washington, USA, was founded in 1975 by Bill Gates and Paul Allen. Microsoft is the world's largest software company.
MMS	Multimedia Message Service, a method of transmitting graphics, video clips, sound files text messages over wireless networks using WAP (Wireless Applications Protocol) .
Moore's Law	A prediction made in 1965 by Gordon Moore, cofounder of Intel, stating the number of transistors occupying a square inch of integrated circuit material had doubled each year since the invention of the integrated circuit and that the multiplication of circuitry would continue. For the most part, the observation held true until the late 1970s when the time span of a year increased to about 18 months.
Mosaic	A GUI which includes several tiles in an array or matrix pattern.
MP3	See .mp3

MPEG (Motion Picture Expert Group)   A proposed International Standards organization (IS) standard for digital video and audio compression for moving images. Responsible for creating standards 1, 2 and 4.

MPEG-2	Similar to MPEG-1, but includes extensions to cover a wider range of applications. MPEG-2 translates to 704 x 480 pixels at 30 frames per second in North America and 704 x 576 fps at 25 fps in Europe. Typically compressed at higher than 5 Mbs. The primary application targeted during the MPEG-2 definition process was the all-digital transmission of broadcast TV quality video.
MTV	Music Television, owned by Viacom.
Multipath	RF signals arriving at a location via different transmission paths, usually referring to a combination of direct and reflected signals. The direct and reflected signals are often opposite in phase, which can result in a significant signal loss due to mutual cancellation in some circumstances. Multipath is most troublesome indoors and in areas where many metallic surfaces are present.
Multiple System Operator (MSO)	Term used often for cable operators that own a number of different networks and services.
Must Carry	A policy, developed by the FCC in the 1960's and codified by Congress in 1992, requiring cable systems to carry the analog signal of a local television station if that broadcaster so chooses. Visit, http://www.fcc.gov for more information.
MVNO	Mobile Virtual Network Operators. A company that buys network capacity from a network operator to offer its own branded mobile subscriptions and value-added services.
MVPDs (Multichannel Video Programming Distributors)	Multichannel Video Program Distributor. All providers of multichannel TV, including MSOs, CLECs and DBS systems.
Napster	Napster, Inc. (formerly Roxio, Inc.) is an online music provider offering a variety of purchase and subscription models. As of 2005, they are arguably the most popular music subscription service, and the second most popular legal music service overall (behind Apple Computer's iTunes Music Store).

National Television Standards Committee (NTSC)   Acronym for National Television Standards Committee, the FCC engineering group formed in 1940 to develop technical standards for black-and-white television (NTSC broadcasting began July 1, 1941) and color television (1953). NTSC developed the video-transmission standard used in the western hemisphere, Japan, and other Asian countries. NTSC standards are 525 lines of resolution transmitted within a 6MHz channel at 30fps.

NBC   The National Broadcasting Company, owned by General Electric.

Netscape   Netscape is a web browser that was originally based on a program called Mosaic. It is a registered trademark of Netscape Communications Corporation.

Network (television)   Group of radio or television outlets linked by cable or microwave that transmit identical programs simultaneously, or the company that produces programs for them.

Networked Television   Group of devices that are connected together for communication or other information sharing.

Nielsen Media Research   Nielsen Media Research (NMR) is a U.S. firm, headquartered in New York City, and operating primarily from Oldsmar, FL, which measures media audiences, including television, radio and newspapers. NMR is best-known for the Nielsen Ratings, a measurement of television viewership.

NTSC   See National Television Standards Committee.

NVOD or NEAR VIDEO ON DEMAND   The service of providing a movie to subscribers on multiple channels and staggering its start time (for example every fifteen minutes). Subscribers can then tune in to the next available showing.

OC-carriers   Optical Carriers — fiber optic data networks

On-demand   Used to describe any system that allows users to request data, video, audio or other content on demand.

Open	A company affiliated with BSkyB's Sky Digital set-top box network in the UK, Open offers viewers a special dedicated channel inside which they can interactively shop, play games, get information about entertainment, travel, and more on the TV screen. Open was originally owned by several companies, but it is now primarily owned by Sky. To use Open, the viewer must click the Interactive button on the remote control, which brings up the Open home page offering various categorized selections. Video clips and audio often accompanies most screens alongside clickable data.
Paramount	A media company owned by Viacom.
Pareto's Law	Italian economist Vilfredo Pareto created a mathematical formula to describe the unequal distribution of wealth in his country. He observed that 20 percent of the people in Italy owned 80 percent of the wealth. In the 1940s, Dr. Joseph M. Juran attributed his own observation of "vital few and trivial many" to the 80/20 rule, which he called "Pareto's Law" or the "Pareto Principle."
Pay TV	Television programming that requires payment upfront usually on a monthly basis as a subscription fee. Cable and satellite operators bundle content programming under packaged names like "Gold," "Silver," and so on.
Pay-per-view	is a service that allows the user to request specific programs for viewing, with a fee charged.
Peer-to-peer networking (P2P)	is an application that runs on a personal computer and shares files with other users across the Internet. P2P networks work by connecting individual computers together to share files instead of having to go through a central server.
Personal Video Recording (PVR)	See Digital Video Recorder.
Phonorecords	A legal term used by the copyright office of the United States to describe physical copies of audio or video content.
Picture-In-Picture (PIP)	The ability to view a video in a small window on top of another video or within a larger interactive interface.
Playlist	A collection of audio or video content.

Playout Software	Software the enables the scheduling and management of video assets for distribution over a network.
Playstation®	Sony's popular console video game system.
Podcast	Podcasting is a portmanteau that combines two words: "iPod" and "broadcasting." It is a misnomer, since neither podcasting nor listening to podcasts requires an iPod or any portable player, and no broadcasting is required. The term has become widely used to describe audio files available on the Internet.
Portal	See Walled Garden.
Prodigy	Prodigy Communications Corporation operated a dialup service (a sort of "mega-BBS") for home computers in the United States before the advent of the Internet. Although Prodigy claimed it was the first consumer online service, CompuServe actually predated it by several years.
Product Placement	The process of integrating an advertiser's product into media settings like TV programs and movies.
Progressive Download	A type of streaming in which the audio or video file begins to play after a certain minimum amount of data has been transferred, rather than requiring the entire file to be downloaded before playback starts.
PVR	See Digital Video Recorder.
QAM	Quadrature amplitude modulation (QAM) is the encoding of information into a carrier wave by variation of the amplitude of both the carrier wave and a 'quadrature' carrier that is 90° out of phase with the main carrier in accordance with two input signals.
QOS	Quality of Service
Qualcomm	Qualcomm is a wireless telecommunications research and development company based in San Diego, California. It was founded in 1985 by Irwin Jacobs and Andrew Viterbi, who previously founded Linkabit.
Quicktime	A digital video file format developed by Apple. It is often used for short, small segments, and can be played on both Macintoshes and PCs. QuickTime has been named as the underlying format for the MPEG 4 standard specification.

Rabbit Ears	Slang for an indoor television antenna.
Random-access	The ability to directly access any portion of data, without having to accept data in sequence.
Rating	Estimated percentage of the universe of TV households (or other specified group) tuned to a program at once. Ratings are expressed as a percent.
RealOne	RealPlayer is a media player, created by RealNetworks, that plays a number of multimedia formats including multiple generations of RealAudio and RealVideo codecs as well as MP3, MPEG-4, QuickTime, etc.
Remote Control	a hand-held device that allows the user to access the functionality of a system from a remote or distant location. Commonly used for the control of home media environments.
RIAA	The Recording Industry Association of America (RIAA) is a trade group representing the U.S. recording industry.
Rich Media	Web pages or ads that contain multi-media components such as audio, video or special effects.
ROI	return on investmentl: (corporate finance) the amount, expressed as a percentage, that is earned on a company's total capital calculated by dividing the total capital into earnings before interest, taxes, or dividends are paid.
RSS	RSS is a protocol, an application of XML, that provides an open method of syndicating and aggregating Web content.
RTSP	Real Time Streaming Protocol. A client/Server communication protocol that simplifies the distribution of multimedia contents on the Internet.
Satellite	Device located in geostationary orbit above the earth which receives transmissions from separate points and retransmits them to cable systems, DBS and others over a wide area.
Satellite Dish	is used to collect signals from a satellite in orbit and focus them to the front of the dish where a feed horn collects them and passes the signals on to the LNB (low-noise blocker) to be amplified and sent to a satellite receiver.

SBC/ATT	The merged telephone/media company created by combining AT&T (formerly an abbreviation for American Telephone and Telegraph) Corporation with SBC Communications is an American telecommunications company based in San Antonio, Texas. According to Daniel Berninger, Vice President and Senior Analyst of Tier1 Research, SBC is as of January, 2005 the largest telecommunications carrier in the United States.
SEM	is the acronym for Search Engine Marketing. SEM a type of marketing which relies on various search engine optimization techniques to achieve its goals.
SEO	the process of choosing targeted keyword phrases related to a site, and ensuring that the site places well when those keyword phrases are part of a Web search.
Set-Top Box (STB)	An electronic device that sits on top of your TV set and allows it to connect to the internet, game systems, or systems operators like cable, telco or satellite.
Share	the percent of households (or persons) using television who are tuned to a specific program, station or network in a specific area at a specific time. (See also, Rating, which represents tuning or viewing as a percent of the entire population being measured.)
Share of Market	A particular product's share of an industry's volume usually expressed in sales or number of units sold
Shelf Space	For the television industry the term refers to the availability of air time for a particular show. For retail, the amount of space that can be allocated to a particular product.
SHVA	The Satellite Home Viewer Act (SHVA) was passed in 1988 and has been updated and reenacted in 1994. The purpose of the Satellite Home Viewer Act is to protect the copyrighted area of local satellite network affiliates. SHVA states that satellite service providers like, DirecTV and DISH Network, can only allow clients with national networks to use their services when the signals from their local network affiliates are not available through the use of a rooftop antenna

Skype	A Voice over Internet Protocol (VoIP) service that uses the public Internet.
Skyscraper	A type of web advertisement that is taller than it is wide. Visit, http://www.iab.org for details.
Smart Card	Plastic cards the viewer can insert in the set-top box, which intelligently trigger the box to decrypt content programming. These cards are a bit thicker than charge cards and sometimes contain special chips or code.
SMS	Short Message Service: available on digital GSM networks allowing text messages of up to 160 characters to be sent and received via the network operator's message center to your mobile phone, or from the Internet, using a so-called "SMS gateway" website. If the phone is powered off or out of range, messages are stored in the network and are delivered at the next opportunity.
Sony	Sony Corporation is a global consumer electronics corporation based in Tokyo, Japan. It is currently one of the world's largest producers of consumer electronics and is one of the biggest corporations in Japan.
Spectrum	The range of electromagnetic radio frequencies used in transmission of voice, data and television.
Spot Cable	refers to commercial schedules placed on local cable systems by national or regional advertisers who often advertise in multiple cable TV markets.
Standard Definition Television (SDTV)	Standard Definition Television refers to digital transmissions over 480-line resolution, either interlaced or progressive scanned formats.
Stream	A contiguous group of data elements being transmitted, or intended for transmission, in character or binary-digit form, using a defined format.
Streamcast	See Streaming Media
Streaming media	Playing video or sound in real time as it is received over a network.
Subscriber	A customer who subscribes to a service. Cable and Satellite companies refer to their customers as subscribers.

Symmetrical Digital Subscriber Line (SDSL)   Symmetric Digital Subscriber Line — A version of DSL where the upload speeds and download speeds are the same. See DSL

Synchronized TV (SyncTV)   Usually called Enhanced TV or "two screen TV," this term defines the simultaneous broadcast and use by the viewer of an Internet application directly related to a regular television broadcast of a show. For example, during the Oscar's in 2000, ABC prepared an application that enabled the home viewer, while watching the program, to play along and vote for their favorite star, movie, or director. Producers "pushed" application content and data updates to all logged in computers. Usage of the application was fairly dynamic with trivia questions, polls, voting, pictures of the reactions of the stars, special offers, chat, and more. SyncTV applications require a complex configuration of standard and proprietary broadcasting and monitoring techniques.

Syndicator   A method of selling a television program to local stations on a market-by-market basis.

Systems Operator   A "catch all" phrase for cable, satellite, telcos and other providers of multiple video, voice, data and wireless services.

Tag   See metatag.

Tag Cloud   A Tag Cloud is a text-based depiction of tags across a body of content to show frequency of tag usage and enable topic browsing. In general, the more commonly used tags are displayed with a larger font or stronger emphasis. Each term in the tag cloud is a link to the collection of items that have that tag.

Tag Cluster   See Tag Cloud.

tcommerce   A word based on "ecommerce," this term describes interactive commerce on television. The word "shopping" also suffices.

TCP/IP   Transmission Control Protocol/Internet Protocol). A communications protocol developed under contract from the US Department of Defense to internetwork dissimilar systems. Invented by Vinton Cerf and Bob Kahn, this de facto UNIX standard is the protocol of the Internet and has become the global standard for communications.

Telecommunications Act Of 1996   U.S. Legislation passed in 1996, which overhauled the telecommunications industry. This bill also put in place important deadlines for the digital transition affecting every commercial and public TV broadcaster in the country.

Terrestrial   Broadcasting analog or digital signal via a large antenna that stands on the ground.

Tile   A small, usually rectangular) area of a screen that contains a graphic or video element.

Time-shifted Television   Used to describe content viewed or used at the temporal discretion of the user.

Transponder   A combination receiver, frequency converter, and transmitter package, physically part of a communications satellite. Transponders have a typical output of five to ten watts, operate over a frequency band with a 36 to 72 megahertz bandwidth in the L, C, Ku, and sometimes Ka Bands or in effect typically in the microwave spectrum, except for mobile satellite communications.

TV Tuner Card   The TV tuner card enables the PC user to receive television signals, which are then converted to digital format for viewing on the computer's monitor or a television monitor (if the card is so equipped).

UHF station   Ultra high frequency, the range used by TV channels 14 through 69.

UI   User Interface. See GUI.

Uniform Resource Locator (URL)   Uniform Resource Locator. An address that specifies the location of a file on the Internet.

Uplink   To transmit analog or digital signal to a satellite so it can then be transmitted back down to earth.

Upstream   The term used to describe traffic and paths that go from the subscriber to the headend. Also known as Reverse Path or Return Path.

URL   See Uniform Resource Locator.

UWB	Ultra Wide Band short-range radio technology, complements other longer range radio technologies such as Wi-Fi*, WiMAX, and cellular wide area communications. It is used to relay data from a host device to other devices in the immediate area (up to 10 meters, or 30 feet) at speeds up to 480 Mbps.
VCR	Video cassette recorder.
Verizon	Verizon Communications is a New York City-based local exchange telephone company formed by the merger of Bell Atlantic, a former Bell Operating Company, and GTE, which was the largest independent local-exchange telephone company in the U.S., with presence in most all of the continental United States and Hawaii.

Vertical Blanking Interval (VBI) Vertical Blanking Interval, comprising lines at the start of a TV signal before the picture area. These lines can contain Teletext, Closed Caption (NTSC only) and other information.

Vertical market	A vertical market is a particular industry or group of enterprises in which similar products or services are developed and marketed using similar methods.

Very High Bit Rate Digital Subscriber Line (VDSL) Stands for Very high rate Digital Subscriber Line, a form of DSL that can transmit up to 52 Mbps downstream and up to 2.3 Mbps upstream, though only over short distances (up to 4500 feet).

VHS	Video Home System, a specification for a consumer VCR. The most popular home video tape format.
Vickery Auctions	Named after the British economist who invented the process and made popular by search engine advertising; It's the type of auctions turned Google into a multi-billion dollar enterprise. No matter how high you bid you only have to pay 1 penny over the next highest bidder. This protects bidders and enables them to bid very high without risk.

Video Game Console a dedicated electronic device designed to play video games. Often the output device is a separate television or a computer monitor. The main input device is a controller. Many current generation game consoles feature media center features, Internet connectivity and home video playback capabilities.

Video-on-Demand (VOD) Video programming that can be requested at any time and is available at the discretion of the end-user.

Viewser A combination of the words viewer and user to denote a person whose behaviors are incorporating the attributes of both types of systems.

Vlog A portmanteau of Video and Blog to describe a video version of a blog.

VoIP Voice over Internet Protocol. The technology used to transmit voice conversations over a data network using the Internet Protocol.

Walled Garden A walled garden, with regards to media content, refers to an closed set of exclusive set of information services provided for users. This is in contrast to providing consumers access to the open Internet for content and e-commerce. The term is often used to describe offerings from cable and satellite operators, interactive television providers or mobile phone operators which provide custom content, and not simply common carrier functions. The term that appeared in the mid- to late 90's to define interactive content offerings contained or walled-off from direct access to Internet users

Walt Disney Company, The The Walt Disney Company (also known as "Disney") is one of the largest media and entertainment corporations in the world. Founded on October 16, 1923 by Walt Disney and his brother Roy Oliver Disney as the Disney Brothers Cartoon Studio, it is today the number two media company in the United States.

Warner Bros. Warner Bros. (an abbreviation for Warner Bros. Entertainment) is one of the world's largest producers of film and television entertainment. It is presently a subsidiary of the Time Warner conglomerate and headquartered in Burbank, California.

Waste Model	advertisers purchase air time based upon a "best guess" of who is watching rather than an actual census or who is watching.
Watchman®	Sony's brand of personal sized, portable televisions.
Watt	A watt is a unit of power equal to one joule of energy per second. The watt was named for the Scottish engineer and inventor James Watt (1736-1819).
Wax Cylinders	The earliest method of recording and reproducing sound was on phonograph cylinders.
WiFi	Short for 'wireless fidelity'. A term for certain types of wireless local area networks (WLAN) that use specifications conforming to IEEE 802.11b-g. WiFi has gained acceptance in many environments as an alternative to a wired LAN. Many airports, hotels, and other services offer public access to WiFi networks so people can log onto the Internet and receive emails on the move. These locations are known as hotspots.
WiMax	WiMAX refers to broadband wireless networks that are based on the IEEE 802.16 standard, which ensures compatibility and interoperability between broadband wireless access equipment.
Windows Media Player	Microsoft's popular audio and video player.
Wireless USB	Wireless USB is a new wireless extension to USB intended to combine the speed and security of wired technology with the ease-of-use of wireless technology. WUSB is based on Ultra Wideband wireless technology (802.15.3a, yet to be accepted), which operates in the range of 3.1 - 10.6 GHz.
Xbox®	Microsoft's popular video game console.
XML	Acronym for Extensible Markup Language. An open standard for exchanging structured documents and data over the Internet that was introduced by the World Wide Web Consortium (W3C) in November 1996

Zipf's Distribution   The simplest case of Zipf's law is a "1/f function". Given a set of Zipfian distributed frequencies, sorted from most common to least common, the second most common frequency will occur ½ as often as the first. The third most common frequency will occur ⅓ as often as the first. The nth most common frequency will occur 1/n as often as the first. However, this cannot hold precisely true, because items must occur an integer number of times: there cannot be 2.5 occurrences of a word. Nevertheless, over fairly wide ranges, and to a fairly good approximation, many natural phenomena obey Zipf's Law.

Cited Works

Adams, Cecil. "Did New York water pressure drop due to toilet flushing after the Super Bowl?" Online Posting. *The Straight Dope.* 13 February 1987. <http://urbanlegends.about.com/gi/dynamic/offsite.htm?z i=1/XJ&sdn = urbanlegends &zu= http%3A% 2F%2Fwww. straightdope.com %2Fclassics%2Fa2_371.html>

Ahment, Phil. "The Gutenberg Bible." *The Great Idea Finder.* ©1997-2005. March 2005. <http://www. ideafinder. com/history/inventions/story040.htm> ... "Alexander Graham Bell."<http://www. ideafinder. com/history/ inventors/bell.htm>

Ayette, Julie, Isabelle Peretz, and Krista Hyde. "A Group Study of Adults Afflicted With A Music-Specific Disorder." *Oxford Journal.*Vol. 125, No. 2, 238-251. February 1, 2002. <http://brain.oxfordjournals. Or g /cgi/content/full/125/2/238>

Bellis, Mary. "Cable Television History." *About.com.* 2005. <http://inventors.about.com/library/inventors/blcabletelevision.htm> ... "The History of Remote Controls." *About.com.* 2005. <http://inventors.about.com/library/inventors/blremotecontrols.htm> ... "Johannes Gutenberg and the Printing Press." *About.com.* 2005. <http://inventors.about.com/library/inventors/blJohannesGutenberg.htm>

Carr, Nichols. "The End of Corporate Computing." *MIT SMR.* Vol. 46, No. 3, pp. 67—73. Spring 2005. <http://sloanreview. mit.edu/smr/issue/2005/spring/13/>

Cisco Systems. "Building the Next Generation Digital Video Network." ©1992-2005. Cisco Systems Inc. <http://www. cisco.com/en/US/netsol/ns341/ns396/ns159/ ns333/networking_solutions_white_paper09186a008017915b.shtml>

Curtin, Michael. "Minow Newton." *Museum of Broadcast Communication*. 2005. <http://www.museum.tv/archives/etv/M/htmlM/minownewton/minownewton.htm>

Decisionmark Corp. *Titan TV*. ©2005. <http://ww2.titantv. com/index.aspx? ReturnUrl= %2fquickguide%2 f quickguide.aspx>

Diosi, Tony. "Virtual Street Reality." *Rense.com*. ©1997-2005. <http://www.rense.com/general67/street.htm>

Federal Communications Commission. "License Broadcast Station Totals in the USA." *FCC*. September 2005. <http://www. fcc. gov/mb/audio/totals/index.html>

Fluxture Advanced Media Inc. *Dynamod Flash*. 2005. <http://www.dynamod.com/>

Genova, Tom. "Television History—the First 75 Years." *TV History.tv*. 2001-2005. <http://www.tvhistory.tv/index.html>

Goff, David. "A Brief History of Fiber Optic Technology." *www.fiberoptics.info*. 2005. <http://www.fiber-optics.info/fiber-history.htm>

Heart Math. "Quotes of the Heart." *Heart Quotes*. ©2004. HeartMath LLC. <http://www.heartquotes.net/Expert.html>

HQ Papermaker. "All About Paper." *HQ Papermaker*. ©Copyright 2004. HQ Group Co. Ltd. <http://www.hqpapermaker.com/paper-history/>

Integrated Imaging. "Mini DV Inforamtion." *Integrated Imaging*. ©1995–2003. <http://www.integratedphoto.com/cgi-bin/infosearch.cgi?MiniDV+ Information&&name>

Interactive TV Dictionary. "2005 Interactive Television Business Index." 2005.date looked at.<http://www.itvdictionary.com/l.html>

Junk Busters Corporation. "A Brief History of Junk." *Junk Busters*. 2005. ©1996-2005. Junk busters Corporation. Reproduced by permission under the GNU General Public License. <http://www.junkbusters.com/variety. html#mail>

Mancusi, Aldo. *Enrico Caruso Museum*. 2005. <http://www.enricocarusomuseum.com/home.html>

Miller, Jeff. "A U.S Television Chronology." *History of American Broadcasting*. 2005. <http://members.aol.com/jeff560/chronotv. html>

Minow, Newton. "Vast Wasteland." *American Government and Politics*. 2001. <http://www.janda.org/b20/News%20articles/vastwastland.htm>

Mobile Tracker "American Idol attracts 41 million text messages" May 27 2005. http://www.mobiletracker.net/archives/2005/05/27/american-idol-sms

Museum of Broadcast Communications. "Standards and Practices." ©2005..<http://www.museum.tv/archives/etv/S/htmlS/standardsand/ standardsand.htm> ..."Must Carry Rules." ©2005. <http://www.museum.tv/archives/etv/M/htmlM/mustcarryru/mustcarryru.htm>

National Cable and Television Association. "Industry Overview." *NCTA*. 23 December 2005. <http://www.ncta.com/Docs/PageContent.cfm?pageID=86>

Nielsen Media Research. "What TV Ratings Really Mean." ©2005. <http://www.nielsenmedia.com/whatratingsmean/>

Paeth, Gregg. "Thanks for Nothing." Cincinnati Press. 13 May 1998. <http://www.cincypost.com/living/1998/jerry051398.html>

PBS Online. "Technology Timeline." *The American Experience*. ©1997-2004 WGBH Educational Foundation. <http://www. pbs.org/wgbh/amex/telephone/ timeline/timeline_text.html>

Productivity Commission. "Broadcasting Inquiry Report." Commonwealth of Australia. 3 March 2000. <http://econwpa. wustl.edu:8089/eps/mic/papers/ 0207/0207004.pdf>

Randolph, P. "Weapons of the Civil War." *Lycos Tripod*. 29 November 2005. <http://members.tripod.com/~ProlificPains/wpns.htm>

Reardon, Marguerite. "The Lowdown on Mobile TV." *Cnet News.com*. 21 October 2005. <http://news. com.com/FAQ+The+ lowdown+on+mobile+TV/2100- 1039_3-5905677.html?tag=nefd.lede>

Robinson, Mark. "Accidental Genius." *Wired.com*. ©1993-2004. The Condé Nast Publications Inc. <http://www. wired. com/wired/archive/10.01/accidental_pr.html>

Rupley, Sebastian "The Biggest Wi-Fi Cloud of All." 16 November 2005. http://www.pcmag.com/article2/0,1759,1884626,00.asp

Sanes, Ken. "War of the Worlds, Orson Welles And The Invasion from Mars." *Transparency*. ©1996-2000. <http://www.transparencynow.com/welles.htm>

Schoenherr, Steven E. "Digital Television." *Recording Technology History*. 6 July 2005. <http://history.acusd.edu/gen/recording/television2.html>

Schoenherr, Steven E. *Recording Technology History*.
   http://history.sandiego.edu/gen/recording/notes.html [July 6, 2005]

Shakesphere, William. "All the World's a Stage." *Art of Europe*.
   <http://www.artofeurope.com/shakespeare/sha9.htm>

Squires, Chase. "TV Taking More of Our Time." *St. Petersburg Times*. 30 September
   2005. <http: //www.sptimes.com/2005/09/30/Artsandentertainment/
   TV_taking_more_of_our.shtml>

Taylor, R. "Postal History" *Images of the World*. ©1998-2005.
   <http://imagesoftheworld.org/stamps/ph-cross-letter.htm>

TV Turnoff Network. "Facts and Figures About Our TV Habit." *TV Turnoff Network*.
   Real Vision 2004. <http://www.tvturnoff.org/factsheets.htm>

Wikipedia. "Suspension of disbelief." *Wkipedia Encyclopedia*. 18 December 2005.
   <http://en.wikipedia.org/wiki/Suspension_of_disbelief>

Van der Bergh, Stefan. "Trompe L'Oeil." *Planet Perplex*. ©2005.
   http://www.planetperplex.com/en/trompe_l_oeil.html

You can find more complete listings of industry statistics and the most up-to-date information about the media and technology industries at www.televisiondisrupted.com